Penny Presses

Mega List of 3,000+ USA Pressed Penny Machines

TABLE OF CONTENTS

AK Alaska 7
AL Alabama 10
AR Arkansas 13
AZ Arizona 15
CA California 22
CO Colorado 42
CT Connecticut 48
DC District of Columbia 49
DE Delaware 51
FL Florida 52
GA Georgia 64
HI Hawaii 68
IA Iowa 70
ID Idaho 72
IL Illinois 74
IN Indiana 80
KS Kansas 84
KY Kentucky 87
LA Louisiana 90
MA Massachusetts 93
MD Maryland 96
ME Maine 100
MI Michigan 101
MN Minnesota 108
MO Missouri 112
MS Mississippi 118
MT Montana 119
NC North Carolina 121
ND North Dakota 129
NE Nebraska 130
NH New Hampshire 132
NJ New Jersey 134
NM New Mexico 137
NV Nevada 141
NY New York 145
OH Ohio 151
OK Oklahoma 157
OR Oregon 160
PA Pennsylvania 164
RI Rhode Island 174
SC South Carolina 175
SD South Dakota 178
TN Tennessee 181
TX Texas 187
UT Utah 198
VA Virginia 202
VT Vermont 208
WA Washington 209
WI Wisconsin 213
WV West Virginia 219
WY Wyoming 221

ACKNOWLEDGEMENTS

I would like to acknowledge the following people for their help in making this book possible:

You. Yes, you. The wonderful PennyPresses.net community for your help in keeping the machine map on the website up to date. By adding new machines that you find in the wild and reporting machines that have gone missing, you have helped countless numbers of pressed coins find a loving home.

ABOUT THIS LIST

(YOU REALLY WANT TO READ THIS)

Pressed pennies have become one of the most common souvenirs purchased from our favorite museums, zoos and landmarks. This book should become your penny "bible" and kept in the glove box of your car. Whenever you hit the road, pull out this reference and find a machine nearby. You'll be surprised at some of the places you've driven by and never knew they had a machine!

A big thank you goes out to the PennyPresses.net and PennyPresses.com community for helping to maintain this pressed penny machine list over the years. Penny seekers have used the website to lookup machines during their penny adventures and have been so kind as to update this list for future hunters.

This book has been organized alphabetically by state and then by city. You should be able to flip through the book easily to find a machine in a nearby town wherever you are. Also, there is a Notes section at the back of this book for you make notes on any new machines, pennies, points of interest, etc. that you may find along the way.

A word of advice: Finding penny machines is kind of like playing whack-a-mole. They're here one day and gone the next. It would be advisable to call a particular location that you plan on visiting to make sure they still have their machine in place.

Here's to many fun and rewarding penny hunts. I hope this guide helps in some way to build your pressed penny collection and help you discover the wonderful places that hold them.

Enjoy!

Stu Hockstein
PennyPresses.net
PennyPresses.com
Smash 'Em If You Got 'Em

			Alaska
AK	Anchorage	Alaska Mint Company	*425 W 4th Ave, Anchorage AK 99501*
AK	Anchorage	Alaska Railroad Corporation	*421 W 1st Ave, Anchorage AK 99501*
AK	Anchorage	Alaska Zoo	*4731 O'Malley Rd, Anchorage AK 99507*
AK	Anchorage	Begich Boggs Visitor Center	*800 Portage Lake Loop, Anchorage AK 99587*
AK	Anchorage	Cabela's Anchorage	*155 W 104th Ave, Anchorage AK 99515*
AK	Anchorage	Exchange	*5800 Westover Ave, Anchorage AK 99506*
AK	Anchorage	Grizzly's Gifts	*501 W 4th Ave, Anchorage AK 99501*
AK	Anchorage	Harbor 360 Hotel	*1400 E 4th Ave, Anchorage AK 99501*
AK	Anchorage	Military Mall	*763C+6P Elmendorf Air Force Base, Anchorage AK 99506*
AK	Anchorage	Polar Bear Gift Shop	*600 W 4th Ave, Anchorage AK 99501*
AK	Anchorage	Polar Bear Gifts	*507 E St STE 206, Anchorage AK 99501*
AK	Anchorage	Polar Bear Gifts	*507 E St STE 206, Anchorage AK 99501*
AK	Denali National Park and Preserve	Canyon Gift Co	*238 Boardwalk Dr, Denali National Park and Preserve AK 99755*
AK	Denali National Park and Preserve	Denali park village	*231 Parks Hwy, Denali National Park and Preserve AK 99755*
AK	Denali National Park and Preserve	Denali River Cabins & Cedars Lodge	*231 Parks Hwy, Denali National Park and Preserve AK 99755*
AK	Fairbanks	Fairbanks Railroad Station	*1031 Alaska Railroad Depot Rd, Fairbanks AK 99701*

AK	Homer	Fish Connection	*4287 Homer Spit Rd #3, Homer AK 99603*
AK	Hoonah	Icy Straits Mall	*108 Cannery Rd, Hoonah AK 99829*
AK	Juneau	AJ Outlet Store	*801 S Franklin St, Juneau AK 99801*
AK	Juneau	Alaska Shirt Company - Juneau	*493 S Franklin St, Juneau AK 99801*
AK	Juneau	Creek Street Chum	*2000 Creek St, Juneau AK 99824*
AK	Juneau	Red Dog Saloon	*200 Admiral Way, Juneau AK 99801*
AK	Ketchikan	Fish Pirate's Saloon	*76 Front St, Ketchikan AK 99901*
AK	Ketchikan	Ketchikan Mining Co	*30 Front St, Ketchikan AK 99901*
AK	Ketchikan	Tongrass Trading Company	*201 Dock St, Ketchikan AK 99901*
AK	Kodiak	(Mack's Sport Shop & Alaskan Gifts) Big Ray's	*212 Lower Mill Bay Rd, Kodiak AK 99615*
AK	North Pole	Santa Claus House	*101 St Nicholas Dr, North Pole AK 99705*
AK	Seward	Alaska Railroad Corporation	*802 Port Ave, Seward AK 99664*
AK	Seward	Alaska SeaLife Center	*Alaska SeaLife Center, Seward AK 99664*
AK	Seward	Kenai Fjords National Park Visitor Center	*1204 "F 4th Ave #2794, Seward AK 99664*
AK	Seward	Seward's Fjords tours	*328 3rd Ave, Seward AK 99664*
AK	Sitka	Russell's	*206 Lincoln St, Sitka AK 99835*
AK	Skagway	Alaska Shirt Company Skagway	*131 Broadway, Skagway AK 99840*
AK	Skagway	Caribou Creek	*565 Broadway, Skagway AK 99840*
AK	Skagway	Skagway Outlet Store	*604B Broadway, Skagway AK 99840*
AK	Talkeetna	Talkeetna Alaska Lodge	*23601 Talkeetna Spur Rd, Talkeetna AK 99676*

AK	Talkeetna	Talkeetna Alaskan Lodge Hotel	*13680 E Main St, Talkeetna AK 99676*
AK	Talkeetna	Talkeetna Train Station	*Talkeetna Train Station, Talkeetna AK 99676*
AK	Tok	Mukluk Land	*Tok Community Park, Tok AK 99780*
AK	Wasilla	Museum of Alaska Transportation	*3800 W Museum Dr, Wasilla AK 99654*
AK	Whittier	Log Cabin Gifts	*6 Harbor Rd, Whittier AK 99693*

Alabama			
AL	Anniston	Anniston Museum of Natural History	*800 Museum Dr, Anniston AL 36206*
AL	Anniston	Anniston Museum of Natural History	*800 Museum Dr, Anniston AL 36206*
AL	Anniston	Anniston Museum of Natural History	*800 Museum Dr, Anniston AL 36206*
AL	Athens	Buc-ee's	*2328 Lindsay Ln S, Athens AL 35613*
AL	Auburn	Buc-ee’s	*2500 Buc-ee's Blvd, Auburn AL 36832*
AL	Bessemer	Alabama Adventure (formerly VisionLand)	*4599 Visionland Pkwy, Bessemer AL 35022*
AL	Bessemer	Alabama Splash Adventure	*4599 Visionland Pkwy, Bessemer AL 35022*
AL	Birmingham	Barber Motorsports Museum	*6030 Barber Motorsports Pkwy, Birmingham AL 35210*
AL	Birmingham	Barber Vintage Motorsports Museum	*6079 Barber Motorsports Pkwy, Birmingham AL 35210*
AL	Birmingham	Birmingham Zoo	*F6PC+RC, Birmingham AL 35223*
AL	Birmingham	Vulcan Park and Museum	*1701 Valley View Dr, Birmingham AL 35209*
AL	Birmingham	Vulcan Park and Museum	*1701 Valley View Dr, Birmingham AL 35209*
AL	Calera	Heart of Dixie Railroad Museum	*1919 9th St, Calera AL 35040*
AL	Calera	Heart of Dixie Railroad Museum	*1919 9th St, Calera AL 35040*
AL	Childersburg	De Soto Caverns Park	*8P3F+H8 Alpine, Childersburg AL 35014*
AL	Childersburg	Desoto Caverns Family Fun Park	*5181 Desoto Caverns Pkwy, Childersburg AL 35044*
AL	Daphne	Bass Pro Shops	*2008 Bass Pro Dr, Daphne AL 36526*

AL	Dauphin Island	Fort Gaines	*51 Bienville Blvd, Dauphin Island AL 36528*
AL	Dauphin Island	The Estuarium at the Dauphin Island Sea Lab	*102 Bienville Blvd, Dauphin Island AL 36528*
AL	Delta	Cheaha State Park	*19 Bunker Loop, Delta AL 36258*
AL	Foley	Lambert's Cafe	*2981 S McKenzie St, Foley AL 36535*
AL	Foley	Lambert's Cafe	*2981 S McKenzie St, Foley AL 36535*
AL	Foley	Tanger Outlet Foley	*2601 S McKenzie St Suite 324, Foley AL 36535*
AL	Foley	Tanger Outlets	*2601 S McKenzie St #224, Foley AL 36535*
AL	Fort Payne	DeSoto State Park	*Screaming Eagle Aerial Adventures at DeSoto Falls State Park, Fort Payne AL 35967*
AL	Fort Payne	Desoto State Park	*Screaming Eagle Aerial Adventures at DeSoto Falls State Park, Fort Payne AL 35967*
AL	Fort Payne	Little River Canyon Center	*4322 Little River Canyon Rim Pkwy, Fort Payne AL 35967*
AL	Fort Rucker	U.S. Army Aviation Museum	*6000 Novosel St, Fort Rucker AL 36362*
AL	Gadsden	Noccalula Falls Park & Campgrounds	*Gorge Trailhead, Gadsden AL 35904*
AL	Gulf Shores	(Lulu's) Homeport Marina	*202 E 25th Ave, Gulf Shores AL 36542*
AL	Gulf Shores	Alabama Gulf Coast Zoo	*1204 Gulf Shores Pkwy, Gulf Shores AL 36542*
AL	Gulf Shores	Fort Morgan State Historic Site Museum	*51 AL-180, Gulf Shores AL 36542*
AL	Gulf Shores	Gulf Shores Souvenirs & Gifts	*301 Gulf Shores Pkwy, Gulf Shores AL 36542*
AL	Gulf Shores	Gulf Shores Souvenirs & Gifts	*301 Gulf Shores Pkwy, Gulf Shores AL 36542*

AL	Gulf Shores	Gulf State Park	*21101 AL-135, Gulf Shores AL 36542*
AL	Gulf Shores	Pirate's Island Adventure Golf	*3201 Gulf Shores Pkwy, Gulf Shores AL 36542*
AL	Gulf Shores	Souvenir City	*217 Gulf Shores Pkwy, Gulf Shores AL 36542*
AL	Gulf Shores	The Hangout	*114 Gulf Ct, Gulf Shores AL 36542*
AL	Guntersville	Lake Guntersville State Park	*Lodge Dr, Guntersville AL 35976*
AL	Huntsville	U.S. Space & Rocket Center	*1 Tranquility Base, Huntsville AL 35805*
AL	Leeds	Bass Pro Shops	*5000 Bass Pro Blvd, Leeds AL 35094*
AL	Lincoln	International Motorsports Hall of Fame	*3198 Speedway Blvd, Lincoln AL 35096*
AL	McCalla	Tannehill Historical State Park	*12632 Confederate Pkwy, McCalla AL 35111*
AL	Mobile	Gulf Coast Exploreum Science Center	*65 Government St, Mobile AL 36602*
AL	Mobile	USS Alabama	*2703 Battleship Pkwy, Mobile AL 36603*
AL	Montgomery	Montgomery Zoo	*2301 Coliseum Pkwy, Montgomery AL 36110*
AL	Orange Beach	Adventure Island	*24559 Perdido Beach Blvd, Orange Beach AL 36561*
AL	Orange Beach	Live Bait Restaurant	*24281 Perdido Beach Blvd, Orange Beach AL 36561*
AL	Pelham	Oak Mountain Petting Farm	*1 John Findley Dr, Pelham AL 35124*
AL	Prattville	Bass Pro Shops	*2553 Rocky Mt Rd, Prattville AL 36066*
AL	Woodville	Cathedral Caverns State Park	*637 Cave Rd, Woodville AL 35776*

			Arkansas
AR	Bull Shoals	Bull Shoals White River	*153 Dam Overlook Ln, Bull Shoals AR 72619*
AR	Conway	Pickles Gap Village	*315 US-65, Conway AR 72032*
AR	Eureka Springs	Razorback Gift Shop	*579 W Van Buren, Eureka Springs AR 72632*
AR	Fort Smith	United States Marshals Museum	*789 Riverfront Dr, Fort Smith AR 72904*
AR	Gilbert	Buffalo Camping & Canoeing	*1 Frost St, Gilbert AR 72636*
AR	Gilbert	Gilbert Cafe	*Parking lot, Gilbert AR 72636*
AR	Gilbert	Gilbert RV Campground	*Parking lot, Gilbert AR 72636*
AR	Hot Springs	Arkansas Alligator Farm	*847 Whittington Ave, Hot Springs AR 71901*
AR	Hot Springs	Hot Springs Mountain Tower	*401 Hot Springs Mountain Dr, Hot Springs AR 71901*
AR	Hot Springs	Josephine Tussaud Wax Museum	*252 AR 7, Hot Springs AR 71901*
AR	Hot Springs	Mid-America Science Museum	*500 Mid America Blvd, Hot Springs AR 71913*
AR	Hot Springs	Pirate's Cove Adventure Golf	*4612 Central Ave, Hot Springs AR 71913*
AR	Little Flock	War Eagle Cavern	*21492 Cavern Dr, Little Flock AR 72756*
AR	Little Rock	Arkansas State Capital	*500 Woodlane St, Little Rock AR 72201*
AR	Little Rock	Little Rock Zoo	*1 Zoo Dr, Little Rock AR 72205*
AR	Little Rock	MacArthur Museum of Arkansas Military History	*503 E 9th St, Little Rock AR 72202*
AR	Little Rock	Museum of Discovery	*500 President Clinton Ave, Little Rock AR 72201*
AR	Little Rock	Old State House Museum	*300 W Markham St, Little Rock AR 72201*

AR	Mammoth Spring	Mammoth Spring State Park	*17 US-63, Mammoth Spring AR 72554*
AR	Mountain View	Ozark Folk Center Auditorium	*1028 Park Ave, Mountain View AR 72560*
AR	Murfreesboro	Crater of Diamonds State Park	*Crater of Diamonds State Park, Murfreesboro AR 71958*
AR	North Little Rock	Arkansas Inland Maritime Museum	*120 Riverfront Park Dr, North Little Rock AR 72114*
AR	Saint Joe	Big Springs Trading Company	*14237 US-65, Saint Joe AR 72675*
AR	Saint Joe	Buffalo River Outfitters	*9664 US-65, Saint Joe AR 72675*
AR	Saint Joe	Fergusons Country Store	*121 AR-333, Saint Joe AR 72675*
AR	Winrock	Petit Jean State Park	*43C8+HW Winrock, Winrock AR 72110*

			Arizona
AZ	Apache Junction	Cantankerous Carl's Hat Store	*4650 N Mammoth Mine Rd, Apache Junction AZ 85119*
AZ	Apache Junction	Goldfield Ghost Town	*4650 N Mammoth Mine Rd, Apache Junction AZ 85119*
AZ	Apache Junction	Goldfield Ghost Town (Cantankerous Carl's Hat Store	*4650 N Mammoth Mine Rd, Apache Junction AZ 85119*
AZ	Apache Junction	Prospector's Palace	*4650 N Mammoth Mine Rd, Apache Junction AZ 85119*
AZ	Ash Fork	Ash Fork Route 66 Museum	*901 Old Rte 66, Ash Fork AZ 86320*
AZ	Benson	Kartchner Caverns State Park	*RJQX+25 Benson, Benson AZ 85602*
AZ	Bisbee	Bisbee Mining & Historical Museum	*10 Tombstone Cn Rd, Bisbee AZ 85603*
AZ	Bisbee	Queen Mine Tour	*478 N Dart Rd, Bisbee AZ 85603*
AZ	Buckeye	White Tank Regional Library and Nature Center	*20298 W Olive Ave, Buckeye AZ 85355*
AZ	Cameron	Cameron Trading Post	*466 US-89, Cameron AZ 86020*
AZ	Camp Verde	Out of Africa Wildlife Park	*3505 AZ-260, Camp Verde AZ 86322*
AZ	Clarkdale	Verde Canyon Railroad	*300 N Broadway 300 n, Clarkdale AZ 86324*
AZ	Dragoon	The Thing	*2631 N Johnson Rd, Dragoon AZ 85609*
AZ	Duncan	Country Chic Art Gallery & Crafters Boutique	*205 SE Old W Hwy, Duncan AZ 85534*
AZ	Flagstaff	Flagstaff Visitor Center	*1 E Rte 66, Flagstaff AZ 86001*
AZ	Flagstaff	Lowell Observatory	*1400 W Mars Hill Rd, Flagstaff AZ 86001*

AZ	Flagstaff	Lowell Observatory	*1400 W Mars Hill Rd, Flagstaff AZ 86001*
AZ	Fredonia	North Rim Country Store	*6051 AZ-67, Fredonia AZ 86022*
AZ	Glendale	Luke Air Force Base Base Exchange	*14185 Falcon St, Glendale AZ 85309*
AZ	Grand Canyon Village	Desert View Watchtower	*906 Desert Vw Rd, Grand Canyon Village AZ 86023*
AZ	Grand Canyon Village	Grand Canyon National Park Grand Canyon Village	*106 S Vlg Lp, Grand Canyon Village AZ 86023*
AZ	Grand Canyon Village	Texaco Tusayan	*439 AZ-64, Grand Canyon Village AZ 86023*
AZ	Holbrook	Crystal Forest Gift Shop & Museum	*6493 Petrified Forest Rd, Holbrook AZ 86025*
AZ	Holbrook	Crystal Forest Museum & Gifts	*9490 US-180, Holbrook AZ 86025*
AZ	Holbrook	Jim Gray's Petrified Wood Co	*147 US-180, Holbrook AZ 86025*
AZ	Holbrook	Navajo County	*294 W Carlos Ave, Holbrook AZ 86025*
AZ	Holbrook	Petrified Forest Gift Shop	*6492 Petrified Forest Rd, Holbrook AZ 86025*
AZ	Jerome	Jerome City Designs	*323 Main St, Jerome AZ 86331*
AZ	Jerome	Jerome State Historic Park	*50 N Jerome State Mine Museum Rd, Jerome AZ 86331*
AZ	Jerome	Tours of Jerome	*110 Jerome Ave, Jerome AZ 86331*
AZ	Jerome	Turquoise Spider	*323 Main St, Jerome AZ 86331*
AZ	Kingman	Mohave Museum of History and Arts	*400 W Beale St, Kingman AZ 86401*
AZ	Kingman	Route 66 Museum	*Powerhouse Visitor Center, Kingman AZ 86401*

AZ	Lake Havasu City	Village Gift & Souvenirs	*81-101 London Bridge Rd, Lake Havasu City AZ 86403*
AZ	Lake Montezuma	Montezuma Castle National Monument	*J568+J2 Lake Montezuma, Lake Montezuma AZ 86335*
AZ	Litchfield Park	Wildlife World Zoo And Aquarium	*16501 W Northern Ave, Litchfield Park AZ 85340*
AZ	Lupton	Teepee Trading Post	*Exit 359, Lupton AZ 86508*
AZ	Mesa	Arizona Museum of Natural History	*53 N Macdonald, Mesa AZ 85201*
AZ	Mesa	Bingham Dermatology	*2855 E Brown Rd #3, Mesa AZ 85213*
AZ	New River	Roadrunner Restaurant	*47801 N Black Canyon Hwy #245, New River AZ 85087*
AZ	North Rim	North Rim General Store	*32 Campground Store Acc Rd, North Rim AZ 86052*
AZ	Oatman	Fast Fanny's Place	*159 Main St, Oatman AZ 86433*
AZ	Oatman	Main Street Emporium	*140 Oatman Hwy, Oatman AZ 86433*
AZ	Oljato-Monument Valley	Monument Valley Trading Post (The View Hotel Gift	*XVJQ+P5 Oljato-Monument Valley, Oljato-Monument Valley AZ 84536*
AZ	Page	Antelope Canyon Tours, Inc.	*22 S Lake Powell Blvd, Page AZ 86040*
AZ	Page	Glen Canyon Dam	*Glen Canyon Dam, Page AZ 86040*
AZ	Payson	Barn Door Books Western Village	*1104 S Beeline Hwy, Payson AZ 85541*
AZ	Peach Springs	Grand Canyon Skywalk	*5001 Eagle Point Service Rd, Peach Springs AZ 86434*
AZ	Phoenix	Arizona Capitol Museum	*1700 W Washington St #403, Phoenix AZ 85007*
AZ	Phoenix	Arizona Science Center	*600 E Washington St, Phoenix AZ 85004*
AZ	Phoenix	Castles N Coasters	*9445 N Metro Pkwy E, Phoenix AZ 85051*

AZ	Phoenix	Phoenix Zoo	*455 N Galvin Pkwy, Phoenix AZ 85008*
AZ	Phoenix	Rosson House Museum at Heritage Square	*113 N 6th St, Phoenix AZ 85004*
AZ	Phoenix	Rustlers Rooste	*8383 S 48th St, Phoenix AZ 85044*
AZ	Phoenix	The Childrens Museum of Phoenix	*215 N 7th St, Phoenix AZ 85034*
AZ	Picacho	Picacho Peak State Park	*15520 Picacho Peak Rd, Picacho AZ 85141*
AZ	Picacho	Rooster Cogburn Ostrich Ranch	*17599 E Peak Ln, Picacho AZ 85141*
AZ	Picture Rocks	Saguaro National Park	*7RWM+M9 Picture Rocks, Picture Rocks AZ 85743*
AZ	Prescott	Fite and Son's Mercantile and Ice Cream	*208 S Montezuma St, Prescott AZ 86303*
AZ	Prescott	Hotel St Michael	*205 W Gurley St, Prescott AZ 86301*
AZ	Quartzsite	Tyson Wells Enterprises Inc	*151 Kuehn St, Quartzsite AZ 85346*
AZ	Scottsdale	Butterfly Wonderland	*9500 East Vía de Ventura, Scottsdale AZ 85250*
AZ	Scottsdale	McCormick-Stillman Railroad Park	*Stillman Station, Scottsdale AZ 85250*
AZ	Scottsdale	OdySea Mirror Maze	*9500 East Vía de Ventura, Scottsdale AZ 85250*
AZ	Scottsdale	Scottsdale Southwest Gifts & Apparel	*3945 N Brown Ave, Scottsdale AZ 85251*
AZ	Scottsdale	Scottsdale Southwest Gifts & Apparel 3937 N Brown Ave	*3937 N Brown Ave, Scottsdale AZ 85251*
AZ	Scottsdale	Southwestern Reflections	*7221 E 1st Ave, Scottsdale AZ 85251*
AZ	Scottsdale	Sugar Drop Candy Shop	*9500 East Via de Ventura E-140, Scottsdale AZ 85256*

AZ	Sedona	Coconino National Forest/Red Rock Visitor Center and Ranger	*Red Rock Information Center, Sedona AZ 86351*
AZ	Sedona	Hangin Tree	*241 N State Rte 89A, Sedona AZ 86336*
AZ	Sedona	Tumbleweed Willies	*252 N State Rte 89A, Sedona AZ 86336*
AZ	Sedona	Western Trading Post	*265 AZ-89A, Sedona AZ 86336*
AZ	Seligman	Deluxe Inn Motel	*22510 Railroad Ave, Seligman AZ 86337*
AZ	Seligman	Grand Canyon Caverns	*115 AZ-66, Seligman AZ 86337*
AZ	Seligman	Historic Route 66 General Store	*22940 Historic Rte 66, Seligman AZ 86337*
AZ	Seligman	Historic Seligman Sundries	*22405 AZ-66 Scenic, Seligman AZ 86337*
AZ	Seligman	J & R	*22855 AZ-66, Seligman AZ 86337*
AZ	Seligman	Ok Saloon & Route 66 Roadkill	*22830 W Old Hwy 66, Seligman AZ 86337*
AZ	Seligman	Route 66 Motoporium	*22390 Historic Rte 66, Seligman AZ 86337*
AZ	Seligman	Rusty Bolt	*22345 W Old hwy, Seligman AZ 86337*
AZ	Sierra Vista	Fort Huachuca Museum	*41401 Grierson Ave, Sierra Vista AZ 85613*
AZ	Tempe	Legoland Discovery Center	*5000 S Arizona Mills Cir Ste 185, Tempe AZ 85282*
AZ	Tempe	Rainforest Cafe	*5000 S Arizona Mills Cir, Tempe AZ 85282*
AZ	Tempe	SEA LIFE Arizona	*5000 S Arizona Mills Cir Suite 145, Tempe AZ 85282*
AZ	Tombstone	O.K. Corral	*326 E Allen St, Tombstone AZ 85638*

AZ	Tombstone	The Bird Cage Theatre	*535 E Allen St, Tombstone AZ 85638*
AZ	Tombstone	Tombstone: Gunfighters Gulch	*524 E Allen St, Tombstone AZ 85638*
AZ	Tombstone	Tombstone: Lilly's Tombstone Memories	*514 E Allen St, Tombstone AZ 85638*
AZ	Tucson	Arizona-Sonora Desert Museum	*Reptiles and Invertebrates, Tucson AZ 85743*
AZ	Tucson	Bookmans East	*6230 E Speedway Blvd, Tucson AZ 85712*
AZ	Tucson	Golf N' Stuff	*6503 E Tanque Verde Rd, Tucson AZ 85715*
AZ	Tucson	International Wildlife Museum	*4800 W Gates Pass Rd, Tucson AZ 85745*
AZ	Tusayan	Tusayan General Store	*577 AZ-64, Tusayan AZ 86023*
AZ	Vail	Colossal Cave Mountain Park	*16721 E Old Spanish Trail, Vail AZ 85641*
AZ	White Hills	Arizona Last Stop	*20606 US-93, White Hills AZ 86445*
AZ	Whitecone	Fred Harvey Painted Desert Gift Shop	*GW28+49 Whitecone, Whitecone AZ 86031*
AZ	Wickenburg	Desert Caballeros Western Museum	*21 N Frontier St, Wickenburg AZ 85390*
AZ	Williams	Addicted To Route 66	*122 Historic Rte 66, Williams AZ 86046*
AZ	Williams	Bearizona Wildlife Park	*1500 Historic Rte 66, Williams AZ 86046*
AZ	Williams	Bedrock City (Yabba-Dabba-Doo)	*AZ-64, Williams AZ 86046*
AZ	Williams	Colors of the West	*112 S 2nd St, Williams AZ 86046*
AZ	Williams	Colors of the West	*112 S 2nd St, Williams AZ 86046*
AZ	Williams	Grand Canyon Railway RV Park	*212 W Franklin Ave, Williams AZ 86046*

AZ	Williams	Grand Canyon Railway Station	*233 N Grand Canyon Blvd, Williams AZ 86046*
AZ	Williams	Grand Depot Cafe	*233 N Grand Canyon Blvd, Williams AZ 86046*
AZ	Williams	Open Road Cowboy	*246 W Rte 66, Williams AZ 86046*
AZ	Williams	Pine Country Restaurant	*107 N Grand Canyon Blvd, Williams AZ 86046*
AZ	Williams	Valle Travel Stop	*257 AZ-64, Williams AZ 86046*
AZ	Williams	Wild West Junction	*321 E Rte 66, Williams AZ 86046*
AZ	Williams	Williams and Forest Service Visitor Center	*200 W Railroad Ave, Williams AZ 86046*
AZ	Window Rock	Navajo Nation Museum	*Hwy 264 and Postal Loop Road, Window Rock AZ 86515*
AZ	Winslow	Meteor Crater, The Museum of Astrogeology	*857C2XHH+25, Winslow AZ 86047*

California			
CA	Alameda	Blue Dot Cafe & Coffee Bar	*1904 Encinal Ave, Alameda CA 94501*
CA	Alameda	Pacific Pinball Museum	*1510 Webster St, Alameda CA 94501*
CA	Alameda	Pacific Pinball Museum	*1510 Webster St, Alameda CA 94501*
CA	Alameda	USS Hornet Museum	*707 W Hornet Ave, Alameda CA 94501*
CA	Amboy	Roy's Motel & Cafe	*87444 National Trails Hwy, Amboy CA 92304*
CA	Anaheim	Angel Stadium of Anaheim	*2000 E Gene Autry Way, Anaheim CA 92806*
CA	Anaheim	Boomer's Free Pressed Penny Offer	*5505 E Santa Ana Canyon Rd #18478, Anaheim CA 92807*
CA	Anaheim	Bubba Gump Shrimp Co.	*321 W Katella Ave STE 101, Anaheim CA 92802*
CA	Anaheim	Disney California Adventure Park	*Disney California Adventure Park, Anaheim CA 92802*
CA	Anaheim	Disney's Grand Californian Hotel & Spa	*1600 Disneyland Dr, Anaheim CA 92802*
CA	Anaheim	Disney's Paradise Pier Hotel	*1717 Disneyland Dr, Anaheim CA 92802*
CA	Anaheim	Disneyland Hotel	*1150 Magic Way, Anaheim CA 92802*
CA	Anaheim	Disneyland Park	*209 Main Street U.S.A., Anaheim CA 92802*
CA	Anaheim	Downtown Disney 1515 Disneyland Dr	*1515 Disneyland Dr, Anaheim CA 92802*
CA	Anaheim	Haunted Mansion	*15 Front Street, Anaheim CA 92802*
CA	Anaheim	It's a Small World Toy Shop	*1313 Disneyland Dr, Anaheim CA 92802*

CA	Anaheim	The Cove on Harbor Market & Cafe	*1540 S Harbor Blvd, Anaheim CA 92802*
CA	Atascadero	Charles Paddock Zoo	*9100 Morro Rd, Atascadero CA 93422*
CA	Avalon	Catalina By the Sea	*407 Crescent Ave, Avalon CA 90704*
CA	Avalon	Island Threadz	*601 Crescent Ave, Avalon CA 90704*
CA	Avila Beach	Central Coast Aquarium	*50 San Juan St, Avila Beach CA 93424*
CA	Avila Beach	Hula Hut	*380 Front St, Avila Beach CA 93424*
CA	Avila Beach	Sea Barn	*444 Front St, Avila Beach CA 93424*
CA	Baker	Alien Fresh Jerky	*72302 Baker Blvd, Baker CA 92309*
CA	Baker	Country Store 76 Gas Station	*92309, Baker CA 92364*
CA	Baker	The World's Tallest Thermometer	*72157 Baker Blvd, Baker CA 92309*
CA	Bakersfield	California Living Museum	*10500 Alfred Harrell Hwy, Bakersfield CA 93306*
CA	Barstow	Barstow Station	*1611 E Main St, Barstow CA 92311*
CA	Big Bear Lake	Brown Bear Gift Shop	*675 Pine Knot Ave, Big Bear Lake CA 92315*
CA	Big Bear Lake	Mountain Room Escapes Big Bear	*40600 Village Dr, Big Bear Lake CA 92315*
CA	Big Bear Lake	Shirt Shanty in The Village	*684 Pine Knot Ave, Big Bear Lake CA 92315*
CA	Big Sur	Big Sur Lodge	*47225 CA-1, Big Sur CA 93920*
CA	Bishop	Laws RailRoad Museum	*147 Silver Canyon Rd, Bishop CA 93514*
CA	Bodega Bay	Fishetarian Fish Market	*599 CA-1, Bodega Bay CA 94923*

CA	Bodega Bay	The Tides Wharf Restaurant & Bar	*835 CA-1, Bodega Bay CA 94923*
CA	Brawley	Shell Gas Station	*610 S Brawley Ave, Brawley CA 92227*
CA	Brawley	Shell Gas Station/ Circle K	*610 S Brawley Ave, Brawley CA 92227*
CA	Buellton	Pea Soup Andersen's	*376 Ave of Flags, Buellton CA 93427*
CA	Buellton	Pea Soup Andersen's (Buellton)	*51 E Hwy 246, Buellton CA 93427*
CA	Buena Park	Knott's Berry Farm	*8039 Beach Blvd, Buena Park CA 90620*
CA	Cabazon	Cabazon Dinosaur Museum	*5090 Seminole Dr, Cabazon CA 92230*
CA	Cabazon	Hadley Fruit Orchards	*47993 Morongo Trail #101, Cabazon CA 92230*
CA	Calistoga	Old Faithful Geyser of California	*1299 Tubbs Ln, Calistoga CA 94515*
CA	Calistoga	The Petrified Forest	*4100 Petrified Forest Rd, Calistoga CA 94515*
CA	Cambria	Old Cambria Marketplace Shell Gas Station	*589 Main St, Cambria CA 93428*
CA	Cambria	The Love Story Project	*734 Main St, Cambria CA 93428*
CA	Capitola	Carousel Taffy	*115 San Jose Ave, Capitola CA 95010*
CA	Carlsbad	Legoland California	*One Legoland Dr, Carlsbad CA 92008*
CA	Carlsbad	Legoland hotel	*One Legoland Dr, Carlsbad CA 92008*
CA	Carlsbad	SEA LIFE Aquarium	*1 Legoland Dr, Carlsbad CA 92008*
CA	Carson	Dreyer's Grand Ice Cream	*20740 S Wilmington Ave, Carson CA 90810*

CA	Cayucos	Pier Gifts On the 1	*137 N Ocean Ave, Cayucos CA 93430*
CA	Chiriaco Summit	General Patton Memorial Museum	*62510 Chiriaco Rd, Chiriaco Summit CA 92201*
CA	Chula Vista	Aquatica, SeaWorld's Water Park San Diego	*2052 Entertainment Cir, Chula Vista CA 91911*
CA	Claremont	Hendricks Pharmacy	*137 Harvard Ave N, Claremont CA 91711*
CA	Coloma	Marshall Gold Discovery State Historic Park	*R422+CG Coloma, Coloma CA 95667*
CA	Columbia	Towle & Leavitt-1853	*22751 Main St, Columbia CA 95310*
CA	Coronado	Coronado Resort Wear Company	*1350 Orange Ave, Coronado CA 92118*
CA	Coronado	Spreckels Sweets And Treats	*1500 Orange Ave, Coronado CA 92118*
CA	Costa Mesa	Centennial Farm	*88 Fair Dr, Costa Mesa CA 92626*
CA	Crescent City	Ocean World	*304 US-101 South, Crescent City CA 95531*
CA	DEATH VALLEY	Stovepipe Wells General Store	*51880 CA-190, DEATH VALLEY CA 92328*
CA	DEATH VALLEY	The Ranch at Furnace Creek	*2 Echo Canyon Rd, DEATH VALLEY CA 92328*
CA	Eureka	Sequoia Park Zoo	*3414 W St, Eureka CA 95503*
CA	Eureka	Sequoia Park Zoo	*3414 W St, Eureka CA 95503*
CA	Fairfield	Jelly Belly	*1 Jelly Belly Ln, Fairfield CA 94533*
CA	Felton	Roaring Camp Railroads	*Roaring Camp, Felton CA 95018*
CA	Ferndale	Ferndale, CA	*580 Main St, Ferndale CA 95536*
CA	Ferndale	Lentz Department Store	*406 Main St Suite #2, Ferndale CA 95536*

CA	Fish Camp	Tenaya Lodge at Yosemite	*1122 CA-41, Fish Camp CA 93623*
CA	Folsom	Folsom City Zoo Sanctuary	*403 Stafford St, Folsom CA 95630*
CA	Fort Bragg	Skunk Train	*100 W Laurel St, Fort Bragg CA 95437*
CA	Fresno	Downing Planetarium	*Downing Planetarium, Fresno CA 93740*
CA	Fresno	Forestiere Underground Gardens	*5021 W Shaw Ave, Fresno CA 93722*
CA	Fresno	Fresno Chaffee Zoo	*Reptile House, Fresno CA 93728*
CA	Fresno	Fresno Coin Gallery Jewelry & Loan	*4616 N Blackstone Ave, Fresno CA 93726*
CA	Fresno	Recyco Inc-Fresno	*4585 E Olive Ave, Fresno CA 93702*
CA	Fresno	Simonian Farms	*2629 S Clovis Ave, Fresno CA 93725*
CA	Garberville	One Log House Espresso & Gifts	*705 US-101, Garberville CA 95542*
CA	Garden Grove	Great Wolf Lodge Garden Grove	*Great Wolf Lodge | Southern California, Garden Grove CA 92840*
CA	Gilroy	Gilroy Gardens Family Theme Park	*3050 Hecker Pass Hwy, Gilroy CA 95020*
CA	Gilroy	Gilroy Welcome Center	*8155 Arroyo Cir Suite A007, Gilroy CA 95020*
CA	Gilroy	Levi's Store Gilroy Premium Outlets	*8375 Arroyo Cir Suite 50, Gilroy CA 95020*
CA	Half Moon Bay	Cameron's Inn	*1410 Cabrillo Hwy S, Half Moon Bay CA 94019*
CA	Half Moon Bay	Half Moon Bay Sportfishing and Tackle	*17 Johnson Pier, Half Moon Bay CA 94019*
CA	Half Moon Bay	Oddyssea	*621 Main St, Half Moon Bay CA 94019*

CA	Hume	Grant Grove Village	*83923 CA-180, Hume CA 93628*
CA	Hume	Hume Lake General Store	*64144 Hume Lake Rd, Hume CA 93628*
CA	Huntington Beach	Huntington Beach Pier Penny Press	*41 Main St, Huntington Beach CA 92648*
CA	Idyllwild-Pine Cove	Idyllwild Gift Shop	*54400 N Circle Dr, Idyllwild-Pine Cove CA 92549*
CA	Julian	Old Julian Garage	*2126 Main St, Julian CA 92036*
CA	Kernville	Eagle Rafting	*11252 Kernville Rd, Kernville CA 93238*
CA	Kings Canyon National Park	Cedar Grove Lodge	*National Pk, Kings Canyon National Park CA 93633*
CA	Klamath	Trees of Mystery	*15500 US-101, Klamath CA 95548*
CA	La Cañada Flintridge	Descanso Gardens	*1418 Descanso Dr, La Cañada Flintridge CA 91011*
CA	Laguna Hills	Moulton Museum	*25256 Cabot Rd, Laguna Hills CA 92653*
CA	Lake Arrowhead	Lake Arrowhead Tattoo	*26744 CA-189, Lake Arrowhead CA 92391*
CA	Lake Arrowhead	Skypark at Santa's Village	*28950 CA-18, Lake Arrowhead CA 92385*
CA	Lakehead	Lake Shasta Caverns National Natural Landmark	*20359 Shasta Caverns Rd, Lakehead CA 96051*
CA	Lee Vining	Nicely's	*24 4th St, Lee Vining CA 93541*
CA	Lee Vining	Whoa Nellie Deli	*22 Vista Point Dr, Lee Vining CA 93541*
CA	Leggett	Confusion Hill	*75150 US-101, Leggett CA 95585*
CA	Leggett	Drive-Thru Tree Park	*65401 Drive Thru Tree Rd, Leggett CA 95585*
CA	Littlerock	Charlie Brown Farms	*8317 Pearblossom Hwy, Littlerock CA 93543*

CA	Long Beach	Aquarium of the Pacific	*100 Aquarium Way, Long Beach CA 90802*
CA	Long Beach	Bubba Gump Shrimp Co.	*87 Aquarium Way, Long Beach CA 90802*
CA	Long Beach	Pirates Cove	*401 Shoreline Village Drive, Long Beach CA 90802*
CA	Long Beach	Raindance	*413 Shoreline Village Dr, Long Beach CA 90802*
CA	Los Angeles	America's Gift Store	*4028 Cahuenga Blvd W, Los Angeles CA 90068*
CA	Los Angeles	Arin Hollywood	*6525 Hollywood Blvd, Los Angeles CA 90028*
CA	Los Angeles	Battleship USS Iowa Museum	*250 S Harbor Blvd, Los Angeles CA 90731*
CA	Los Angeles	Bubba Gump Shrimp Co.	*1000 Universal Studios Blvd, Los Angeles CA 91608*
CA	Los Angeles	Cabrillo Marine Aquarium	*3720 Stephen M White Dr, Los Angeles CA 90731*
CA	Los Angeles	California Science Center	*700 Exposition Park Dr, Los Angeles CA 90037*
CA	Los Angeles	Casa California Inc	*620 N Main St, Los Angeles CA 90012*
CA	Los Angeles	Discovery Cube Los Angeles	*11794 Foothill Blvd, Los Angeles CA 91342*
CA	Los Angeles	Exposition Park	*Exposition Park Fountain, Los Angeles CA 90037*
CA	Los Angeles	Gifts of Hollywood	*6801 Hollywood Blvd, Los Angeles CA 90028*
CA	Los Angeles	Highland Market	*Parking lot, Los Angeles CA 90028*
CA	Los Angeles	Hollywood Bazaar	*6701 Hollywood Blvd, Los Angeles CA 90028*
CA	Los Angeles	Hollywood Happyland	*6725 Hollywood Blvd, Los Angeles CA 90028*
CA	Los Angeles	LA BREA TAR PITS	*5801 Wilshire Blvd, Los Angeles CA 90036*

CA	Los Angeles	Los Angeles Farmers Market	*6333 W 3rd St Suite 110, Los Angeles CA 90036*
CA	Los Angeles	Los Angeles Kings Hockey STAPLES Center	*1111 S Figueroa St, Los Angeles CA 90015*
CA	Los Angeles	Los Angeles Zoo	*5333 Zoo Dr, Los Angeles CA 90027*
CA	Los Angeles	Madame Tussauds Hollywood	*6933 Hollywood Blvd, Los Angeles CA 90028*
CA	Los Angeles	Pirate Tattoo Themed Souvenir Coins	*11038 Ventura Blvd, Los Angeles CA 91604*
CA	Los Angeles	San Pedro Fish Market and Restaurant	*1112 Nagoya Way, Los Angeles CA 90731*
CA	Los Angeles	Souvenir Outlet	*6408 1/2 Hollywood Blvd, Los Angeles CA 90028*
CA	Los Angeles	The Autry	*Griffith Park, Los Angeles CA 90027*
CA	Los Angeles	Travel Town Museum	*5200 Zoo Dr, Los Angeles CA 90027*
CA	Los Angeles	Universal Studios Hollywood	*100 Universal City Plaza, Los Angeles CA 91608*
CA	Los Angeles	USC Bookstores	*848 Childs Way, Los Angeles CA 90089*
CA	Los Angeles	Whistful Thinking at Hammer Museum	*10899 Wilshire Blvd., Los Angeles CA 90025*
CA	Mammoth Lakes	ATS Another T-Shirt Shop	*437 Old Mammoth Rd, Mammoth Lakes CA 93546*
CA	Manteca	Bass Pro Shops	*1356 Bass Pro Dr, Manteca CA 95337*
CA	Manteca	Great Wolf Lodge	*2500 Daniels St, Manteca CA 95337*
CA	March Air Reserve Base	March Field Air Museum	*Corvettes Wings and Wheels Carshow, March Air Reserve Base CA 92518*
CA	Mariposa	Yosemite Gifts	*5023 CA-140, Mariposa CA 95338*

CA	Mariposa	Yosemite Gifts	*5023 CA-140, Mariposa CA 95338*
CA	Mariposa County	Yosemite National Park	*8592VF86+2M, Mariposa County CA*
CA	Menlo Park	Stanford Linear Accelerator Center (SLAC)	*2575 Sand Hill Rd, Menlo Park CA 94025*
CA	Monterey	After the Quake	*643 Cannery Row, Monterey CA 93940*
CA	Monterey	American Revival Co	*711 Cannery Row # C4, Monterey CA 93940*
CA	Monterey	Bubba Gump Shrimp Co.	*720 Cannery Row, Monterey CA 93940*
CA	Monterey	Candy Factory	*685 Cannery Row, Monterey CA 93940*
CA	Monterey	Candy Land	*685 Cannery Row Suite L, Monterey CA 93940*
CA	Monterey	Five & Dime General Store	*685 Cannery Row #113, Monterey CA 93940*
CA	Monterey	Jerkyville USA	*700 Cannery Row, Monterey CA 93940*
CA	Monterey	Kristonio's	*750 Cannery Row, Monterey CA 93940*
CA	Monterey	Mackerel Jack's Trading Co	*799 Cannery Row, Monterey CA 93940*
CA	Monterey	Ocean Front	*15 Fishermans Wharf, Monterey CA 93940*
CA	Monterey	Old Fisherman's Grotto	*39 Old Fisherman's Wharf, Monterey CA 93940*
CA	Monterey	Sea Otter Shirts	*810 Cannery Row, Monterey CA 93940*
CA	Monterey	Steinbeck Wax Museum	*700 Cannery Row, Monterey CA 93940*
CA	Morro Bay	Carousel Taffy	*845 Embarcadero # A, Morro Bay CA 93442*

CA	Morro Bay	Crazy Otters	*845 Embarcadero, Morro Bay CA 93442*
CA	Morro Bay	Crills Saltwater Taffy	*1247 Embarcadero, Morro Bay CA 93442*
CA	Morro Bay	Dutchman's Seafood House	*701 Embarcadero, Morro Bay CA 93442*
CA	Morro Bay	Farmer's Kites Surreys & More	*1108 Front St, Morro Bay CA 93442*
CA	Morro Bay	Morro Bay Aquarium and Gift Shop	*595 Embarcadero, Morro Bay CA 93442*
CA	Murphys	Mercer Caverns	*1665 Sheep Ranch Rd, Murphys CA 95247*
CA	Murphys	Murphy's Historic Hotel	*457 Main St, Murphys CA 95247*
CA	Murphys	Murphys Historic Hotel	*457 Main St, Murphys CA 95247*
CA	Nevada City	Nevada City Chocolate Shoppe	*233 Broad St, Nevada City CA 95959*
CA	Newport Beach	Bay Arcade	*706 E Bay Ave, Newport Beach CA 92661*
CA	Newport Beach	Mothman Museum	*801 E Balboa Blvd, Newport Beach CA 92661*
CA	Norwalk	Golf N Stuff	*10555 Firestone Blvd, Norwalk CA 90650*
CA	Oakland	Chabot Space & Science Center	*10000 Skyline Blvd, Oakland CA 94619*
CA	Oakland	Children's Fairyland	*696 Bellevue Ave, Oakland CA 94610*
CA	Oakland	Oakland Museum of California	*Oakland Museum of California, Oakland CA 94607*
CA	Oakland	Oakland Zoo - lower entrance	*9777 Golf Links Rd, Oakland CA 94605*
CA	Oceanside	California Welcome Center, Oceanside	*928 N Coast Hwy, Oceanside CA 92054*
CA	Ojai	Treasures of Ojai	*110 N Signal St, Ojai CA 93023*

CA	Ontario	Rainforest Cafe Ontario	*4810 Mills Cir, Ontario CA 91764*
CA	Pacific Grove	Candy World	*111-125 Ocean View Blvd, Pacific Grove CA 93950*
CA	Palm Desert	The Living Desert Zoo & Gardens	*47908 Portola Ave, Palm Desert CA 92260*
CA	Palm Springs	Palm Springs Aerial Tramway	*1 Tramway Rd, Palm Springs CA 92262*
CA	Palm Springs	Palm Springs Air Museum	*745 N Gene Autry Trail, Palm Springs CA 92262*
CA	Palmdale	DryTown Water Park	*Avenue S & 10th Street East, Palmdale CA 93550*
CA	Pasadena	California Institute of Technology	*1200 E California Blvd, Pasadena CA 91125*
CA	Pasadena	Universal Coin Galleries	*1188 E Walnut St, Pasadena CA 91106*
CA	Pasadena	Vroman's Bookstore	*695 E Colorado Blvd, Pasadena CA 91101*
CA	Pismo Beach	Boardwalk Plaza - BeachWest Casual Wear	*1 Pier Ave, Pismo Beach CA 93449*
CA	Pismo Beach	F. McLintocks Saloon and Dining House	*750b Mattie Rd, Pismo Beach CA 93449*
CA	Pismo Beach	Pier Gifts	*195 Pomeroy Ave, Pismo Beach CA 93449*
CA	Pismo Beach	Point Break LLC	*175 Pomeroy Ave, Pismo Beach CA 93449*
CA	Pismo Beach	Tomasko Salt Water Taffy	*711 Dolliver St, Pismo Beach CA 93449*
CA	Placerville	Placerville True Value Hardware	*441 Main St, Placerville CA 95667*
CA	Point Arena	Point Arena Lighthouse and Museum	*45500 Lighthouse Rd, Point Arena CA 95468*
CA	Ragged Point	Ragged Point Inn & Resort	*19019 CA-1, Ragged Point CA 93452*

CA	Rancho Cucamonga	Bass Pro Shops	*7777 Victoria Gardens Ln, Rancho Cucamonga CA 91739*
CA	Redcrest	Ancient Redwoods RV Park	*28101 Avenue of the Giants, Redcrest CA 95569*
CA	Redcrest	Redcrest Resort	*26454 Avenue of the Giants, Redcrest CA 95569*
CA	Redding	Turtle Bay Exploration Park Museum Store (Next to Sundial Br	*848 Sundial Bridge Drive, Redding CA 96001*
CA	Riverbank	Funworks Modesto	*4307 Coffee Rd, Riverbank CA 95367*
CA	Riverside	Car Craft	*1006 W La Cadena Dr, Riverside CA 92507*
CA	Sacramento	California Automobile Museum	*2206 Front St, Sacramento CA 95818*
CA	Sacramento	California State Capitol Museum	*California State Capitol Museum, Sacramento CA 95814*
CA	Sacramento	California State Railroad Museum	*125 I St, Sacramento CA 95814*
CA	Sacramento	Candy Barrell	*1008 2nd St, Sacramento CA 95814*
CA	Sacramento	Candy Heaven	*1201 Front St, Sacramento CA 95814*
CA	Sacramento	Esquire IMAX Theatre	*1217 K St, Sacramento CA 95814*
CA	Sacramento	Fairytale Town	*Fairytale Town, Sacramento CA 95822*
CA	Sacramento	Munchies	*122 J St, Sacramento CA 95814*
CA	Sacramento	Powerhouse Science Center - Discovery Campus	*3615 Auburn Blvd, Sacramento CA 95821*
CA	Sacramento	Sacramento History Museum	*101 I St, Sacramento CA 95814*

CA	Sacramento	Sacramento Zoo	*3930 W Land Park Dr, Sacramento CA 95822*
CA	Sacramento	Sam's Cafe	*910 2nd St #2201, Sacramento CA 95814*
CA	Sacramento	Turtles	*900 I St, Sacramento CA 95814*
CA	Salinas	National Steinbeck Center	*1 Main St, Salinas CA 93901*
CA	San Diego	Balboa Park Visitors Center	*1549 El Prado Suite 4, San Diego CA 92101*
CA	San Diego	Belmont Park	*3146 Mission Blvd, San Diego CA 92109*
CA	San Diego	Birch Aquarium at Scripps Institution of Oceanogra	*2300 Expedition Way, San Diego CA 92037*
CA	San Diego	Cabrillo National Monument	*1800 Cabrillo Memorial Dr, San Diego CA 92106*
CA	San Diego	Cafe Coyote	*2461 San Diego Ave # 204, San Diego CA 92110*
CA	San Diego	Corvette Diner	*2965 Historic Decatur Rd, San Diego CA 92106*
CA	San Diego	Fiesta De Reyes/Casa de Reyes	*2754 Calhoun St Ste G, San Diego CA 92110*
CA	San Diego	Five & Dime	*2501 San Diego Ave, San Diego CA 92110*
CA	San Diego	Inka's Art	*2543 San Diego Ave, San Diego CA 92110*
CA	San Diego	Marine Corps Recruit Depot San Diego	*1600 Henderson Ave Building 31, San Diego CA 92140*
CA	San Diego	Maritime Museum of San Diego	*1492 N Harbor Dr, San Diego CA 92101*
CA	San Diego	Mex-Expressions (Old Town)	*2505 San Diego Ave, San Diego CA 92110*
CA	San Diego	Old Town - Cielito Lindo	*2491-97 San Diego Ave, San Diego CA 92110*

CA	San Diego	Old Town Market	*2612 San Diego Ave, San Diego CA 92110*
CA	San Diego	Old Town Trolley Tours San Diego	*4010 Twiggs St, San Diego CA 92110*
CA	San Diego	Reuben H. Fleet Science Center	*1875 El Prado, San Diego CA 92101*
CA	San Diego	San Diego Air & Space Museum	*2001 Pan American Plaza, San Diego CA 92101*
CA	San Diego	San Diego Automotive Museum	*2080 Pan American Plaza, San Diego CA 92101*
CA	San Diego	San Diego Model Railroad Museum	*1649 El Prado, San Diego CA 92101*
CA	San Diego	San Diego Natural History Museum	*1788 El Prado, San Diego CA 92101*
CA	San Diego	San Diego Zoo	*4 Front St, San Diego CA 92101*
CA	San Diego	San Diego Zoo	*1111 Sixth Ave ste 550, San Diego CA 92101*
CA	San Diego	San Diego Zoo Safari Park	*32W3+XP San Pasqual Valley, San Diego CA 92027*
CA	San Diego	San Diego's Best	*2415 San Diego Ave #102, San Diego CA 92110*
CA	San Diego	Seaport Village - Eclipse Eyewear	*817 W Harbor Dr, San Diego CA 92101*
CA	San Diego	SeaWorld San Diego	*500 Sea World Dr., San Diego CA 92109*
CA	San Diego	USS Midway Museum	*Parking lot, San Diego CA 92132*
CA	San Diego	Wings Beachwear - San Diego, CA (Ocean Beach) #103	*4948 Newport Ave, San Diego CA 92107*
CA	San Francisco	111 Minna Gallery	*140 2nd St #600, San Francisco CA 94105*
CA	San Francisco	Asian Image	*778 Clay St, San Francisco CA 94108*

CA	San Francisco	Asian Trends	*752 Grant Ave, San Francisco CA 94108*
CA	San Francisco	Bay City Bike Rentals & Tours	*Jones St & Beach St, San Francisco CA 94133*
CA	San Francisco	Bubba Gump Shrimp Co. Gift Shop	*BLDG M, San Francisco CA 94133*
CA	San Francisco	Cable Car Museum	*1120 Washington St, San Francisco CA 94108*
CA	San Francisco	California Academy of Sciences	*55 Music Concourse Dr, San Francisco CA 94118*
CA	San Francisco	Camera Empire	*799 Beach St, San Francisco CA 94109*
CA	San Francisco	Chen Tseng Trading Co LTD	*833 Washington St #300, San Francisco CA 94108*
CA	San Francisco	Children's Creativity Carousel	*Leroy King Carousel, San Francisco CA 94103*
CA	San Francisco	China Bazaar	*665-669 Grant Ave, San Francisco CA 94108*
CA	San Francisco	Chinatown - Far East Flea Market	*729 Grant Ave, San Francisco CA 94108*
CA	San Francisco	Chinatown Kite Shop	*899-867 Clay St, San Francisco CA 94108*
CA	San Francisco	Coit Tower	*Coit Tower, San Francisco CA 94133*
CA	San Francisco	Ess Eff Gift Shop	*43 1/2 The Embarcadero, San Francisco CA 94133*
CA	San Francisco	Franks Fisherman	*366 Jefferson St, San Francisco CA 94133*
CA	San Francisco	Katachi	*1660 Geary Blvd, San Francisco CA 94115*
CA	San Francisco	KHC Plaza	*445 Grant Ave, San Francisco CA 94108*
CA	San Francisco	Lefty's	*1 Pier 39, San Francisco CA 94133*
CA	San Francisco	Madame Tussauds San Francisco	*145 Jefferson St Suite 500, San Francisco CA 94133*

CA	San Francisco	Magnetron	*The Embarcadero & Beach St, San Francisco CA 94133*
CA	San Francisco	Musee Mecanique	*45 Sausalito - San Francisco Pier 41, San Francisco CA 94133*
CA	San Francisco	New Peking Gift Shop	*747 Grant Ave, San Francisco CA 94108*
CA	San Francisco	New Shanghai Enterprise	*857-867 Grant Ave, San Francisco CA 94108*
CA	San Francisco	Only In Chinatown	*864 Washington St, San Francisco CA 94108*
CA	San Francisco	S F Fashion House	*420 Grant Ave, San Francisco CA 94108*
CA	San Francisco	San Francisco Carousel at Pier 39	*39 Pier 39, San Francisco CA 94133*
CA	San Francisco	San Francisco Kite Company	*41 Vallejo - San Francisco Pier 41, San Francisco CA 94133*
CA	San Francisco	San Francisco Zoo	*San Francisco Zoo, San Francisco CA 94132*
CA	San Francisco	SS Jeremiah O'Brien	*99 Fishermans Wharf, San Francisco CA 94133*
CA	San Francisco	StoGies	*542 Beach St, San Francisco CA 94133*
CA	San Francisco	The Bagel Bakery	*153 Townsend St, San Francisco CA 94107*
CA	San Francisco	The Bay Company	*496 Jefferson St, San Francisco CA 94109*
CA	San Francisco	The San Francisco Dungeon	*145 Jefferson St Suite 500, San Francisco CA 94133*
CA	San Francisco	USS Pampanito	*Pier 45 Seafood, San Francisco CA 94133*
CA	San Francisco	Wharf Central	*3600 Baker St, San Francisco CA 94123*
CA	San Jose	Children's Discovery Museum of San Jose	*160 Woz Way, San Jose CA 95110*

CA	San Jose	Happy Hollow Park & Zoo	*748 Story Rd, San Jose CA 95112*
CA	San Jose	Plaza De Cesar Chavez Park	*194 S Market St, San Jose CA 95113*
CA	San Jose	The Tech Museum of Innovation	*201 S Market St floor b1, San Jose CA 95113*
CA	San Jose	Winchester Mystery House	*Winchester Mystery House, San Jose CA 95128*
CA	San Juan Capistrano	Ortega's Capistrano Trading	*31741 Camino Capistrano, San Juan Capistrano CA 92675*
CA	San Juan Capistrano	San Juan Capistrano Mission	*26801 Ortega Hwy., San Juan Capistrano CA 92675*
CA	San Luis Obispo	clothing store next to Bubblegum Alley	*737 Higuera St, San Luis Obispo CA 93401*
CA	San Luis Obispo	The Madonna Inn	*100 Madonna Rd, San Luis Obispo CA 93405*
CA	San Simeon	Hearst Castle Visitor Center	*Hearst Castle Visitor Center, San Simeon CA 93452*
CA	Sanger	Pine Flat Lake	*27866 Pine Flat Rd, Sanger CA 93657*
CA	Santa Ana	Discovery Cube Orange County	*2500 N Main St, Santa Ana CA 92705*
CA	Santa Ana	Santa Ana Zoo	*Santa Ana Zoo, Santa Ana CA 92701*
CA	Santa Barbara	Old Wharf Trading Co	*217A Stearns Wharf, Santa Barbara CA 93101*
CA	Santa Barbara	Santa Barbara Museum Of Natural History	*2559 Puesta Del Sol, Santa Barbara CA 93105*
CA	Santa Barbara	Santa Barbara Museum of Natural History Sea Center	*211 Stearns Wharf, Santa Barbara CA 93101*
CA	Santa Barbara	Santa Barbara Zoo	*500 Ninos Dr, Santa Barbara CA 93103*
CA	Santa Barbara	The Historic Mausoleum at Old Mission Santa Barbar	*2201 Laguna St, Santa Barbara CA 93105*

CA	Santa Clarita	Six Flags Hurricane Harbor - LA	*26101 Magic Mountain Pkwy, Santa Clarita CA 91355*
CA	Santa Cruz	Santa Cruz Beach Boardwalk	*400 Beach St, Santa Cruz CA 95060*
CA	Santa Cruz	The Mystery Spot	*465 Mystery Spot Rd, Santa Cruz CA 95065*
CA	Santa Monica	Bubba Gump Shrimp Co.	*301 Santa Monica Pier Building 9, Santa Monica CA 90401*
CA	Santa Monica	Pacific Park	*380 Santa Monica Pier, Santa Monica CA 90401*
CA	Santa Monica	PLAYLAND ARCADE	*350 Santa Monica Pier, Santa Monica CA 90401*
CA	Santa Monica	Santa Monica Pier Bait and tackle	*401 Santa Monica Pier, Santa Monica CA 90401*
CA	Santa Nella	Pea Soup Andersen's	*12411 CA-33, Santa Nella CA 95322*
CA	Santa Rosa	Charles M. Schulz Museum and Research Center	*2301 Hardies Ln, Santa Rosa CA 95403*
CA	Santa Rosa	Snoopy's Gallery & Gift Shop	*1665 W Steele Ln, Santa Rosa CA 95403*
CA	Sebastopol	Sebastopol Hardware Ctr	*Hardware Center, Sebastopol CA 95472*
CA	sequoia national park	Lodgepole Village & Market	*63204 Lodgepole Rd, sequoia national park CA 93262*
CA	Sequoia National Park	Stony Creek Lodge	*65569 Generals Hwy, Sequoia National Park CA 93262*
CA	Sequoia National Park	Wuksachi Lodge	*64740 Wuksachi Way, Sequoia National Park CA 93262*
CA	Solvang	Copenhagen T's & Gifts	*1687 Copenhagen Dr, Solvang CA 93463*
CA	Solvang	La Bella Rosa Fashion	*1618 Copenhagen Dr, Solvang CA 93463*
CA	Solvang	Nativo Art	*485 Alisal Rd, Solvang CA 93463*

CA	Solvang	Ostrichland USA	*610 E Hwy 246, Solvang CA 93463*
CA	Solvang	Solvang Gift & Souvenirs	*444 Alisal Rd, Solvang CA 93463*
CA	Solvang	The Right Gift	*436 Alisal Rd, Solvang CA 93463*
CA	Solvang	Wishing Well	*444 Alisal Rd, Solvang CA 93463*
CA	Soquel	Ocean Honda	*3801 Soquel Dr, Soquel CA 95073*
CA	South Lake Tahoe	Lakeside Landing	*4039 Lake Tahoe Blvd, South Lake Tahoe CA 96150*
CA	South Lake Tahoe	Tahoe T-Shirts Outlet	*3465 Lake Tahoe Blvd, South Lake Tahoe CA 96150*
CA	Tahoe City	Cabin Fever	*531 N Lake Blvd #201, Tahoe City CA 96145*
CA	Tahoe City	NAPA Auto Parts - North Lake Auto Parts	*295 N Lake Blvd, Tahoe City CA 96145*
CA	Tamalpais-Homestead Valley	Muir Woods National Monument	*VCWC+4Q Tamalpais-Homestead Valley, Tamalpais-Homestead Valley CA 94941*
CA	Temecula	Coin-Op Game Room Temecula	*28588 Old Town Front St, Temecula CA 92590*
CA	Temecula	Old Town Sweet Shop	*28545 Old Town Front St #204, Temecula CA 92590*
CA	Three Rivers	Three Rivers Museum	*42268 Sierra Dr, Three Rivers CA 93271*
CA	Vallejo	Six Flags Discovery Kingdom	*1001 Fairgrounds Dr, Vallejo CA 94589*
CA	Vallejo	Vallejo Naval and Historical Museum	*734 Marin St, Vallejo CA 94590*
CA	Ventura	Golf N' Stuff	*5555 Walker St, Ventura CA 93003*
CA	Ventura	Ventura Village Carousel	*1567 Spinnaker Dr #105, Ventura CA 93001*

CA	Walnut Creek	Lindsay Wildlife Experience	*1931 1st Ave, Walnut Creek CA 94597*
CA	Warner Valley	Kohm Yah-mah-nee Visitor Center Lassen CafÃ© & Gift	*FHXH+3P Warner Valley, Warner Valley CA 96020*
CA	Wheatland	Bishop's Pumpkin Farm	*1415 Pumpkin Ln, Wheatland CA 95692*
CA	Willits	Lumberjack Restaurant	*1740 S Main St, Willits CA 95490*
CA	Willits	Lumberjack's Restaurant - Willits	*1740 S Main St, Willits CA 95490*
CA	Willits	Skunk Train	*299 E Commercial St, Willits CA 95490*
CA	Willits	The Skunk Train	*299 E Commercial St, Willits CA 95490*
CA	Yermo	Calico Ghost Tours	*36600 Ghost Town Rd, Yermo CA 92398*
CA	Yorba Linda	The Richard Nixon Library & Museum	*18001 Yorba Linda Blvd, Yorba Linda CA 92886*
CA	Yosemite Valley	Yosemite National Park	*Half Dome Village, Yosemite Valley CA 95389*
CA	Yucaipa	Los Rios Rancho	*39611 Oak Glen Rd, Yucaipa CA 92399*

Colorado

CO	Air Force Academy	United States Air Force Academy	*X4XQ+8F Air Force Academy, Air Force Academy CO 80840*
CO	Antonito	Conejos County Museum	*5250 US Hwy 285, Antonito CO 81120*
CO	Antonito	Conejos County Museum	*5250 US Hwy 285, Antonito CO 81120*
CO	Antonito	Cumbres &Toltec Scenic Railroad	*5234 US Hwy 285, Antonito CO 81120*
CO	Breckenridge	Peak a Boo Toys	*117 S Main St, Breckenridge CO 80424*
CO	Breckenridge	Skinny Winter	*123 S Main St, Breckenridge CO 80424*
CO	Cascade-Chipita Park	North Pole Colorado Santas Workshop	*5050 Pikes Peak Hwy, Cascade-Chipita Park CO 80809*
CO	Cascade-Chipita Park	Pikes Peak - America's Mountain	*5069 Pikes Peak Hwy, Cascade-Chipita Park CO 80809*
CO	Cañon City	Kaleidoscope Inspiration	*602 Main St, Cañon City CO 81212*
CO	Cañon City	Royal Gorge Bridge and Park	*4218 Royal Gorge Bridge, Cañon City CO 81212*
CO	Cañon City	Royal Gorge Route Railroad	*330 Royal Gorge Blvd, Cañon City CO 81212*
CO	Colorado Springs	American Numismatic Association	*818 N Cascade Ave, Colorado Springs CO 80903*
CO	Colorado Springs	Cave of the Winds	*100 Cave of the Winds Rd, Colorado Springs CO 80809*
CO	Colorado Springs	Cheyenne Mountain Zoo	*700 Cheyenne Mountain Hwy, Colorado Springs CO 80906*
CO	Colorado Springs	Children's Smile Center	*7770 N Union Blvd Suite B, Colorado Springs CO 80920*

CO	Colorado Springs	Fargo's Pizza Co	*2910 E Platte Ave, Colorado Springs CO 80909*
CO	Colorado Springs	Garden of the Gods - Visitor Center	*1805 N 30th St, Colorado Springs CO 80904*
CO	Colorado Springs	George Orthodontics	*7770 N Union Blvd Suite B, Colorado Springs CO 80920*
CO	Colorado Springs	Seven Falls	*8 Lake Ave, Colorado Springs CO 80906*
CO	Colorado Springs	Western Museum of Mining and Industry	*225 North Gate Blvd, Colorado Springs CO 80921*
CO	Creede	Downstream Gas & Mercantile	*117 E 7th St, Creede CO 81130*
CO	Cripple Creek	Cripple Creek and Victor Narrow Gauge Railroad	*520 E Carr Ave, Cripple Creek CO 80813*
CO	Denver	Aramark	*1499 Delaware St, Denver CO 80204*
CO	Denver	Aramark at the US Mint Denver	*1499 Delaware St, Denver CO 80204*
CO	Denver	Bass Pro Shops	*7970 E Northfield Blvd, Denver CO 80238*
CO	Denver	Children's Museum of Denver at Marsico Campus	*2121 Children's Museum Dr, Denver CO 80211*
CO	Denver	Coors Field	*2001 Blake St, Denver CO 80205*
CO	Denver	Denver Firefighters Museum	*1326 Tremont Pl, Denver CO 80204*
CO	Denver	Denver Museum of Nature & Science	*2001 Colorado Blvd, Denver CO 80205*
CO	Denver	Denver Zoo	*3200 E 23rd Ave, Denver CO 80205*
CO	Denver	Downtown Aquarium	*700 Water St, Denver CO 80211*
CO	Denver	Downtown Aquarium	*700 Water St, Denver CO 80211*
CO	Denver	Elitch Gardens	*299 Walnut St, Denver CO 80204*

CO	Denver	Forney Museum of Transportation	*4303 Brighton Blvd, Denver CO 80216*
CO	Denver	Hammond's Candies	*5735 Washington St, Denver CO 80216*
CO	Divide	Mueller State Park	*21045 CO-67, Divide CO 80814*
CO	Durango	Durango & Silverton Narrow Gauge Railroad & Museum	*479 Main Ave, Durango CO 81301*
CO	Englewood	Candy Cane Lane	*500 W Grand Ave, Englewood CO 80110*
CO	Estes Park	Beef Jerky Experience - Machine 1	*131 Virginia Dr, Estes Park CO 80517*
CO	Estes Park	Fall River Visitor Center	*B 2000 Fall River Rd, Estes Park CO 80517*
CO	Estes Park	Mad Moose	*900 Moraine Ave, Estes Park CO 80517*
CO	Fairplay	South Park Pottery	*417 Front St, Fairplay CO 80440*
CO	Fort Collins	Colorado Candy Company	*814 S College Ave, Fort Collins CO 80524*
CO	Fort Collins	Totally 80s Pizza & Museum - Machine 1	*2567 S Shields St, Fort Collins CO 80526*
CO	Fort Collins	Wadoo Home and Gifts	*200 S College Ave, Fort Collins CO 80524*
CO	Fruita	Colorado National Monument Visitor Center	*1750 Rimrock Dr, Fruita CO 81521*
CO	Glenwood Springs	Downtown Drug	*825 Grand Ave, Glenwood Springs CO 81601*
CO	Glenwood Springs	Glenwood Caverns Adventure Park	*51000 Two Rivers Plaza Road, Glenwood Springs CO 81601*
CO	Golden	Buffalo Bill Memorial Museum	*987 1/2 Lookout Mountain Rd, Golden CO 80401*
CO	Golden	Colorado Railroad Museum	*491 W 44th Ave, Golden CO 80403*

CO	Golden	Coors Brewery Tour	*1313 Ford St, Golden CO 80401*
CO	Golden	Red Rocks Amphitheatre	*2901 Ship Rock Rd, Golden CO 80401*
CO	Grand Junction	Cabela's	*Sola Salons, Grand Junction CO 81505*
CO	Grand Junction	Grand Junction Amtrak Station	*339 S 1st St, Grand Junction CO 81501*
CO	Grand Lake	Quacker Gift Shop Grand Lake	*1034 Grand Ave, Grand Lake CO 80447*
CO	Greeley	Centennial Village Museum: Living Heritage Experie	*1401 A St, Greeley CO 80631*
CO	Greeley	Colorado Model Railroad Museum	*680 10th St, Greeley CO 80631*
CO	Gypsum	Eagle County Regional Airport	*217 Eldon Wilson Rd, Gypsum CO 81637*
CO	Hugo	Main Street Mama's	*329 4th St, Hugo CO 80821*
CO	Idaho Springs	Beau Jo's Idaho Springs	*1517 Miner St, Idaho Springs CO 80452*
CO	Idaho Springs	Echo Lake Lodge	*13264 CO-103, Idaho Springs CO 80452*
CO	Idaho Springs	Margie's Place Custom Tee Shirt	*1534 Miner St, Idaho Springs CO 80452*
CO	Johnstown	Buc-ee's	*5201 Nugget Rd, Johnstown CO 80534*
CO	Julesburg	Colorado Welcome Center	*20934 Co Rd 28, Julesburg CO 80737*
CO	Keenesburg	The Wild Animal Sanctuary	*1942 Co Rd 53, Keenesburg CO 80643*
CO	La Junta	Koshare Indian Museum & Trading Post	*Koshare Kiva, La Junta CO 81050*
CO	Lakewood	Casa Bonita	*6719 W Colfax Ave, Lakewood CO 80214*
CO	Leadville	Leadville , Colorado & Southern Railroad	*324 E 7th St, Leadville CO 80461*

CO	Leadville	National Mining Hall of Fame and Museum	*821 Harrison Ave, Leadville CO 80461*
CO	Littleton	Littleton Museum	*6028 S Gallup St, Littleton CO 80120*
CO	Lone Tree	Cabela's	*10670 Cabela Dr, Lone Tree CO 80124*
CO	Loveland	Loveland Museum/Gallery	*503 N Lincoln Ave, Loveland CO 80537*
CO	Loveland	The Dam Store	*11 River Hollow Ln, Loveland CO 80538*
CO	Manitou Springs	Arcade Amusements Inc.	*9 Arcade St, Manitou Springs CO 80829*
CO	Manitou Springs	Garden of the Gods Trading Post	*324 Beckers Ln, Manitou Springs CO 80829*
CO	Manitou Springs	Manitou Cliff Dwellings	*10 Sunshine Trail, Manitou Springs CO 80829*
CO	Manitou Springs	Manitou Outpost	*807 Manitou Ave, Manitou Springs CO 80829*
CO	Manitou Springs	Manitou Springs Cliff Dwellings	*10 Cliff Rd, Manitou Springs CO 80829*
CO	Manitou Springs	Quacker Gift Shop Manitou	*738 Manitou Ave, Manitou Springs CO 80829*
CO	Manitou Springs	The Broadmoor Pikes Peak Cog Railway	*515 Ruxton Ave, Manitou Springs CO 80829*
CO	Manitou Springs	White Bear	*935A Manitou Ave, Manitou Springs CO 80829*
CO	Mesa Verde National Park	Mesa Verde National Park	*6GJQ+87 Mesa Verde National Park, Mesa Verde National Park CO 81330*
CO	Montrose	Black Canyon Corner Store	*72381 US-50, Montrose CO 81401*
CO	Morrison	Dinosaur Ridge	*16831 W Alameda Pkwy, Morrison CO 80465*
CO	Mosca	Colorado Gators Reptile Park	*9162 Ln 9 N, Mosca CO 81146*

CO	Mosca	Great Sand Dunes Visitor Center	*11999 CO-150, Mosca CO 81146*
CO	Nederland	Carousel of Happiness	*20 Lakeview Dr, Nederland CO 80466*
CO	Ouray	Bachelor Syracuse Mine Tour	*95 Gold Mountain Trl, Ouray CO 81427*
CO	Ouray	Gator Emporium	*610 Main St, Ouray CO 81427*
CO	Pueblo	El Pueblo History Museum	*211 Victoria Ave, Pueblo CO 81003*
CO	Pueblo	Pueblo Zoo	*3455 Nuckolls Ave, Pueblo CO 81005*
CO	Red Feather Lakes	Red Feathers Trading Post	*41 Main St, Red Feather Lakes CO 80545*
CO	Salida	Kaleidoscope Toys	*116 F St, Salida CO 81201*
CO	Silver Plume	Georgetown Loop Railroad	*825 Railroad Avenue, Silver Plume CO 80476*
CO	Silverton	San Juan County Historical Society	*1557 Greene Street •, Silverton CO 81433*
CO	Silverton	Shady Lady	*1159 Blair St, Silverton CO 81433*
CO	Silverton	Silverton Trading Post (Silverton Train Depot)	*1101 Cement St, Silverton CO 81433*
CO	Thornton	Cabela's	*14050 Lincoln St, Thornton CO 80023*
CO	Thornton	Cabela's	*14050 Lincoln St, Thornton CO 80023*
CO	Vail	Lionshead Village Welcome Center	*395 E Lionshead Cir, Vail CO 81657*
CO	Westminster	Butterfly Pavilion	*6252 W 104th Ave, Westminster CO 80020*
CO	Winter Park	B Jammin'/Imaginations Toy Store	*47 Cooper Creek Way, Winter Park CO 80482*
CO	Woodland Park	Rocky Mountain Dinosaur Resource Center	*201 S Fairview St, Woodland Park CO 80863*

Connecticut			
CT	Bridgeport	Connecticut's Beardsley Zoo	*1875 Noble Ave, Bridgeport CT 06610*
CT	Bridgeport	Connecticut's Beardsley Zoo	*1 Beardsley Park Terrace, Bridgeport CT 06610*
CT	East Hartford	Cabela's	*615 Silver Ln, East Hartford CT 06118*
CT	East Haven	Shore Line Trolley Museum	*17 River St, East Haven CT 06512*
CT	Groton	Mystic Pizza	*56 W Main St, Groton CT 06355*
CT	Groton	USS Nautilus	*1 Crystal Lake Rd, Groton CT 06340*
CT	Hartford	Connecticut Science Center	*250 Columbus Blvd, Hartford CT 06103*
CT	Montville	Nature's Art	*1650 Hartford-New London Turnpike, Montville CT 06370*
CT	Montville	The Dinosaur Place at Nature's Art Village	*1650 Hartford-New London Turnpike, Montville CT 06370*
CT	Orange	PEZ Candy Inc	*35 Prindle Hill Road, Orange CT 06477*
CT	Rocky Hill	Dinosaur State Park and Arboretum	*400 West St, Rocky Hill CT 06067*
CT	Stonington	Mystic Aquarium	*55 Coogan Blvd, Stonington CT 06355*
CT	Stonington	Mystic Seaport	*Mystic Seaport, Stonington CT 06355*

			District of Columbia
DC	Washington	Ford's Theater	*511 10th St NW, Washington DC 20004*
DC	Washington	Hard Rock Cafe	*999 E St NW, Washington DC 20463*
DC	Washington	International Spy Museum	*700 L'Enfant Plaza SW, Washington DC 20024*
DC	Washington	National Building Museum	*401f Street NW, Washington DC 20001*
DC	Washington	National Geographic Museum	*1145 17th St NW, Washington DC 20036*
DC	Washington	National Geographic Museum	*1145 17th St NW, Washington DC 20036*
DC	Washington	Smithsonian American Art Museum	*8th St NW & G St NW, Washington DC 20001*
DC	Washington	Smithsonian National Air and Space Museum	*655 Jefferson Dr SW, Washington DC 20004*
DC	Washington	Smithsonian National Air and Space Museum	*655 Jefferson Dr SW, Washington DC 20004*
DC	Washington	Smithsonian National Museum of American History	*1300 Constitution Ave. NW, Washington DC 20004*
DC	Washington	Smithsonian National Museum of Natural History	*1010 Madison Dr NW, Washington DC 20004*
DC	Washington	Smithsonian National Postal Museum	*2 Massachusetts Ave NE, Washington DC 20002*
DC	Washington	Smithsonian National Zoological Park	*3001 Connecticut Ave NW, Washington DC 20008*
DC	Washington	The White House Historical Association - The Peoples House	*1700 Pennsylvania Ave NW, Washington DC 20006*
DC	Washington	U.S. Navy Museum	*736 Sicard St SE, Washington DC 20374*
DC	Washington	Union Station	*40 Massachusetts Ave NE, Washington DC 20002*
DC	Washington	Washington National Cathedral	*3101 Wisconsin Ave, Washington DC 20016*

DC	Washington	Washington National Cathedral	*3101 Wisconsin Ave, Washington DC 20016*
DC	Washington	Washington Welcome Center / Trolley Tour	*1001 E St NW, Washington DC 20004*
DC	Washington	White House Visitor Center	*Herbert C. Hoover Building, Washington DC 20004*

			Delaware
DE	Bethany Beach	Bethany Beach Boardwalk	*676 Half Moon Dr, Bethany Beach DE 19930*
DE	Brookside	Delaware Welcome Visitors Center	*M865+VW Brookside, Brookside DE 19713*
DE	Dover	Air Mobility Command Museum	*1301 Perimeter Rd, Dover DE 19902*
DE	Fenwick Island	SEA SHELL CITY	*708 Coastal Hwy, Fenwick Island DE 19944*
DE	Fenwick Island	Sea Shell City Inc	*708 Coastal Hwy, Fenwick Island DE 19944*
DE	Lewes	Cape May-Lewes Ferry, Lewes Terminal	*43 Cape Henlopen Dr, Lewes DE 19958*
DE	Newark	Cabela's	*1100 Christiana Mall, Newark DE 19702*
DE	Rehoboth Beach	Funland	*6 Delaware Ave, Rehoboth Beach DE 19971*
DE	Rehoboth Beach	Snyder's Candy	*58 Rehoboth Ave, Rehoboth Beach DE 19971*
DE	Wilmington	Greater Wilmington Convention and Visitor's Bureau	*100 W 10th St #309, Wilmington DE 19801*
DE	Wilmington	Hagley Museum	*200 Hagley Creek Rd, Wilmington DE 19807*

Florida			
FL	Apalachicola	Apalachicola Bay Chamber of Commerce	*17 Avenue E, Apalachicola FL 32320*
FL	Apollo Beach	Manatee Viewing Center Gift Shop	*6998 Dickman Rd, Apollo Beach FL 33572*
FL	Apopka	WEKIWA SPRINGS STATE PARK	*1800 Wekiwa Cir, Apopka FL 32712*
FL	Arcadia	Peace River Campground	*2998 FL-70, Arcadia FL 34266*
FL	Bay Lake	Disney Boardwalk Screen Door	*Boardwalk Hotel, Bay Lake FL 34747*
FL	Bay Lake	Disney's Animal Kingdom Theme Park	*Wildlife Express Train - Harambe, Bay Lake FL 34747*
FL	Bay Lake	Disney's BoardWalk Villas	*Boardwalk Hotel, Bay Lake FL 34747*
FL	Bay Lake	Disney's Caribbean Beach Resort	*Disney's Riviera Resort, Bay Lake FL 32830*
FL	Bay Lake	Disney's Grand Floridian Resort & Spa	*Disney's Grand Floridian Resort & Spa (Gold Launch), Bay Lake FL 32836*
FL	Bay Lake	Disneys Grand Floridian Resort & Spa	*Disney's Grand Floridian Resort & Spa, Bay Lake FL 32836*
FL	Bay Lake	Walt Disney World Resort	*9CPP+3F Bay Lake, Bay Lake FL 32836*
FL	Bay Lake	Walt Disney World, Boardwalk Inn Resort	*9C8W+43 Bay Lake, Bay Lake FL 34747*
FL	Boca Grande	Pink Pony Ice Cream Shop	*471 Park Ave, Boca Grande FL 33921*
FL	Bradenton Beach	Fish Hole Mini Golf	*117 Bridge St, Bradenton Beach FL 34217*
FL	Cape Canaveral	Carnival Cruise Line	*9245 Charles M Rowland Dr, Cape Canaveral FL 32920*
FL	Cape Canaveral	Disney Cruise Lines	*9155 Charles M Rowland Dr, Cape Canaveral FL 32920*
FL	Celebration	ESPN Wide World of Sports Complex	*8CQX+48 Celebration, Celebration FL 34747*

FL	Christmas	Jungle Adventures Nature Park and Zoo	*26205 E Colonial Dr, Christmas FL 32709*
FL	Clearwater	Clearwater Beach Pier 60	*1101 Pier 60, Clearwater FL 33767*
FL	Clearwater	Clearwater marine aquarium	*249 Windward Passage, Clearwater FL 33767*
FL	Clearwater	Sunsets At Pier 60	*1101 Pier 60, Clearwater FL 33767*
FL	Clermont	Show Case of Citrus	*5010 US-27, Clermont FL 34714*
FL	Cocoa Beach	Marlin's Bar & Grille	*401 Meade Ave, Cocoa Beach FL 32931*
FL	Cocoa Beach	Pelicans Bar & Grill	*401 Meade Ave, Cocoa Beach FL 32931*
FL	Cocoa Beach	Trader Ricky's Ice Cream	*401 Meade Ave, Cocoa Beach FL 32931*
FL	Crawfordville	Edward Ball Wakulla Springs State Park	*465 Wakulla Park Dr, Crawfordville FL 32327*
FL	Dania Beach	Bass Pro Shops	*220 Gulf Stream Way, Dania Beach FL 33004*
FL	Dania Beach	Jaxson's Ice Cream Parlour & Restaurant	*126 S Federal Hwy # 202, Dania Beach FL 33004*
FL	Davie	Flamingo Gardens	*3750 S Flamingo Rd, Davie FL 33330*
FL	Daytona Beach	Beach Bazaar	*203 N Atlantic Ave, Daytona Beach FL 32118*
FL	Daytona Beach	Beach Express	*101 S Atlantic Ave, Daytona Beach FL 32118*
FL	Daytona Beach	Big Shark	*2715 N Atlantic Ave, Daytona Beach FL 32118*
FL	Daytona Beach	Buccee's	*2340 Gateway N Dr, Daytona Beach FL 32117*
FL	Daytona Beach	Daytona 500 Experience	*1801 W International Speedway Blvd, Daytona Beach FL 32114*
FL	Daytona Beach	Museum of Arts and Sciences Daytona Beach	*352 S Nova Rd, Daytona Beach FL 32114*

FL	Daytona Beach	Ocean Walk	*250 N Atlantic Ave #131, Daytona Beach FL 32118*
FL	De Leon Springs	De Leon Springs State Park	*601 Ponce Deleon Blvd, De Leon Springs FL 32130*
FL	DeBary	Blue Spring State Park	*WMX5+HV DeBary, DeBary FL 32713*
FL	Delray Beach	The Girls Strawberry U-pick	*14466 S Military Trl, Delray Beach FL 33484*
FL	Destin	Bass Pro Shops	*Parking lot, Destin FL 32541*
FL	Destin	Harry T's Lighthouse	*34 Harbor Blvd #110, Destin FL 32541*
FL	Destin	McGuire's Irish Pub	*33 US-98, Destin FL 32541*
FL	Dunedin	Honeymoon Island State Park	*Honeymoon Island State Park, Dunedin FL 34698*
FL	Eglin Air Force Base	Air Force Armament Museum	*Building 2938, Eglin Air Force Base FL 32542*
FL	Fernandina Beach	Amelia Island Museum of History	*233 S 3rd St, Fernandina Beach FL 32034*
FL	Fernandina Beach	Corner-Copia	*212 Centre St, Fernandina Beach FL 32034*
FL	Fernandina Beach	Fort Clinch State Park	*2601 Atlantic Ave, Fernandina Beach FL 32034*
FL	Fort Lauderdale	Royal Caribbean Cruises Ltd.	*2025 Eller Dr, Fort Lauderdale FL 33316*
FL	Fort Myers	Bass Pro Shops	*10040 Gulf Center Dr, Fort Myers FL 33913*
FL	Fort Myers	Calusa Nature Center & Planetarium	*Iona House, Fort Myers FL 33905*
FL	Fort Myers	Edison & Ford Winter Estates	*Tickets & Museum Store, Fort Myers FL 33901*
FL	Fort Myers Beach	Cheap Beach Stuff	*320 San Carlos Blvd, Fort Myers Beach FL 33931*
FL	Fort Myers Beach	Shipwreck Motel	*245 San Carlos Blvd, Fort Myers Beach FL 33931*

FL	Fort Walton Beach	Gulfarium Marine Adventure Park	*1010 Miracle Strip Pkwy SE, Fort Walton Beach FL 32548*
FL	Gainesville	Florida Museum of Natural History	*Powell Hall, Gainesville FL 32608*
FL	Gainesville	Satchel's Pizza	*1800 NE 23rd Ave, Gainesville FL 32609*
FL	Gulf Breeze	Gulf Breeze Zoo	*5701 Gulf Breeze Pkwy, Gulf Breeze FL 32563*
FL	Homosassa	Ellie Schiller Homosassa Springs Wildlife State Park	*4150 S Suncoast Blvd, Homosassa FL 34446*
FL	Homosassa	Ellie Schiller Homosassa Springs Wildlife State Park West En	*9350 W Fishbowl Dr, Homosassa FL 34448*
FL	Islamorada	Bass Pro Shops	*81576 Overseas Hwy, Islamorada FL 33036*
FL	Islamorada	Florida National High Adventure Sea Base, Boy Scou	*73800 Overseas Hwy, Islamorada FL 33036*
FL	Jacksonville	Jacksonville Zoo and Gardens Entrance	*370 FL-105, Jacksonville FL 32218*
FL	Jacksonville	Jacksonville Zoo and Gardens Rear Gift Shop	*370 FL-105, Jacksonville FL 32218*
FL	Jacksonville	MOSH	*1051 Gulf Life Dr, Jacksonville FL 32207*
FL	Juno Beach	Loggerhead Marine Life Center	*14200 U.S. Hwy 1, Juno Beach FL 33408*
FL	Key Largo	Shell World Florida Keys	*97600 Overseas Hwy, Key Largo FL 33037*
FL	Key West	Conch Tour Train	*501 Front St, Key West FL 33040*
FL	Key West	Conch Tour Train Depot	*100 Duval St, Key West FL 33040*
FL	Key West	Key West Aquarium	*1 Whitehead St, Key West FL 33040*
FL	Key West	Mel Fisher Maritime Museum	*200 Greene St, Key West FL 33040*

FL	Key West	Turtle Cannery Museum	*901 Caroline St, Key West FL 33040*
FL	Kissimmee	(Old Town Leather Shop) Gavere Leather	*5770 W Irlo Bronson Memorial Hwy, Kissimmee FL 34746*
FL	Kissimmee	Black Market Minerals	*5770 W Irlo Bronson Memorial Hwy, Kissimmee FL 34746*
FL	Kissimmee	Blizzard Beach	*1675 Buena Vista Dr, Kissimmee FL 34747*
FL	Kissimmee	Disney's All-Star Movies Resort	*Cinema Hall, Kissimmee FL 34747*
FL	Kissimmee	Disney's All-Star Music Resort	*Disney's All-Star Music Resort, Kissimmee FL 34747*
FL	Kissimmee	Disney's All-Star Sports Resort	*Disney's All-Star Sports Resort, Kissimmee FL 34747*
FL	Kissimmee	Main Gate Flea Market	*5407 W Irlo Bronson Memorial Hwy, Kissimmee FL 34746*
FL	Kissimmee	Winter Summerland Miniature Golf	*1320 W Buena Vista Dr, Kissimmee FL 34747*
FL	Lake Buena Vista	Disney Springs, Marketplace Stage	*1503 C E, Lake Buena Vista FL 32830*
FL	Lake Buena Vista	Disney's Animal Kingdom Lodge	*2901 Osceola Pkwy, Lake Buena Vista FL 32830*
FL	Lake Buena Vista	Disney's Art of Animation Resort	*The Little Mermaid - Building 7, Lake Buena Vista FL 32830*
FL	Lake Buena Vista	Disney's Beach Club Resort	*Beach Club Resort, Lake Buena Vista FL 32830*
FL	Lake Buena Vista	Disney's Coronado Springs Resort	*1001 W Buena Vista Dr, Lake Buena Vista FL 32830*
FL	Lake Buena Vista	Disney's Days of Christmas	*Disney Springs, Lake Buena Vista FL 32830*
FL	Lake Buena Vista	Disney's Pin Traders	*1486 E Buena Vista Dr, Lake Buena Vista FL 32830*
FL	Lake Buena Vista	DisneyQuest Indoor Interactive Theme Park	*1486 E Buena Vista Dr, Lake Buena Vista FL 32830*
FL	Lake Buena Vista	Disneys Pop Century Resort	*1050 Century Dr, Lake Buena Vista FL 32807*

FL	Lake Buena Vista	Disneys Port Orleans Resort - Riverside	*1251 Riverside Dr, Lake Buena Vista FL 32830*
FL	Lake Buena Vista	Disneys Saratoga Springs Resort & Spa	*1960 Broadway, Lake Buena Vista FL 32830*
FL	Lake Buena Vista	Disneys Typhoon Lagoon Water Park	*Disney's Typhoon Lagoon Water Park, Lake Buena Vista FL 32830*
FL	Lake Buena Vista	Disneys Yacht Club Resort	*1700 Epcot Resorts Blvd, Lake Buena Vista FL 32830*
FL	Lake Buena Vista	Epcot	*200 Epcot Center Dr, Lake Buena Vista FL 32830*
FL	Lake Buena Vista	House of Blues Orlando	*1490 E Lake, Lake Buena Vista FL 32830*
FL	Lake Buena Vista	La Nouba Theater	*1478 Buena Vista Dr, Lake Buena Vista FL 32830*
FL	Lake Buena Vista	Magic Kingdom Park	*1365 Monorail Way, Lake Buena Vista FL 32830*
FL	Lake Buena Vista	Marvel Super Hero Headquarters	*1486 Buena Vista Dr, Lake Buena Vista FL 32830*
FL	Lake Buena Vista	Once Upon a Toy (store)	*1486 Buena Vista Dr, Lake Buena Vista FL 32830*
FL	Lake Buena Vista	Rainforest Cafe	*1520 Marketplace, Lake Buena Vista FL 32830*
FL	Lake Buena Vista	Star Wars Trading Post	*1770 E Buena Vista Dr, Lake Buena Vista FL 32830*
FL	Lake Buena Vista	Star Warsâ„¢ Galactic Outpost	*1486 East Buena Vista Drive, Lake Buena Vista FL 32830*
FL	Lake Buena Vista	T-Rex Cafe	*1780 E Buena Vista Dr, Lake Buena Vista FL 32830*
FL	Lake Buena Vista	Tinker Bell's Treasures	*1180 Seven Seas Drive, Lake Buena Vista FL 32830*
FL	Lake Buena Vista	World of Disney Store	*Marketplace, Lake Buena Vista FL 32830*
FL	Marianna	Florida Caverns State Park	*RQ79+7H Marianna, Marianna FL 32448*
FL	Melbourne	Brevard Zoo	*8225 N Wickham Rd, Melbourne FL 32940*

FL	Merritt Island	Kennedy Space Center Visitor Complex	*405 Nasa Pkwy W, Merritt Island FL 32953*
FL	Miami	Bubba Gump Shrimp Co.	*401 Biscayne Blvd, Miami FL 33132*
FL	Miami	Jungle Island	*1111 Parrot Jungle Trail, Miami FL 33132*
FL	Miami	Miami Seaquarium	*PRMP+63 Miami, Miami FL 33149*
FL	Miami	Norwegian Cruise Line	*1509 N Cruise Blvd, Miami FL 33132*
FL	Miami	Norwegian Cruise Line	*1509 N Cruise Blvd, Miami FL 33132*
FL	Naples	Naples Zoo at Caribbean Gardens	*1590 Goodlette-Frank Rd, Naples FL 34102*
FL	Naples	Tin City Shops	*1200 5th Ave S, Naples FL 34102*
FL	Ocala	Don Garlits Museum of Drag Racing	*13700 SW 17th Ct, Ocala FL 34491*
FL	Ocala	Ocala/Marion County Visitors and Convention Bureau	*123 FL-40, Ocala FL 34471*
FL	Orlando	Aquatica, SeaWorld's Waterpark Orlando	*5800 Water Play Way, Orlando FL 32821*
FL	Orlando	Disney's Contemporary Resort	*Monorail Station - Disney's Contemporary Resort, Orlando FL 32836*
FL	Orlando	Disney's Earport @ MCO (Orlando International Airport)	*9450 Jeff Fuqua Blvd, Orlando FL 32827*
FL	Orlando	Disney's Hollywood Studios	*14351 Seth Rd, Orlando FL 32824*
FL	Orlando	Disney's Polynesian Village Resort	*1600 Seven Seas Drive, Orlando FL 32830*
FL	Orlando	Disneys Fantasia Gardens Miniature Golf Course	*1209 Epcot Resorts Blvd, Orlando FL 32830*
FL	Orlando	Disneys Old Key West Resort	*Building 27, Orlando FL 32830*

FL	Orlando	Gatorland	*14501 S Orange Blossom Trl, Orlando FL 32837*
FL	Orlando	Goofy's Candy Company	*1772 E Buena Vista Dr, Orlando FL 32830*
FL	Orlando	Machine my test	*9412 Jeff Fuqua Blvd, Orlando FL 32827*
FL	Orlando	Madame Tussauds Orlando	*8361 International Dr, Orlando FL 32819*
FL	Orlando	One Fat Frog Penny Press	*2416 Sand Lake Rd, Orlando FL 32809*
FL	Orlando	Orlando Science Center	*777 E Princeton St, Orlando FL 32803*
FL	Orlando	Orlando Science Center	*777 E Princeton St, Orlando FL 32803*
FL	Orlando	Polynesian Resort	*1600 Seven Seas Drive, Orlando FL 32830*
FL	Orlando	Rainforest Cafe	*Rainforest Cafe - Disney Animal Kingdom, Orlando FL 32830*
FL	Orlando	Ripley's Believe It or Not - Orlando	*8245 International Dr, Orlando FL 32819*
FL	Orlando	SEA LIFE Orlando Aquarium	*8449 International Dr, Orlando FL 32819*
FL	Orlando	Sea World Adventure Park	*7007 Sea World Dr, Orlando FL 32821*
FL	Orlando	SKELETONS: Museum Of Osteology	*8457 International Dr, Orlando FL 32819*
FL	Orlando	The Campsites at Disneys Fort Wilderness Resort	*Disney's Fort Wilderness Resort and Campground Entrance, Orlando FL 32836*
FL	Orlando	The Wheel at ICON Parkâ„¢ (Orlando Eye)	*8401 International Dr, Orlando FL 32819*
FL	Orlando	Universal Studios	*5000 Universal Studios Plaza, Orlando FL 32819*
FL	Orlando	Universal Studios CityWalk - Bubba Gump Shrimp Company	*6000 Universal Blvd Suite 735, Orlando FL 32819*

FL	Orlando	Universal Studios CityWalk - Hard Rock Cafe	*6050 Universal Blvd, Orlando FL 32819*
FL	Orlando	Universal Studios CityWalk - Margaritaville	*6000 Universal Studios Plaza #704, Orlando FL 32819*
FL	Orlando	Universal Studios CityWalk - Universal Studio Store	*6000 Universal Blvd, Orlando FL 32819*
FL	Orlando	Universal Studios CityWalk - Universalâ„¢ Cinemark	*6000 Universal Blvd, Orlando FL 32819*
FL	Orlando	Universal Studios CityWalk - Voodoo Doughnut	*6000 Universal Blvd, Orlando FL 32819*
FL	Orlando	Universal Studios Store	*6000 Universal Blvd, Orlando FL 32819*
FL	Orlando	Universal Studios Store at Universal CityWalk Orlando	*6000 Universal Blvd, Orlando FL 32819*
FL	Orlando	Universal's Islands of Adventure	*FGCH+F9 Orlando, Orlando FL 32819*
FL	Orlando	Wilderness Lodge Resort	*901 Timberline Dr, Orlando FL 32830*
FL	Orlando	WonderWorks	*9067 International Dr, Orlando FL 32819*
FL	Palm Beach	Henry Morrison Flagler Museum	*1 Whitehall Way, Palm Beach FL 33480*
FL	Panama City Beach	Fun land	*9954 S Thomas Dr, Panama City Beach FL 32408*
FL	Panama City Beach	Gulf World Marine Park	*15412 Front Beach Rd, Panama City Beach FL 32413*
FL	Panama City Beach	Pineapple Willy's Restaurant	*9875 S Thomas Dr, Panama City Beach FL 32408*
FL	Panama City Beach	Pirates Island Adventure Golf	*9518 Front Beach Rd, Panama City Beach FL 32407*
FL	Panama City Beach	Ripley's Believe It or Not! Odditorium	*9907 Front Beach Rd, Panama City Beach FL 32407*

FL	Panama City Beach	Shell Port	*9949 Thomas Dr, Panama City Beach FL 32408*
FL	Panama City Beach	Zoltar Penny Press	*701 S Pier Park Dr #107, Panama City Beach FL 32413*
FL	Pensacola	National Naval Aviation Museum	*1750 Radford Blvd, Pensacola FL 32508*
FL	Pensacola	Pensacola Welcome Center	*42 E Cervantes St, Pensacola FL 32501*
FL	Pensacola	Visit Pensacola Welcome Center	*1401 E Gregory St, Pensacola FL 32502*
FL	Plant City	Dinosaur World	*5145 Harvey Tew Rd, Plant City FL 33565*
FL	Polk City	Fantasy of Flight	*1400 Broadway Blvd SE, Polk City FL 33868*
FL	Ponce Inlet	Ponce de Leon Inlet Lighthouse & Museum	*Kay and Ayres Davies Lighthouse Park, Ponce Inlet FL 32127*
FL	Port Orange	Racing's North Turn Bar	*4511 S Atlantic Ave, Port Orange FL 32127*
FL	Sarasota	Beach Bazaar	*5216 Ocean Blvd, Sarasota FL 34242*
FL	Sarasota	Mote Marine Laboratory	*1600 Ken Thompson Pkwy, Sarasota FL 34236*
FL	Sarasota	Sarasota Jungle Gardens	*Sarasota Jungle Gardens, Sarasota FL 34234*
FL	Sky Lake	Crayola Experience, Orlando FL	*CJV5+X7 Sky Lake, Sky Lake FL 32809*
FL	Sky Lake	M&M's World	*CJV4+Q8 Sky Lake, Sky Lake FL 32809*
FL	Spring Hill	Weeki Wachee Springs State Park	*6131 Commercial Way, Spring Hill FL 34606*
FL	St. Augustine	Anastasia State Park	*VPPF+89 Anastasia, St. Augustine FL 32080*
FL	St. Augustine	Coat of Arms Shoppe	*113 St George St, St. Augustine FL 32084*
FL	St. Augustine	Flagler College	*74 King St, St. Augustine FL 32084*

FL	St. Augustine	Heritage Walk Shopping Village	*57 Treasury St, St. Augustine FL 32084*
FL	St. Augustine	Marineland Dolphin Adventure	*9600 N Ocean Shore Blvd, St. Augustine FL 32080*
FL	St. Augustine	Old City Gates	*102 Orange St, St. Augustine FL 32084*
FL	St. Augustine	Old Jail	*167 San Marco Ave, St. Augustine FL 32084*
FL	St. Augustine	Ponce de Leon's Fountain of Youth Archaeological	*11 Magnolia Ave, St. Augustine FL 32084*
FL	St. Augustine	Potter's Wax Museum	*31 Orange St, St. Augustine FL 32084*
FL	St. Augustine	Ripley's Believe It or Not	*19 San Marco Ave, St. Augustine FL 32084*
FL	St. Augustine	St George St & Orange St	*102 Orange St, St. Augustine FL 32084*
FL	St. Augustine	St. Augustine Alligator Farm Zoological Park	*999 Anastasia Blvd, St. Augustine FL 32080*
FL	St. Augustine	St. Augustine Lighthouse	*St. Augustine Lighthouse, St. Augustine FL 32080*
FL	St. Augustine	St. Augustine Visitor Information Center	*10 S Castillo Dr, St. Augustine FL 32084*
FL	St. Augustine	St. Georges Row Shops	*105 St George St, St. Augustine FL 32084*
FL	Sunrise	Rainforest Cafe	*12801 W Sunrise Blvd, Sunrise FL 33323*
FL	Tallahassee	Museum of Florida History	*R.A. Gray Building, Tallahassee FL 32399*
FL	Tallahassee	Tallahassee Museum	*3945 Museum Rd, Tallahassee FL 32310*
FL	Tampa	Busch Gardens	*3000 E Busch Blvd, Tampa FL 33612*
FL	Tampa	Florida Aquarium	*701 Channelside Dr, Tampa FL 33602*
FL	Tampa	Florida Aquarium (token machine)	*701 Channelside Dr, Tampa FL 33602*

FL	Tampa	Glazer Children's Museum	*110 W Gasparilla Plaza, Tampa FL 33602*
FL	Tampa	Museum Of Science & Industry	*4801 E Fowler Ave, Tampa FL 33617*
FL	Tampa	Tampa's Lowry Park Zoo Machine # 9	*1311 W Sligh Ave, Tampa FL 33604*
FL	Tampa	The Florida Aquarium	*701 Channelside Dr, Tampa FL 33602*
FL	Tarpon Springs	Aquarium Tarpon Springs	*850 Dodecanese Blvd, Tarpon Springs FL 34689*
FL	The Acreage	Lion Country Safari	*2000 Lion Country Safari Rd, The Acreage FL 33470*
FL	Titusville	Apollo/Saturn V Center	*Kennedy Pkwy N, Titusville FL 32780*
FL	Upper Grand Lagoon	ZooWorld Zoological and Botanical Conservatory	*Front Beach Rd. & Allison Ave., Upper Grand Lagoon FL 32408*
FL	Vero Beach	Disney's Vero Beach Resort	*1450 W Island Club Square, Vero Beach FL 32963*
FL	West Palm Beach	Manatee Lagoon	*5915 N Flagler Dr, West Palm Beach FL 33407*
FL	West Palm Beach	Palm Beach Zoo & Conservation Society	*SUMMIT BLVD at DREHER TRL N, West Palm Beach FL 33405*
FL	West Palm Beach	South Florida Science Center and Aquarium	*Estación tren de Miami, West Palm Beach FL 33401*

Georgia			
GA	Acworth	Cabela's	*152 Northpoint Pkwy, Acworth GA 30102*
GA	Albany	All American Fun Park	*2608 N Slappey Blvd, Albany GA 31701*
GA	Albany	Flint RiverQuarium	*101 Pine Ave, Albany GA 31701*
GA	Atlanta	Bodies The Exhibition Atlanta	*264 19th St NW Suite #2220, Atlanta GA 30363*
GA	Atlanta	CNN Center	*190 Marietta St NW, Atlanta GA 30303*
GA	Atlanta	Fernbank Museum of Natural History	*767 Clifton Rd N E, Atlanta GA 30307*
GA	Atlanta	LEGOLAND Discovery Center Atlanta	*3500 Peachtree Rd NE, Atlanta GA 30326*
GA	Atlanta	Only You Tattoo	*401 Memorial Dr SE k, Atlanta GA 30312*
GA	Atlanta	Zoo Atlanta	*800 Cherokee Ave SE, Atlanta GA 30308*
GA	Augusta	Cabela's	*833 Cabela Dr, Augusta GA 30909*
GA	Augusta	Georgia Visitor Information Center, Augusta	*18 Park Pl Cir, Augusta GA 30909*
GA	Austell	Six Flags Over Georgia	*275 Riverside Pkwy, Austell GA 30168*
GA	Blue Ridge	Blue Ridge Scenic Railway	*241 Depot St, Blue Ridge GA 30513*
GA	Calhoun	Buc-ee's	*430 Union Grove Rd SE, Calhoun GA 30701*
GA	Cartersville	Booth Western Art Museum	*501 N Museum Dr, Cartersville GA 30120*
GA	Cartersville	Tellus Science Museum	*100 Tellus Dr, Cartersville GA 30120*
GA	Columbus	Giant Screen Theater at the National Infantry Muse	*1775 Legacy Way, Columbus GA 31903*

GA	Columbus	National Civil War Naval Museum	*1002 Victory Dr, Columbus GA 31901*
GA	Dahlonega	Consolidated Gold Mine	*185 Consolidated Gold Mine Rd, Dahlonega GA 30533*
GA	Dahlonega	Dahlonega General Store	*200 Choice Ave, Dahlonega GA 30533*
GA	Dahlonega	Dahlonega Gold Museum Historic Site	*1 Public Square N, Dahlonega GA 30533*
GA	Dawsonville	Amicalola Falls State Park	*418 Amicalola Falls State Park Rd, Dawsonville GA 30534*
GA	Dawsonville	Amicalola Falls State Park & Lodge	*418 Amicalola Falls State Park Rd, Dawsonville GA 30534*
GA	Decatur	Fernbank Science Center	*144 Heaton Park Dr, Decatur GA 30030*
GA	Duluth	Bass Pro Shops	*XWJ8+F9 Duluth, Duluth GA 30043*
GA	Duluth	Southeastern Railway Museum	*3595 Buford Hwy, Duluth GA 30096*
GA	Emerson	Red Top Mountain State Park Visitors Center	*47XW+47 Emerson, Emerson GA 30121*
GA	Fort Valley	Buc-ee's Warner Robins	*7001 Russell Pkwy, Fort Valley GA 31030*
GA	Hampton	Atlanta Motor Speedway	*1500 Tara Pl, Hampton GA 30228*
GA	Hiawassee	Creekside General Store	*1710 Bearmeat Rd, Hiawassee GA 30546*
GA	Kennesaw	Southern Museum of Civil War and Locomotive History	*2829 Cherokee St NW, Kennesaw GA 30144*
GA	Lake Park	Georgia Visitor Information Center	*I-75, Lake Park GA 31636*
GA	Lakeview	Lake Winnepesaukah Amusement Park	*XQG3+HM Lakeview, Lakeview GA 30741*
GA	Lavonia	Georgia Welcome Center i85	*938 Co Rd 84, Lavonia GA 30553*
GA	Lookout Mountain	Rock City Gardens	*1400 Patten Rd, Lookout Mountain GA 30750*

GA	Macon	Bass Pro Shops	*5000 Bass Pro Blvd, Macon GA 31210*
GA	Macon	Museum of Arts and Sciences	*Sweet Gum Trail, Macon GA 31210*
GA	Marietta	Kennesaw Mountain National Battlefield Park	*XC23+82 Marietta, Marietta GA 30064*
GA	Marietta	Six Flags White Water	*250 Cobb Pkwy N, Marietta GA 30062*
GA	McCaysville	Nature's Collectibles	*6 Toccoa Ave, McCaysville GA 30555*
GA	Plains	Plain Peanuts	*231 Main St, Plains GA 31780*
GA	Ringgold	Cabela's	*350 Cobb Pkwy, Ringgold GA 30736*
GA	Ringgold	Georgia Visitor Information Center	*2726 I-75, Ringgold GA 30736*
GA	Rising Fawn	Cloudland Canyon State Park	*122 Cloudland Canyon Park Rd, Rising Fawn GA 30738*
GA	Savannah	Bass Pro Shops	*14045 Abercorn St #1503, Savannah GA 31419*
GA	Savannah	Cinnamon Bear Country Store	*205 E River St, Savannah GA 31401*
GA	Savannah	Cinnamon Bear Country Store	*33 Jefferson St, Savannah GA 31401*
GA	Savannah	Fannies Your Aunt	*305 E River St, Savannah GA 31401*
GA	Savannah	Five & Dime General Store	*417 E River St, Savannah GA 31401*
GA	Savannah	Georgia Welcome Center Southbound	*I-95, Savannah GA 31408*
GA	Savannah	Leopold 's Ice Cream	*210 E Broughton St, Savannah GA 31401*
GA	Savannah	Mini Leopold's Ice Cream	*Savannah/Hilton Head International Airport (SAV), Savannah GA 31408*
GA	Savannah	River Street Sweets	*13 E River St, Savannah GA 31401*

GA	Savannah	The Pirates House	*20 E Broad St, Savannah GA 31401*
GA	Savannah	True Grits	*105 E River St, Savannah GA 31401*
GA	St. Marys	Georgia Visitor Information Center	*100 St Marys Rd, St. Marys GA 31558*
GA	St. Simons Island	Frederica Station	*209 Mallery St, St. Simons Island GA 31522*
GA	Stone Mountain	Escape the Netherworld	*2076 W Park Pl. Blvd, Stone Mountain GA 30087*
GA	Stone Mountain	Stone Mountain Park	*RV33+GR Stone Mountain, Stone Mountain GA 30087*
GA	Stone Mountain	Stone Mountain Sky Ride - BOTTOM OF RIDE	*2003 Robert E Lee Blvd, Stone Mountain GA 30086*
GA	Stone Mountain	Stone Mountain SkyRide - TOP OF RIDE	*Confederate Memorial Carving, Stone Mountain GA 30087*
GA	Tallapoosa	Georgia Visitor Information Center	*MMHH+4W Tallapoosa, Tallapoosa GA 30182*
GA	Tallapoosa	Georgia Visitor Information Center - Tallapoosa	*I-20, Tallapoosa GA 30176*
GA	Tallulah Falls	Tallulah Gorge Interpretive Center	*338 Jane Hurt Yarn Dr, Tallulah Falls GA 30573*
GA	Thomasville	Illuminated Wooden Cabinet	*101 N Broad St, Thomasville GA 31792*
GA	Thomasville	The Big Oak	*119 N Broad St, Thomasville GA 31792*
GA	Tybee Island	Island Style	*502 1st St, Tybee Island GA 31328*
GA	Tybee Island	Tybee Island Lighthouse and Museum	*30 Meddin Dr, Tybee Island GA 31328*
GA	Tybee Island	Waves Beach Wear Surf & Gifts	*704 1st St, Tybee Island GA 31328*
GA	Waycross	Okefenokee Swamp Park	*5700 Okefenokee Swamp Park Rd, Waycross GA 31503*
GA	West Point	West Point Lake	*500 Resource Management Rd, West Point GA 31833*

Hawaii			
HI	Haleiwa	Aloha General Store	*66-250 Kamehameha Hwy # G130, Haleiwa HI 96712*
HI	Haleiwa	Waimea Valley	*43 Waimea Valley Trail, Haleiwa HI 96712*
HI	Honolulu	Aloha Tower Marketplace?Navatek Cruises	*1 Aloha Tower Dr, Honolulu HI 96813*
HI	Honolulu	Battleship Missouri Memorial	*63 Cowpens St, Honolulu HI 96818*
HI	Honolulu	Honolulu Zoo	*2760 Monsarrat Ave, Honolulu HI 96815*
HI	Honolulu	Iolani Palace	*364 S King St, Honolulu HI 96813*
HI	Honolulu	Pacific Aviation Museum Pearl Harbor	*319 Lexington Blvd, Honolulu HI 96818*
HI	Honolulu	Rainbow Drive-In	*3308 Kanaina Ave, Honolulu HI 96815*
HI	Honolulu	The Navy Exchange Mall at Pearl Harbor	*4725 Bougainville Dr, Honolulu HI 96818*
HI	Honolulu	Waikiki Food Pantry	*Perry's smorgy restaurants in Honolulu, Honolulu HI 96815*
HI	Honolulu	Waiola Shave Ice	*2135 Waiola St, Honolulu HI 96826*
HI	Honolulu	World War II Valor in the Pacific National Monumen	*1 Arizona Memorial Pl, Honolulu HI 96818*
HI	Kahului	Kahului Airport	*VHW8+PR Kahului, Kahului HI 96732*
HI	Kalaheo	Kauai Coffee Company	*870 Halewili Rd, Kalaheo HI 96741*
HI	Kalaheo	The Right Slice, Kauai Fresh Pies	*2-2459 Kaumualii Hwy, Kalaheo HI 96741*
HI	Kaneohe	Coral Kingdom Inc	*49-140 Kamehameha Hwy, Kaneohe HI 96744*
HI	Kaneohe	Kualoa Ranch & Zipline	*49-049 Kamehameha Hwy, Kaneohe HI 96744*

HI	Kaneohe	The Byodo-In Temple	*Byodo-In Temple, Kaneohe HI 96744*
HI	Kapolei	Wet'n'Wild Hawaii	*400 Farrington Hwy, Kapolei HI 96707*
HI	Lahaina	Bubba Gump Shrimp Co.	*889 Front St, Lahaina HI 96761*
HI	Lahaina	Olowalu General Store	*820 Olowalu Village Rd, Lahaina HI 96761*
HI	Lahaina	Whalers Village	*2435 Kaanapali Pkwy, Lahaina HI 96761*
HI	Laie	Polynesian Cultural Center	*5 Iosepa St, Laie HI 96762*
HI	Lihue	Lihue Airport	*3901 Mokulele Loop, Lihue HI 96766*
HI	Pāhoa	Volcano House	*1 Crater Rim Drive, Pāhoa HI 96718*
HI	Volcano	Akatsuka Orchid Gardens	*11-3051 Old Volcano Rd, Volcano HI 96785*
HI	Wahiawa	Dole Plantation	*64-1550 Kamehameha Hwy, Wahiawa HI 96786*
HI	Wailuku	Maui Ocean Center	*192 Maalaea Rd, Wailuku HI 96793*
HI	Wailuku	Maui Tropical Plantation	*1670 HI-30, Wailuku HI 96793*
HI	Waimanalo	Sea Life Park Hawaii	*41-202 Kalaniana'ole Hwy, Waimanalo HI 96795*
HI	Waimea	Kokee Natural History Museum	*3600 Kokee Rd, Waimea HI 96796*

Iowa			
IA	Altoona	Adventureland	*3200 Adventureland Dr, Altoona IA 50009*
IA	Amana	Amana Colonies - General Store	*4423 220th Trail, Amana IA 52203*
IA	Ankeny	Saylorville Lake Visitor Center	*8200 NW 37th St, Ankeny IA 50023*
IA	Arnolds Park	Arnolds Park	*200 W Broadway St, Arnolds Park IA 51331*
IA	Bettendorf	Family Museum	*2900 Learning Campus Dr, Bettendorf IA 52722*
IA	Boone	Boone & Scenic Valley Railroad	*225 10th St, Boone IA 50036*
IA	Boone	Boone & Scenic Valley Railroad and James H. Andrew	*225 10th St, Boone IA 50036*
IA	Burlington	Kenny's Roller Ranch	*8985 Koestner St, Burlington IA 52601*
IA	Center Point	Center Point Foods	*800 Ford Ln, Center Point IA 52213*
IA	Council Bluffs	Bass Pro Shops Outdoor World	*2901 Bass Pro Dr, Council Bluffs IA 51501*
IA	Council Bluffs	Union Pacific Railroad Museum	*200 Pearl St, Council Bluffs IA 51503*
IA	Davenport	Putnam Museum & Science Center	*1717 W 12th St, Davenport IA 52804*
IA	Des Moines	Blank Park Zoo	*7401 SW 9th St, Des Moines IA 50315*
IA	Des Moines	Blank Park Zoo Gift Shop	*7401 SW 9th St, Des Moines IA 50315*
IA	Des Moines	Iowa Hall of Pride	*700 3rd St, Des Moines IA 50309*
IA	Des Moines	Iowa State Fair	*3000 E Grand Ave, Des Moines IA 50317*
IA	Des Moines	The Wyoming Territorial Prison State Historic Site	*1111 6th Ave, Des Moines IA 50314*

IA	Dubuque	Crystal Lake Cave	*6686 Crystal Lake Cave Rd, Dubuque IA 52003*
IA	Dubuque	National Mississippi River Museum & Aquarium	*350 E 3rd St, Dubuque IA 52001*
IA	Iowa City	University of Iowa Museum of Natural History	*17 N. Clinton St., Iowa City IA 52240*
IA	Marion	Hills Bank and Trust	*3207 7th Ave, Marion IA 52302*
IA	Mount Pleasant	Midwest Old Threshers Heritage Museum	*2438 S Locust St, Mount Pleasant IA 52641*
IA	Oskaloosa	Penn Central Mall	*200 High Ave W # 7, Oskaloosa IA 52577*
IA	Prairie City	Neal Smith National Wildlife Refuge	*12230 S 102nd Ave W, Prairie City IA 50228*
IA	Urbandale	Living History Farm	*11121 Hickman Rd, Urbandale IA 50322*
IA	Walcott	Iowa 80 trucking museum	*505 Sterling Dr, Walcott IA 52773*
IA	Walcott	Iowa 80 Truckstop	*755 W Iowa 80 Rd, Walcott IA 52773*
IA	Walcott	Worlds Largest Truck Stop	*103 S Main St, Walcott IA 52773*
IA	Winterset	John Wayne birthplace museum	*205 S John Wayne Dr, Winterset IA 50273*

Idaho			
ID	Ammon	Cabela's	*3693 S 25th E, Ammon ID 83406*
ID	Ammon	Cabela's	*3693 S 25th E, Ammon ID 83406*
ID	Athol	Silverwood Theme Park	*5787 E Bunco Rd, Athol ID 83801*
ID	Blackfoot	Idaho Potato Museum	*130 NW Main St, Blackfoot ID 83221*
ID	Blaine County	Craters of the Moon National Monument & Preserve	*85M86F4X+8W, Blaine County ID*
ID	Boise	Aquarium of Boise	*64 N Cole Rd, Boise ID 83704*
ID	Boise	Goody's Soda Fountain	*1502 N 13th St, Boise ID 83702*
ID	Boise	MK Nature Center (Idaho Fish and Game)	*MK Nature Center - Idaho Fish and Game, Boise ID 83712*
ID	Boise	Pojos Family Fun Center	*7736 Fairview Ave, Boise ID 83704*
ID	Boise	Zoo Boise	*355 Julia Davis Dr, Boise ID 83702*
ID	Caldwell	Babby Farms	*5900 El Paso Rd, Caldwell ID 83607*
ID	Coeur d'Alene	Memory Lane Gems	*210 E Sherman Ave Unit 161, Coeur d'Alene ID 83814*
ID	Coeur d'Alene	Museum of North Idaho	*115 Northwest Blvd, Coeur d'Alene ID 83814*
ID	Harrison	Gozzer Ranch Golf & Lake Club	*5854 S Grainger Ct, Harrison ID 83833*
ID	Idaho Falls	Idaho Falls Zoo at Tautphaus Park	*425 Soft Ball Dr, Idaho Falls ID 83402*
ID	Idaho Falls	Idaho Falls Zoo at Tautphaus Park	*425 Soft Ball Dr, Idaho Falls ID 83402*
ID	Idaho Falls	Museum of Idaho	*200 N Eastern Ave, Idaho Falls ID 83402*
ID	Montpelier	National Oregon/California Trail Center	*320 N 4th St, Montpelier ID 83254*
ID	Post Falls	Cabela's	*101 N Cabela Way, Post Falls ID 83854*
ID	Rexburg	Yellowstone Bear World	*6010 S 4300 W, Rexburg ID 83440*

ID	Sandpoint	Cedar Street Bridge Public Market	*334 N 1st Ave #105A, Sandpoint ID 83864*
ID	Stanley	Redfish Lake Lodge	*405 Redfish Ldg Rd, Stanley ID 83278*
ID	Twin Falls	Herrett Center	*315 Falls Ave, Twin Falls ID 83301*
ID	Twin Falls	Magic Valley Regional Airport	*FGJ7+QH Twin Falls, Twin Falls ID 83301*
ID	Twin Falls	Shoshone Falls on the Snake River	*3300 Shoshone Falls Grade Rd, Twin Falls ID 83301*
ID	Wallace	The Center of the Universe	*631699 The Harry F. Magnuson Wy, Wallace ID 83873*

Illinois			
IL	Amboy	O'Connell's Yogi Bear Park	*970 Green Wing Rd, Amboy IL 61310*
IL	Arcola	Rockome Garden	*127a N Co Rd 425E, Arcola IL 61910*
IL	Arcola	Rockome Garden Foods	*127a N Co Rd 425E, Arcola IL 61910*
IL	Aurora	Phillips Park Zoo	*1000 Ray Moses Dr, Aurora IL 60505*
IL	Aurora	Phillips Park Zoo	*901 Ray Moses Dr, Aurora IL 60505*
IL	Bishop Hill	Bishop Hill Colony Store	*302 E Main St, Bishop Hill IL 61419*
IL	Bloomington	Grady's Family Fun Park	*1501 Morrissey Dr, Bloomington IL 61701*
IL	Bloomington	Grady's Family Fun Park, Morrissey Drive, Blooming	*1501 Morrissey Dr, Bloomington IL 61701*
IL	Bloomington	McLean County Museum of History	*200 N Main St, Bloomington IL 61701*
IL	Bloomington	McLean County Museum of History, North Main Street	*200 N Main St, Bloomington IL 61701*
IL	Bloomington	Miller Park Zoo	*911 W Wood St, Bloomington IL 61701*
IL	Bloomington	Miller Park Zoo	*Miller Park Zoo, Bloomington IL 61701*
IL	Bolingbrook	Bass Pro Shop Outdoor World	*709 Janes Ave, Bolingbrook IL 60440*
IL	Bolingbrook	Bass Pro Shops	*709 Janes Ave, Bolingbrook IL 60440*
IL	Brookfield	Brookfield Zoo	*8400 31st St, Brookfield IL 60513*
IL	Chester	Chester Illinois Welcome Center	*10 Bridge Bypass Rd, Chester IL 62233*
IL	Chicago	Adler Planetarium	*1300 S DuSable Lake Shore Dr, Chicago IL 60605*

IL	Chicago	Chicago Children's Museum	*700 E Grand Ave, Chicago IL 60611*
IL	Chicago	Chicago Sports Museum	*835 Michigan Ave # 209, Chicago IL 60611*
IL	Chicago	Chicago Sports Museum	*875 N Michigan Ave # 1351, Chicago IL 60611*
IL	Chicago	Chicago Sports Museum Store	*835 N Michigan Ave, Chicago IL 60611*
IL	Chicago	Harry Caray's Tavern	*Navy pier, Chicago IL 60611*
IL	Chicago	John Hancock Center	*875 N Michigan Ave # 1351, Chicago IL 60611*
IL	Chicago	Lincoln Park Zoo	*2101 N Lincoln Park W, Chicago IL 60614*
IL	Chicago	Lincoln Park Zoo	*2234 N Cannon Dr, Chicago IL 60614*
IL	Chicago	Museum of Science and Industry	*5700 S DuSable Lake Shore Dr, Chicago IL 60637*
IL	Chicago	Museum of Science and Industry Chicago	*5700 S DuSable Lake Shore Dr, Chicago IL 60637*
IL	Chicago	Shedd Aquarium	*1200 S DuSable Lake Shore Dr, Chicago IL 60605*
IL	Chicago	Shedd Aquarium	*1200 S DuSable Lake Shore Dr, Chicago IL 60605*
IL	Chicago	Shedd Aquarium	*1200 S DuSable Lake Shore Dr, Chicago IL 60605*
IL	Chicago	Sports World Chicago, North Clark Street, Chicago,	*1045 W Addison St, Chicago IL 60613*
IL	Chicago	The Field Museum	*Field Museum, Chicago IL 60605*
IL	Chicago	Wild Things gift shop at Lincoln Park Zoo	*2234 N Cannon Dr, Chicago IL 60614*
IL	Chicago	Wrigley Field	*1060 W Addison St, Chicago IL 60613*
IL	Chicago	Wrigley Field, West Addison Street, Chicago, IL, U	*1060 W Addison St, Chicago IL 60613*

IL	Coal Valley	Niabi Zoo	*13010 Niabi Zoo Rd, Coal Valley IL 61240*
IL	Collinsville	Cahokia Mounds Museum Society	*30 Ramey St, Collinsville IL 62234*
IL	Decatur	Children's Museum of Illinois	*55 S Country Club Rd, Decatur IL 62521*
IL	Decatur	Scovill Children's Zoo	*71 S Country Club Rd, Decatur IL 62521*
IL	Decatur	Scovill Zoo	*71 S Country Club Rd, Decatur IL 62521*
IL	Dixon	John Deere Historic Site, South Clinton Street, Di	*8334 S Clinton St, Dixon IL 61021*
IL	East Dundee	Sants's Village Azoosment Park	*601 Dundee Ave, East Dundee IL 60118*
IL	East Moline	John Deere	*GHG7+MV East Moline, East Moline IL 61244*
IL	East Moline	John Deere Harvester Works, 13th Avenue, East Moli	*GHG7+MV East Moline, East Moline IL 61244*
IL	Edwards	Wildlife Prairie Park	*P7M4+Q9 Edwards, Edwards IL 61528*
IL	Edwards	Wildlife Prairie Park -	*P7M4+Q9 Edwards, Edwards IL 61528*
IL	Glenview	The Grove	*The Grove, Glenview IL 60025*
IL	Grayslake	Lake County Fair Association	*1060 E Peterson Rd, Grayslake IL 60030*
IL	Gurnee	Great wolf lodge Indoor Waterpark Resort	*1700 Nations Dr, Gurnee IL 60031*
IL	Gurnee	Rainforest Cafe	*6170 W Grand Ave, Gurnee IL 60031*
IL	Gurnee	Six Flags Great America	*1 Great America Parkway, Gurnee IL 60031*
IL	Gurnee	TILT Studio Family Entertainment Center & Rink Sid	*6152 Grand Ave, Gurnee IL 60031*

IL	Gurnee	Tilt Studio Gurnee	*6152 Grand Ave, Gurnee IL 60031*
IL	Hoffman Estates	Cabela's	*5225 Prairie Stone Pkwy, Hoffman Estates IL 60192*
IL	Homer Glen	Bengston's Pumpkin Farm	*13341 W 151st St, Homer Glen IL 60491*
IL	Homer Glen	Bengtson's Pumpkin Farm and Fall Fest	*13341 W 151st St, Homer Glen IL 60491*
IL	Homer Glen	Konow's Corn Maze	*16849 S Cedar Rd, Homer Glen IL 60491*
IL	Homer Glen	Konow's Corn Maze, South Cedar Road, Homer Glen, I	*16849 S Cedar Rd, Homer Glen IL 60491*
IL	Karbers Ridge	Garden of the Gods Outpost	*281 Karbers Ridge Rd, Karbers Ridge IL 62955*
IL	Makanda	Makanda Boardwalk	*520 Makanda Rd Suite 1, Makanda IL 62958*
IL	Makanda	Makanda Trading Company	*520 Makanda Rd Ste. #3, Makanda IL 62958*
IL	Marion	17th Street Barbecue	*2700 17th St, Marion IL 62959*
IL	Marion	17th Street Barbecue, 17th Street, Marion, IL, Uni	*2700 17th St, Marion IL 62959*
IL	Metropolis	The Super Man Museum	*523 Market St, Metropolis IL 62960*
IL	Metropolis	The Superman Museum	*517 Market St, Metropolis IL 62960*
IL	Moline	John Deere Pavilion	*1400 River Dr, Moline IL 61265*
IL	Naperville	Naper Settlement	*523 S Webster St, Naperville IL 60540*
IL	Naperville	Naper Settlement	*523 S Webster St, Naperville IL 60540*
IL	Nauvoo	Nauvoo Historical Society	*1380 Mulholland St, Nauvoo IL 62354*
IL	Nauvoo	The Allyn House	*1420 Mulholland St, Nauvoo IL 62354*

IL	Nauvoo	The Allyn House	*1400 Mulholland St, Nauvoo IL 62354*
IL	North Utica	Starved Rock State Park Visitor Center	*2678 Illinois 178, North Utica IL 61373*
IL	Pekin	Gethsemane Church	*1601 Fredrick Dr, Pekin IL 61554*
IL	Peoria	Freedom Ink Tattoos	*760 SW Washington St, Peoria IL 61602*
IL	Peoria	Louisville Slugger Sports Complex	*8400 Orange Prairie Rd, Peoria IL 61615*
IL	Peoria	Peoria Riverfront Museum	*222 SW Washington St, Peoria IL 61602*
IL	Peoria	Peoria Zoo	*2320 N Prospect Rd, Peoria IL 61603*
IL	Peoria Heights	Tower Park	*Tower Park, Peoria Heights IL 61616*
IL	Petersburg	Lincolns New Salem State Park	*107 S 7th St, Petersburg IL 62675*
IL	Rockford	Discovery Center Museum, North Main Street, Rockfo	*711 N Main St, Rockford IL 61103*
IL	Rockford	Nicholas Conservatory	*Nicholas Conservatory & Gardens, Rockford IL 61107*
IL	Round Lake Beach	Kristof's Entertainment Center	*421 W Rollins Rd, Round Lake Beach IL 60073*
IL	Round Lake Beach	Kristofs World of Fun Entertainment Center	*421 W Rollins Rd, Round Lake Beach IL 60073*
IL	Schaumburg	LEGOLAND Discovery Center	*601 N Martingale Rd, Schaumburg IL 60173*
IL	Schaumburg	LEGOLAND Discovery Center Chicago	*601 N Martingale Rd, Schaumburg IL 60173*
IL	Schaumburg	Woodfield Mall - Rainforest Cafe	*D121 Woodfield Mall, Schaumburg IL 60173*
IL	Springfield	Abraham Lincoln Presidential Library	*112 N 6th St, Springfield IL 62701*
IL	Springfield	Cafe Andiamo	*204 1 S 6th St, Springfield IL 62701*

IL	Springfield	Henson Robinson Zoo	*1100 E Lake Shore Dr, Springfield IL 62712*
IL	Springfield	Illinois State Museum, South Spring Street, Spring	*502 S Spring St, Springfield IL 62706*
IL	Springfield	Lincoln's Tomb Souvenir & Gift Shop	*1500 Monument Avenue Cemetery, Springfield IL 62702*
IL	Springfield	Lincoln's Tomb Souvenir & Gift Shop	*1410 Monument Ave, Springfield IL 62702*
IL	Springfield	Mr Lincoln's Souvenirs & Gifts	*603 S 7th St, Springfield IL 62703*
IL	Springfield	Washington Park Botanical Garden	*Washington Park Botanical Garden, Springfield IL 62704*
IL	Springfield	Washington Park Botanical Garden	*Washington Park Botanical Garden, Springfield IL 62704*
IL	Vandalia	Vandalia Statehouse	*300 W Gallatin St, Vandalia IL 62471*
IL	Volo	Volo Auto Museum	*27640 Volo Village Rd, Volo IL 60073*
IL	Wheaton	Cosley Zoo	*1356 N Gary Ave, Wheaton IL 60187*
IL	Wheaton	Cosley Zoo	*1356 N Gary Ave, Wheaton IL 60187*
IL	Wilmington	Launching Pad Drive-In	*810 E Baltimore St, Wilmington IL 60481*

Indiana			
IN	Anderson	Uranus Fudge Factory	*1423 W 53rd St, Anderson IN 46013*
IN	Auburn	National Automotive & Truck Museum	*1000 Gordon M Buehrig Pl, Auburn IN 46706*
IN	Bloomingdale	Gobbler's Knob Country Store	*7479 N US Highway 41, Bloomingdale IN 47832*
IN	Bloomington	Wonderlab Science Museum	*308 W 4th St, Bloomington IN 47404*
IN	Bristol	Bonneyville Mill County Park	*53373 Co Rd 131, Bristol IN 46507*
IN	Brookville	Wolf Creek Habitat & Rescue	*14099 Wolf Creek Rd, Brookville IN 47012*
IN	Carmel	Carmel Christkindlmarkt	*10 Carter Green, Carmel IN 46032*
IN	Clarksville	Bass Pro Shops	*951 E Lewis and Clark Pkwy, Clarksville IN 47129*
IN	Clarksville	Falls of the Ohio State Park	*76CQ+XJ Clarksville, Clarksville IN 47129*
IN	Connersville	Whitewater Valley Railroad	*455 Market St, Connersville IN 47331*
IN	Elkhart	George Craig Travel Plaza	*2971 Moose Trl Dr, Elkhart IN 46514*
IN	Elkhart	Henry F. Schricker Travel Plaza	*28054 - 2 C.R. 4 West, Elkhart IN 46514*
IN	Elkhart	Henry Schricker Travel Plaza	*52019 Co Rd 5, Elkhart IN 46514*
IN	Evansville	Mesker Park Zoo	*Amazonia, Evansville IN 47712*
IN	Fair Oaks	Fair Oaks Farms	*816 N 600 E, Fair Oaks IN 47943*
IN	Fishers	Conner Prairie Interactive History Park	*Conner Prairie, Fishers IN 46038*
IN	Fort Wayne	Crazy Pinz Entertainment Center	*1414 Northland Blvd, Fort Wayne, IN 46825, Fort Wayne IN 46825*
IN	Fort Wayne	Fort Wayne Children's Zoo	*3411 Sherman Blvd, Fort Wayne IN 46808*

IN	Fort Wayne	Hopscotch House	*1301 Broadway, Fort Wayne IN 46802*
IN	Fort Wayne	Science Central	*1950 N Clinton St, Fort Wayne IN 46805*
IN	Fort Wayne	The History Center	*Fort Wayne Old City Hall Bldg, Fort Wayne IN 46802*
IN	Franklin	Festival Country Indiana Visitor Center	*66 S Water St, Franklin IN 46131*
IN	Greenfield	Riley Home Museum	*250 W Main St, Greenfield IN 46140*
IN	Howe	Ernie Pyle Travel Plaza	*5000 E 750 N, Howe IN 46746*
IN	Indianapolis	Indiana Historical Society	*450 W Ohio St, Indianapolis IN 46202*
IN	Indianapolis	Indiana State Museum	*650 W Washington St, Indianapolis IN 46204*
IN	Indianapolis	Indianapolis Colts Traveling Museum	*500 S Capitol Ave, Indianapolis IN 46225*
IN	Indianapolis	Indianapolis Motor Speedway (Traveling Exhibit)	*4790 W 16th St, Indianapolis IN 46222*
IN	Indianapolis	Indianapolis Motor Speedway Museum	*4750 W 16th St, Indianapolis IN 46222*
IN	Indianapolis	Indianapolis Zoo	*Simon Skjodt International Orangutan Center, Indianapolis IN 46222*
IN	Indianapolis	The Children's Museum of Indianapolis	*3000 N Meridian St, Indianapolis IN 46208*
IN	Jasper	The Schnitzelbank Restaurant	*393 Third Ave, Jasper IN 47546*
IN	Jeffersonville	Schimpff's Confectionery LLC	*347 Spring St, Jeffersonville IN 47130*
IN	Laurel	Family Touch Primitive Treasures and Cafe	*11261 Little Duck Creek Rd, Laurel IN 47024*
IN	Marengo	Marengo Cave U.S. National Landmark	*400 IN-64, Marengo IN 47140*
IN	Mauckport	Squire Boone Caverns	*300 Squire Boone Rd SW, Mauckport IN 47142*

IN	Michigan City	Washington Park Zoo	*115 Lake Shore Dr, Michigan City IN 46360*
IN	Mitchell	Spring Mill Inn	*3333 IN-60, Mitchell IN 47446*
IN	Mitchell	Spring mill state park	*3333 IN-60, Mitchell IN 47446*
IN	Monroeville	Monroeville Community Park	*421 Monroe St., Monroeville IN 46773*
IN	Monticello	Indiana Beach	*5224 E Indiana Beach Rd, Monticello IN 47960*
IN	Nashville	Millers Ice Cream House Inc	*61 W Main St, Nashville IN 47448*
IN	Nashville	Primitives and PInecones	*76 E Main St, Nashville IN 47448*
IN	Nashville	Rhonda Kay's	*77 N Van Buren St, Nashville IN 47448*
IN	Noblesville	Cabellas	*13725 Cabela Pkwy, Noblesville IN 46060*
IN	Noblesville	Old picket Fence	*894 Logan St, Noblesville IN 46060*
IN	Peru	Grissom air museum	*1000 W Hoosier Blvd, Peru IN 46970*
IN	Portage	Bass Pro Shops	*6425 Daniel Burnham Dr, Portage IN 46368*
IN	Porter	Indiana Dunes Visitor Center	*1215 N State Rd 49, Porter IN 46304*
IN	Richmond	Uranus Fudge Factory	*6400 National Rd E, Richmond IN 47374*
IN	Rockville	Aunt Patty's On the Square	*101 W High St, Rockville IN 47872*
IN	Santa Claus	Holiday World & Splashing Safari	*Gobbler Getaway, Santa Claus IN 47579*
IN	Santa Claus	Lake Rudolph Campground & RV Resort	*Sun Outdoors Lake Rudolph, Santa Claus IN 47579*
IN	South Bend	Potawatomi Zoo	*500 S Greenlawn Ave, South Bend IN 46615*
IN	South Bend	South Bend International Airport	*PM4H+Q2 South Bend, South Bend IN 46628*

IN	Spencer	Spencer Pride CommUnity Center	*17 E Franklin St, Spencer IN 47460*
IN	Terre Haute	Terre Haute Children's Museum	*727 Wabash Ave, Terre Haute IN 47807*
IN	West Lafayette	Neil Armstrong Hall of Engineering at Purdue University	*Neil Armstrong Hall of Engineering, West Lafayette IN 47907*

Kansas			
KS	Abilene	Dwight D. Eisenhower Presidential Library & Museum	*Place of Meditation, Abilene KS 67410*
KS	Abilene	Eisenhower Center	*200 S E 4th St, Abilene KS 67410*
KS	Abilene	Eisenhower Center	*200 S E 4th St, Abilene KS 67410*
KS	Atchison	Amelia Earhart Birthplace Museum	*223 N Terrace St, Atchison KS 66002*
KS	Atchison	Amelia Earhart Hangar Museum	*16701 286th Rd, Atchison KS 66002*
KS	Augusta	World Famous Sugar Shane's Cafe	*430 State St, Augusta KS 67010*
KS	Baxter Springs	SACS 66	*1143 Military Ave, Baxter Springs KS 66713*
KS	Clay Center	Clay County Museum Penny Press	*518 Lincoln Ave, Clay Center KS 67432*
KS	Coffeyville	Coffeyville Area Chamber of Commerce	*807 S Walnut St, Coffeyville KS 67337*
KS	Coffeyville	Old Condon Bank	*807 S Walnut St, Coffeyville KS 67337*
KS	Coffeyville	White Mountain Trading Post	*2473 County Rd 3900, Coffeyville KS 67337*
KS	Dodge City	Boot Hill Museum	*500 W Wyatt Earp Blvd, Dodge City KS 67801*
KS	Dodge City	Boot Hill Museum	*636 Wyatt Earp Blvd, Dodge City KS 67801*
KS	Garden City	Lee Richardson Zoo	*312 E Finnup Dr, Garden City KS 67846*
KS	Goddard	Tanganyika Wildlife Park	*Tanganyika Wildlife Park, Goddard KS 67052*
KS	Great Bend	Kansas Wetlands Education Center	*593 KS-156, Great Bend KS 67530*
KS	Greensburg	Big Well Museum	*315 S Sycamore St, Greensburg KS 67054*

KS	Hedville	Rolling Hills Zoo	*V63P+83 Hedville, Hedville KS 67401*
KS	Hiawatha	Citizens State Bank & Trust Co	*602 Oregon St, Hiawatha KS 66434*
KS	Hutchinson	Cosmosphere	*Richard E. Smith Science Center, Hutchinson KS 67501*
KS	Hutchinson	Strataca	*3650 E Ave G, Hutchinson KS 67501*
KS	Independence	FOOD PANTRY Waikiki Kuhio	*319 W Laurel St, Independence KS 67301*
KS	Independence	Lake Dardanelle State Park	*319 W Laurel St, Independence KS 67301*
KS	Independence	Museum of Aviation	*319 W Laurel St, Independence KS 67301*
KS	Kansas City	Great Wolf Lodge Kansas City	*10401 Cabela Dr, Kansas City KS 66111*
KS	Lawrence	Local Crush - migratory press currently at Waxman Candles	*608 N 2nd St, Lawrence KS 66044*
KS	Leavenworth	C. W. Parker Carousel Museum	*320 S Esplanade St, Leavenworth KS 66048*
KS	Leavenworth	Fort Leavenworth Post Exchange (PX)	*330 Iowa Ave Bldg 700, Leavenworth KS 66027*
KS	Liberal	Seward County Historical Society - Dorothy's House	*567 E Cedar St, Liberal KS 67901*
KS	Manhattan	Sunset Zoo	*5CG3+QP Manhattan, Manhattan KS 66502*
KS	Olathe	Bass Pro Shops	*12051 Bass Pro Dr, Olathe KS 66061*
KS	Overland Park	Deanna Rose Children's Farmstead	*Deanna Rose Children's Farmstead, Overland Park KS 66221*
KS	Phillipsburg	C&R Railroad Museum	*875 Park St, Phillipsburg KS 67661*
KS	Topeka	Combat Air Museum	*7022 SE Forbes Ave, Topeka KS 66619*
KS	Topeka	Topeka Zoo	*635 SW Gage Blvd, Topeka KS 66606*

KS	Wichita	Cabela's	*2427 N Greenwich Rd, Wichita KS 67226*
KS	Wichita	Exploration Place	*300 N McLean Blvd, Wichita KS 67203*
KS	Wichita	Exploration Place	*300 N McLean Blvd, Wichita KS 67203*
KS	Wichita	Museum of World Treasures	*835 E 1st St N, Wichita KS 67202*
KS	Wichita	Sedgwick County Zoo	*Cargill Learning Center, Wichita KS 67212*
KS	Wichita	Sedgwick County Zoo	*Cargill Learning Center, Wichita KS 67212*
KS	Wichita	Third Planet	*7700 E. Kellogg K-06, Wichita KS 67207*

			Kentucky
KY	Bowling Green	Bowling Green Corvette Plant	*551 Corvette Dr, Bowling Green KY 42101*
KY	Campbellsville	Green River Lake Visitor Center	*495 Lake Rd, Campbellsville KY 42718*
KY	Cave City	Big Mike's Rock & Gift Shop	*566 Old Mammoth Cave Rd, Cave City KY 42127*
KY	Cave City	Dinosaur World	*105 Mammoth Cave Rd, Cave City KY 42127*
KY	Cave City	Mammoth Cave Wildlife Museum	*409-A E Happy Valley St, Cave City KY 42127*
KY	Cave City	Olde General Store	*802 Mammoth Cave Rd, Cave City KY 42127*
KY	Fort Knox	Patton Museum of Cavalry and Armor	*4554 Fayette Ave, Fort Knox KY 40121*
KY	Frankfort	Kentucky State Capitol Building	*100 Capital Ave, Frankfort KY 40601*
KY	Frankfort	Rebecca Ruth Chocolates	*116 E 2nd St, Frankfort KY 40601*
KY	Frankfort	Salato Wildlife Education Center	*1 Sportsman's Ln, Frankfort KY 40601*
KY	Glasgow	South Central Kentucky Cultural Center	*200 W Water St, Glasgow KY 42141*
KY	Golden Pond	Land Between the Lakes National Recreation Area	*238 Visitor Center Dr, Golden Pond KY 42211*
KY	Hodgenville	The Lincoln Museum	*66 Lincoln Square, Hodgenville KY 42748*
KY	Horse Cave	Kentucky Down Under	*3700 L and N Turnpike Rd, Horse Cave KY 42749*
KY	Jamestown	Wolf Creek National Fish Hatchery	*50 Kendall Rd, Jamestown KY 42629*
KY	Lexington	Barrel House Distilling Co. / Elkhorn Tavern	*1200 Manchester St, Lexington KY 40504*
KY	Lexington	Cabela's	*1510 Conservation Wy, Lexington KY 40509*

KY	Lexington	Street Scene Vintage	*2571 Regency Rd, Lexington KY 40503*
KY	Louisville	Cabela's	*5100 Norton Healthcare Blvd, Louisville KY 40241*
KY	Louisville	Kentucky Derby Museum	*704 Central Ave, Louisville KY 40208*
KY	Louisville	Kentucky Derby Museum	*704 Central Ave, Louisville KY 40208*
KY	Louisville	Kentucky Kingdom	*937 Phillips Ln, Louisville KY 40209*
KY	Louisville	Kentucky Science Center	*727 W Main St, Louisville KY 40202*
KY	Louisville	Kentucky State Fair Ground	*937 Phillips Ln, Louisville KY 40209*
KY	Louisville	Louisville Mega Cavern	*1841 Taylor Ave, Louisville KY 40213*
KY	Louisville	Louisville Slugger Museum & Factory	*810 W Main St, Louisville KY 40202*
KY	Louisville	Louisville Zoo	*3915 Illinois Ave, Louisville KY 40213*
KY	Mammoth Cave	Mammoth	*Quarters 43, Mammoth Cave KY 42259*
KY	Mammoth Cave	Mammoth Cave Hotel	*Quarters 43, Mammoth Cave KY 42259*
KY	Mammoth Cave	Mammoth Cave National Park Visitor Center	*Quarters 43, Mammoth Cave KY 42259*
KY	New Haven	Kentucky Train Museum	*136 S Main St, New Haven KY 40051*
KY	Newport	Newport Aquarium	*1 Levee Wy #3104, Newport KY 41071*
KY	Newport	Newport on the Levee	*1 Aquarium Way, Newport KY 41071*
KY	Paducah	River Discovery Center	*117 S Water St, Paducah KY 42001*
KY	Park City	Historic Diamond Caverns	*1900 Mammoth Cave Pkwy, Park City KY 42160*
KY	Petersburg	Creation Museum	*2800 Bullittsburg Church Rd, Petersburg KY 41080*
KY	Richmond	Buc-ee's	*1013 Buc-ee's Blvd, Richmond KY 40475*

KY	Slade	Boone Forest Shop	*1200 Natural Bridge Rd, Slade KY 40376*
KY	Slade	Natural Bridge Skylift & Gift Shop	*607 Skylift Dr, Slade KY 40376*
KY	Williamstown	The Ark Encounter	*1 Ark Encounter Dr, Williamstown KY 41097*

Louisiana			
LA	Alexandria	Alexandria Zoo	*3016 Masonic Dr, Alexandria LA 71301*
LA	Alexandria	Alexandria Zoological Park	*3016 Masonic Dr, Alexandria LA 71301*
LA	Alexandria	Silver Dollar Pawn & Jewelry	*2417 Lee St, Alexandria LA 71301*
LA	Avery Island	Jungle Gardens	*W36P+9X Camellias, Avery Island LA 70513*
LA	Avery Island	McIlhenny Company	*6040 Avery Island Rd, Avery Island LA 70513*
LA	Avery Island	Tobasco Factory	*32 Wisteria Rd, Avery Island LA 70513*
LA	Baton Rouge	BREC's Baton Rouge Zoo	*12343 Gibbens Rd, Baton Rouge LA 70807*
LA	Baton Rouge	State Capitol Welcome Center	*1051 N 3rd St, Baton Rouge LA 70802*
LA	Baton Rouge	USS KIDD Veterans Museum	*Coast Guard Cutter WHITE ALDER Memorial, Baton Rouge LA 70802*
LA	Bossier City	Bass Pro Shops	*110 Bass Pro Dr, Bossier City LA 71111*
LA	Bossier City	Bass Pro Shops	*100 Bass Pro Dr, Bossier City LA 71111*
LA	Bossier City	Louisiana Boardwalk Outlets	*2 River Colony Dr, Bossier City LA 71111*
LA	Bossier City	Regal Cinemas Louisiana Boardwalk 14 & IMAX	*798-700, Bossier City LA 71111*
LA	Broussard	Zoosiana	*5601 Hwy 90 E, Broussard LA 70518*
LA	Denham Springs	Bass Pro Shops	*175 Bass Pro Blvd, Denham Springs LA 70726*
LA	Gonzales	Cabela's	*Gonzales Cabela'S, Gonzales LA 70737*
LA	Greenwood	Gators and Friends	*11435 US-80, Greenwood LA 71033*

LA	Henderson	Pat's Fisherman's Wharf Restaurant	*1008 Henderson Levee Rd, Henderson LA 70517*
LA	Kinder	Fausto's Family Restaurant	*14514 US-165, Kinder LA 70648*
LA	Lafayette	Children's Museum of Acadiana	*201 E Congress St, Lafayette LA 70501*
LA	Many	Fisherman's Galley	*14934 Texas Hwy, Many LA 71449*
LA	Metairie	Clearview Mall	*4436 Veterans Memorial Blvd, Metairie LA 70006*
LA	Monroe	Louisiana Purchase Gardens & Zoo	*1405 Bernstein Park Dr, Monroe LA 71202*
LA	Natchitoches	Bayou Pierre Alligator Park	*380 Old Bayou Pierre Rd, Natchitoches LA 71457*
LA	Natchitoches	Southern Necessities	*616 Front St, Natchitoches LA 71457*
LA	New Iberia	El Chile Verde of New Iberia	*2714b LA-14, New Iberia LA 70560*
LA	New Orleans	Audubon Zoo	*WVF9+9F, New Orleans LA 70118*
LA	New Orleans	Cafe Du Monde French Market	*800 Decatur St, New Orleans LA 70116*
LA	New Orleans	Gumbo File Gift Shop	*439 Decatur St, New Orleans LA 70130*
LA	New Orleans	Hard Rock Cafe - Penny Machines USA	*125 Bourbon St, New Orleans LA 70112*
LA	New Orleans	Jackson Brewhouse	*620 Decatur St, New Orleans LA 70130*
LA	New Orleans	Jazz Funeral Store #2	*405 Bourbon St, New Orleans LA 70130*
LA	New Orleans	Louisiana Children's Museum	*420 Julia St, New Orleans LA 70130*
LA	New Orleans	Mardi Gras World	*1380 Port of New Orleans Pl, New Orleans LA 70130*
LA	New Orleans	World War II Museum	*945 Magazine St, New Orleans LA 70130*
LA	Pineville	Gone Wild Safari	*805 Hooper Rd, Pineville LA 71360*

LA	Ponchatoula	Berryland Campers	*42775 Pleasant Ridge Ext, Ponchatoula LA 70454*
LA	Roanoke	Peto's Travel Center	*15125 LA-395, Roanoke LA 70581*
LA	Robert	Yogi Bear's Jellystone Park	*23 Jellystone Park, Robert LA 70455*
LA	Shreveport	Sci-Port: Louisiana's Science Center	*80798 Common St, Shreveport LA 71101*
LA	Shreveport	Shreveport Aquarium	*104 Lafayette St, Shreveport LA 71107*
LA	Springfield	Tickfaw State Park	*27265 Patterson Rd, Springfield LA 70462*
LA	Uneedus	Global Wildlife Center	*JPH7+C7 Uneedus, Uneedus LA 70437*
LA	Vacherie	Oak Alley Plantation	*3645 LA-18, Vacherie LA 70090*
LA	West Monroe	Duck Commander	*117 Kings Ln, West Monroe LA 71292*

			Massachusetts
MA	Agawam	Six Flags New England	*1623 Main St, Agawam MA 01001*
MA	Barnstable	Kandy Korner	*474 Main St, Barnstable MA 02601*
MA	Boston	Boston Children's Museum	*308 Congress St, Boston MA 02210*
MA	Boston	Boston South Station	*South Station, Boston MA 02110*
MA	Boston	Boston Tea Party Ships & Museum	*306 Congress St, Boston MA 02210*
MA	Boston	Fenway Park	*4 Jersey St, Boston MA 02215*
MA	Boston	Museum of Science	*1 Museum Of Science Driveway, Boston MA 02114*
MA	Boston	Quincy Market- Boston	*Faneuil Hall Marketplace, Boston MA 02109*
MA	Boston	Skywalk Observatory	*800 Boylston St Suite 2520, Boston MA 02199*
MA	Boston	USS Constitution Museum	*Building 22, Boston MA 02129*
MA	Boston	Zoo New England	*1 Franklin Park Rd, Boston MA 02121*
MA	Bourne	Island Home Ferry	*Cataumet Motel/Steamship Authority Cataumet Parking Lot, Bourne MA 02534*
MA	Carver	Jellystone Parkâ„¢ Cranberry Acres	*V73C+XM Carver, Carver MA 02330*
MA	Charlton	Charlton Service Plaza Eastbound	*166 Sturbridge Rd, Charlton MA 01507*
MA	Charlton	Charlton Service Plaza Westbound	*6 Massachusetts Tpke, Charlton MA 01507*
MA	Charlton	McDonald's	*6 Massachusetts Tpke, Charlton MA 01507*
MA	Deerfield	Magic Wings Butterfly Conservatory	*281 Greenfield Rd, Deerfield MA 01373*
MA	Deerfield	Yankee Candle	*25 Greenfield Rd, Deerfield MA 01373*
MA	Essex	Woodman's of Essex	*119 Main St, Essex MA 01929*

MA	Fall River	USS Massachusetts BB59	*5 Water St, Fall River MA 02721*
MA	Falmouth	Steamship Authority	*17 Albatross St, Falmouth MA 02543*
MA	Fitchburg	Great Wolf Lodge New England	*150 Great Wolf Dr, Fitchburg MA 01420*
MA	Foxborough	Bass Pro Shops	*2 Patriot Pl, Foxborough MA 02035*
MA	Lancaster	Johnny Appleseed Visitor Center	*1000 MA-2, Lancaster MA 01523*
MA	Lee	Lee Service Plaza	*370 Stockbridge Rd, Lee MA 01238*
MA	Lee	Lee Service Plaza Eastbound	*1 E Massachusetts Tpke, Lee MA 01238*
MA	Ludlow	Mass Pike East Travel Plaza	*862 Massachusetts Tpke, Ludlow MA 01104*
MA	Mendon	Southwick's Zoo	*5 Southwick St, Mendon MA 01756*
MA	New Bedford	Buttonwood Park	*425 Hawthorn St, New Bedford MA 02740*
MA	Oak Bluffs	Flying Horses	*15 Lake Ave, Oak Bluffs MA 02557*
MA	Plymouth	Plimoth Plantation	*137 Warren Ave, Plymouth MA 02360*
MA	Provincetown	Lopes Square Variety Store	*307 Commercial St, Provincetown MA 02657*
MA	Provincetown	Provincetown Chamber Of Commerce Inc.	*307 Commercial St, Provincetown MA 02657*
MA	Provincetown	Shirts N Stuff	*329 Commercial St, Provincetown MA 02657*
MA	Provincetown	Whalers Wharf	*239 Commercial St, Provincetown MA 02657*
MA	Quincy	Boston Tea Party Ships & Museum	*42 Saville Ave, Quincy MA 02169*
MA	Rockport	BearskinNeck.net	*46 Bearskin Neck, Rockport MA 01966*
MA	Salem	Salem Historical Tours/Haunted Footsteps Ghost Tour	*8 Central St, Salem MA 01970*
MA	Salem	Salem Wax Museum	*288 Derby St, Salem MA 01970*

MA	Salem	Salem Witch Museum	*19 1/2 N Washington Square, Salem MA 01970*
MA	Salem	Salem Witch Village	*278-282 Derby St, Salem MA 01970*
MA	Salem	Witch Way Gifts	*155 Derby St, Salem MA 01970*
MA	Springfield	Naismith Memorial Basketball Hall of Fame	*1000 Hall of Fame Ave, Springfield MA 01105*
MA	Springfield	Springfield Science Museum	*21 Edwards St, Springfield MA 01103*
MA	Stoneham	Stone Zoo	*149 Pond St, Stoneham MA 02180*
MA	Sturbridge	Old Sturbridge Village	*1 Old Sturbridge Village Rd, Sturbridge MA 01566*
MA	Wellfleet	Riley's $2 T-shirt Shop	*464 State, Wellfleet MA 02667*
MA	Westford	The Butterfly Place	*120 Tyngsboro Rd, Westford MA 01886*
MA	Westport	WISCO	*1219 Main Rd, Westport MA 02790*
MA	Worcester	EcoTarium	*222 Harrington Way, Worcester MA 01604*
MA	Worcester	Worcester Historical Museum	*30 Elm St #2, Worcester MA 01609*
MA	Yarmouth	Skull Island Sports World	*934 MA-28, Yarmouth MA 02664*

Maryland			
MD	Aberdeen	Maryland House Rest Area	*Maryland Hse, Aberdeen MD 21001*
MD	Annapolis	A L Goodies Northside Inc	*112 Main St #3, Annapolis MD 21401*
MD	Annapolis	A L Goodies Northside Inc	*112 Main St, Annapolis MD 21401*
MD	Baltimore	B & O Railroad Museum	*901 W Pratt St, Baltimore MD 21223*
MD	Baltimore	Babe Ruth Birthplace and Museum	*216 Emory St, Baltimore MD 21230*
MD	Baltimore	Baltimore & Ohio Railroad Museum	*901 W Pratt St, Baltimore MD 21223*
MD	Baltimore	Baltimore Maritime Museum	*802 S Caroline St Suite A, Baltimore MD 21231*
MD	Baltimore	Fort McHenry	*1401 Constellation Plaza, Baltimore MD 21230*
MD	Baltimore	Fort McHenry National Monument and Historic Shrine	*1401 Constellation Plaza, Baltimore MD 21230*
MD	Baltimore	Historic Ships in Baltimore	*Harborplace, Baltimore MD 21230*
MD	Baltimore	Maryland Science Center	*601 Light St, Baltimore MD 21230*
MD	Baltimore	National Aquarium	*501 E Pratt St, Baltimore MD 21202*
MD	Baltimore	Oriole Park at Camden Yards	*333 W Camden St, Baltimore MD 21201*
MD	Baltimore	Oriole Park at Camden Yards	*333 W Camden St, Baltimore MD 21201*
MD	Baltimore	Point 28	*211 E Lombard St, Baltimore MD 21202*
MD	Baltimore	Ripley's Believe It or Not	*301 Light St, Baltimore MD 21202*
MD	Baltimore	Ripley's Believe It or Not Baltimore	*301 Light St # 1445, Baltimore MD 21202*
MD	Baltimore	The Maryland Zoo in Baltimore	*1 Safari Pl, Baltimore MD 21217*

MD	Baltimore	The Maryland Zoo in Baltimore	*1 Safari Pl, Baltimore MD 21217*
MD	Baltimore	The Walters Art Museum	*600 N Charles St, Baltimore MD 21201*
MD	Berlin	Frontier Town OC	*8428 Stephen Decatur Hwy, Berlin MD 21811*
MD	Berlin	Frontier Town OC	*8428 Stephen Decatur Hwy, Berlin MD 21811*
MD	Bowie	Six Flags America	*13710 Central Ave, Bowie MD 20721*
MD	College Park	Cherry Hill Park	*9800 Cherry Hill Rd, College Park MD 20740*
MD	College Park	Cherry Hill Park	*9832 Cherry Hill Rd, College Park MD 20740*
MD	Cumberland	Western Maryland Scenic Railroad	*13 Canal St 2nd Floor, Cumberland MD 21502*
MD	Emmitsburg	National Fallen Firefighters Memorial	*16825 S Seton Ave, Emmitsburg MD 21727*
MD	Emmitsburg	National Fallen Firefighters Memorial	*16825 S Seton Ave, Emmitsburg MD 21727*
MD	Hagerstown	Discovery Station At Hagerstown Inc	*105 W Washington St, Hagerstown MD 21740*
MD	Hagerstown	Discovery Station At Hagerstown Inc	*101 W Washington St, Hagerstown MD 21740*
MD	Laurel	The Johns Hopkins University Applied Physics Laboratory	*7288 Sanner Rd, Laurel MD 21029*
MD	Lutherville	Fire Museum of Maryland	*1301-R York Rd, Lutherville MD 21093*
MD	McHenry	Pine Lodge Steakhouse	*1520 Deep Creek Dr, McHenry MD 21541*
MD	McHenry	Smiley's Fun Zone	*25 Cedar Shores Dr, McHenry MD 21541*
MD	Monrovia	Adventure Park Academy	*11936 E Baldwin Rd, Monrovia MD 21770*

MD	Mount Savage	Western Maryland Scenic Railroad	*11622 Woodcock Hollow Rd NW, Mount Savage MD 21545*
MD	New Market	Adventure Park USA	*11113 Baldwin Rd, New Market MD 21774*
MD	North East	Chesapeake House	*965 John F Kennedy Memorial Hwy, North East MD 21901*
MD	North East	Elk Neck State Park	*95 Campground Rd, North East MD 21901*
MD	Oakland	The Tourist Trap	*19895 Garrett Hwy, Oakland MD 21550*
MD	Ocean City	Dead Freddies Island Grill	*105 64th St, Ocean City MD 21842*
MD	Ocean City	Dead Freddies Island Grill	*105 64th St, Ocean City MD 21842*
MD	Ocean City	Dead Freddies Island Grill	*105 64th St, Ocean City MD 21842*
MD	Ocean City	Dolle's Candyland Inc.	*500 S Atlantic Ave, Ocean City MD 21842*
MD	Ocean City	Fun City Arcade	*100 S Atlantic Ave, Ocean City MD 21842*
MD	Ocean City	Fun City Arcade	*6 Caroline St, Ocean City MD 21842*
MD	Ocean City	Funcade	*905 Boardwalk, Ocean City MD 21842*
MD	Ocean City	Inlet Bar and Grill	*804 S Atlantic Ave, Ocean City MD 21842*
MD	Ocean City	Marty's Playland	*5 Worcester St, Ocean City MD 21842*
MD	Ocean City	Old Pro Golf	*13603 Coastal Hwy, Ocean City MD 21842*
MD	Ocean City	Ripley's Believe It or Not	*401 S Atlantic Ave, Ocean City MD 21842*
MD	Ocean City	The Kite Loft	*511 Boardwalk, Ocean City MD 21842*
MD	Ocean City	Trimper's Rides (Haunted House)	*720 S Atlantic Ave, Ocean City MD 21842*
MD	Port Deposit	Chesapeake House Travel Plaza	*10670 I-95, Port Deposit MD 21904*

MD	Salisbury	Salisbury Zoological Park	*755 S Park Dr, Salisbury MD 21804*
MD	Salisbury	Salisbury Zoological Park	*755 S Park Dr, Salisbury MD 21804*
MD	Scotland	Point Lookout State Park	*3M67+92 Scotland, Scotland MD 20687*
MD	Scotland	Point Lookout State Park	*3M57+X6 Scotland, Scotland MD 20687*
MD	Severn	Bass Pro Shops	*7000 Arundel Mills Cir, Severn MD 21076*
MD	Severn	Bass Pro Shops	*7000 Arundel Mills Dr, Severn MD 21076*
MD	Severn	Bass Pro Shops	*7000 Arundel Mills Dr, Severn MD 21076*
MD	Upper Marlboro	Six Flags America	*Grand Theater, Upper Marlboro MD 20774*
MD	Williamsport	Yogi Bear's Jellystone Park In Williamsport MD	*9546 Jellystone Pk Wy, Williamsport MD 21795*

Maine			
ME	Bangor	Maine Discovery Museum	*72 Main St, Bangor ME 04401*
ME	Bar Harbor	Acadia Outdoors	*45 Main St, Bar Harbor ME 04609*
ME	Bar Harbor	Jordan Pond Ice Cream and Fudge shop - Downtown Bar Harbor	*45 Main St, Bar Harbor ME 04609*
ME	Belfast	Harborwalk Cafe.	*31 Front St, Belfast ME 04915*
ME	Boothbay Harbor	shirts by the Bay	*33 Commercial St, Boothbay Harbor ME 04538*
ME	Gray	Maine Wildlife Park	*Maine Wildlife Park, Gray ME 04039*
ME	Kittery	Kittery Trading Post	*301 U.S. Rte 1 One, Kittery ME 03904*
ME	Mount Desert	Acadia Jordan Pond House Shop	*2928 Park Loop Rd, Mount Desert ME 04675*
ME	Old Orchard Beach	Old orchard beach maine	*2 Old Orchard St, Old Orchard Beach ME 04064*
ME	Waterville	Hive Medicinal	*210 College Ave, Waterville ME 04901*
ME	Wells	Maine Diner	*2247 Post Rd, Wells ME 04090*
ME	Wells	Ogunquit Trading Post	*97 Post Rd, Wells ME 04090*
ME	York	York's Wild Kingdom	*23 Railroad Ave, York ME 03909*

			Michigan
MI	Alpena	Great Lakes Maritime Heritage Center	*318 W Fletcher St, Alpena MI 49707*
MI	Alpena	Great Lakes Maritime Heritage Center	*500 W Fletcher St, Alpena MI 49707*
MI	Alto	Boulder Ridge Wild Animal Park	*8198 Pratt Lake Ave SE, Alto MI 49302*
MI	Alto	Boulder Ridge Wild Animal Park	*8313 Pratt Lake Ave SE, Alto MI 49302*
MI	Ann Arbor	Ann Arbor Hands-On Museum	*220 E Ann St, Ann Arbor MI 48104*
MI	Ann Arbor	Dixboro General Store	*5206 Plymouth Rd, Ann Arbor MI 48105*
MI	Auburn Hills	Bass Pro Shops	*4500 Baldwin Rd, Auburn Hills MI 48326*
MI	Auburn Hills	Legoland	*4500 Baldwin Rd, Auburn Hills MI 48326*
MI	Auburn Hills	Rainforest Cafe	*4310 Baldwin Rd, Auburn Hills MI 48326*
MI	Auburn Hills	SEA LIFE Michigan Aquarium	*4316 Baldwin Rd, Auburn Hills MI 48326*
MI	Battle Creek	Binder Park Zoo	*Smith Wildlife Discovery Theater, Battle Creek MI 49014*
MI	Battle Creek	Binder Park Zoo Discovery Station	*10808 Gorsline Rd, Battle Creek MI 49014*
MI	Bloomfield Hills	Cranbrook Institute of Science	*10 Cranbrook Ln, Bloomfield Hills MI 48304*
MI	Boyne Falls	Boyne Mountain Resort	*1 Mountain Road, Boyne Falls MI 49713*
MI	Boyne Falls	Mountain Grand Lodge and Spa	*537C+92 Boyne Falls, Boyne Falls MI 49713*
MI	Buchanan	Niles Scream Park	*855 Mayflower Rd, Buchanan MI 49107*
MI	Charlevoix	The Taffy Barrel	*211B Bridge St, Charlevoix MI 49720*

MI	Copper Harbor	Fort Wilkins State Park	*Fort Wilkins State Park Store, Copper Harbor MI 49918*
MI	Copper Harbor	Last Frontier	*550 Gratiot St, Copper Harbor MI 49918*
MI	Davison	Outdoor Adventures Lake Shore Resort	*Outdoor Adventures Information Center, Davison MI 48423*
MI	Dearborn	Ford Rouge Factory Tour	*Ford Rouge Factory, Dearborn MI 48120*
MI	Dearborn	Greenfield Village	*Ford Home, Dearborn MI 48124*
MI	Dearborn	The Henry Ford Museum	*20900 Oakwood Blvd, Dearborn MI 48124*
MI	Dearborn	The Henry Ford Museum	*20900 Oakwood Blvd, Dearborn MI 48124*
MI	Detroit	Detroit Historical Society	*5401 Woodward Ave, Detroit MI 48202*
MI	Detroit	Michigan Science Center	*5020 John R St, Detroit MI 48202*
MI	Dundee	Cabela's	*110 Cabela Blvd E, Dundee MI 48131*
MI	East Tawas	Mooney's Ben Franklin	*138 Newman St, East Tawas MI 48730*
MI	East Tawas	Tawas Point State Park	*Tawas Point Lighthouse, East Tawas MI 48730*
MI	Farmington Hills	Marvin's Marvelous Mechanical Museum	*31005 A Orchard Lake Rd, Farmington Hills MI 48334*
MI	Fayette	Fayette Historic State Park	*P88J+XP, Fayette MI 49835*
MI	Flint	Crossroads Village & Huckleberry Railroad	*6140 N Bray Rd, Flint MI 48505*
MI	Frankenmuth	Bavarian Belle Riverboat (The Michigan Shoppe)	*925 S Main St, Frankenmuth MI 48734*
MI	Frankenmuth	Bavarian Inn Lodge	*1 Covered Bridge Ln, Frankenmuth MI 48734*
MI	Frankenmuth	Bavarian Inn Restaurant	*713 S Main St, Frankenmuth MI 48734*
MI	Frankenmuth	Bronner's CHRISTmas Wonderland	*25 Christmas Ln, Frankenmuth MI 48734*

MI	Frankenmuth	Covered Bridge & Leather Gift Shop	*775 S Main St, Frankenmuth MI 48734*
MI	Frankenmuth	Frankenmuth Cheese Haus	*561 S Main St, Frankenmuth MI 48734*
MI	Frankenmuth	Frankenmuth River Place Shops, Bee Bee's Fun Place	*925 S Main St D1, Frankenmuth MI 48734*
MI	Frankenmuth	Frankenmuth Yogi Bear's Jellystone Park	*Frankenmuth Mini Golf, Frankenmuth MI 48734*
MI	Frankenmuth	Rau's Country Store	*656 S Main St, Frankenmuth MI 48734*
MI	Frankenmuth	Zehnder's of Frankenmuth	*730 S Main St, Frankenmuth MI 48734*
MI	Grand Rapids	Grand Rapids Public Museum	*272 Pearl St NW, Grand Rapids MI 49504*
MI	Grand Rapids	John Ball Zoo	*John Ball Park Ballroom, Grand Rapids MI 49504*
MI	Grandville	Cabela's	*3020 44th St SW, Grandville MI 49418*
MI	Hancock	Quincy Mine Tours	*49750 US-41, Hancock MI 49930*
MI	Holland	Nelis' Dutch Village	*12350 James St, Holland MI 49424*
MI	Houghton	Houghton Coins	*200 Shelden Ave, Houghton MI 49931*
MI	Indian River	Big Bear Adventures	*4271 S Straits Hwy, Indian River MI 49749*
MI	Indian River	Cross In the Woods	*7078 M-68, Indian River MI 49749*
MI	Indian River	Indian River Trading Post Inc	*6225 M-68, Indian River MI 49749*
MI	Kalamazoo	Kalamazoo Valley Museum	*230 N Rose St World Works, Kalamazoo MI 49007*
MI	Kimball	Port Huron KOA Resort	*5111 Lapeer Rd, Kimball MI 48074*
MI	Lansing	Impression 5	*200 Museum Dr, Lansing MI 48933*
MI	Lansing	Michigan History Center	*702 W Kalamazoo St, Lansing MI 48909*

MI	Lansing	Potter Park Zoo	*1301 S Pennsylvania Ave, Lansing MI 48912*
MI	Ludington	S.S. Badger	*701 Maritime Dr, Ludington MI 49431*
MI	Ludington	S.S. Badger Carferry	*701 Maritime Dr, Ludington MI 49431*
MI	Ludington	Sloaney's LLC	*200 W Ludington Ave, Ludington MI 49431*
MI	Ludington	White pine village	*White Pine Village, Ludington MI 49431*
MI	Mackinac Island	Balsam Shops Inc	*7400 Main St, Mackinac Island MI 49757*
MI	Mackinac Island	Carriage Stables Gift Shop?Grand Hotel Stables	*7528 Carriage Rd, Mackinac Island MI 49757*
MI	Mackinac Island	Fort Mackinac Museum	*7127 Huron Rd, Mackinac Island MI 49757*
MI	Mackinac Island	Island Bookstore	*7372-106 Main St, Mackinac Island MI 49757*
MI	Mackinac Island	Mackinac Island State Parks Visitor's Center/ Muse	*V99C+8X Mackinac Island, Mackinac Island MI 49757*
MI	Mackinac Island	Star Line Mackinac Island	*7463 Main St, Mackinac Island MI 49757*
MI	Mackinaw City	A cats grin	*209 E Central Ave, Mackinaw City MI 49701*
MI	Mackinaw City	Fort Fudge Shop	*113 Straits Ave, Mackinaw City MI 49701*
MI	Mackinaw City	Mackinaw Crossings Games Stores	*136 S Huron Ave, Mackinaw City MI 49701*
MI	Mackinaw City	Mama Mia's Pizza	*227 E Central Ave, Mackinaw City MI 49701*
MI	Mackinaw City	Marshall's Fudge & Candy Co	*312 E Central Ave, Mackinaw City MI 49701*
MI	Mackinaw City	Mystery Town, USA	*200 S Nicolet St, Mackinaw City MI 49701*

MI	Mackinaw City	O'Brien's Shirt Shop	*222 E Central Ave, Mackinaw City MI 49701*
MI	Mackinaw City	Star Line Ferry - Mackinaw City Dock #1	*801 S Huron Ave, Mackinaw City MI 49701*
MI	Mackinaw City	Treasure Chest Gifts	*226 E Central Ave Units 7 8 9 10, Mackinaw City MI 49701*
MI	Mackinaw City	Windjammer Gifts	*327 E Central Ave, Mackinaw City MI 49701*
MI	Marshall	Cornwell's Turkeyville	*18935 15 1/2 Mile Rd, Marshall MI 49068*
MI	Mason	Shawhaven Farm	*1826 Rolfe Rd, Mason MI 48854*
MI	Mears	Mac Wood's Dune Rides	*629 N 18th Ave, Mears MI 49436*
MI	Mears	Silver Lake Tees	*8432 Silver Lake Rd, Mears MI 49436*
MI	Midland	Midland Center for the Arts	*1801 St Andrews St, Midland MI 48640*
MI	Mount Pleasant	Ziibiwing Center	*6650 E Broadway Rd, Mount Pleasant MI 48858*
MI	Munising	Pictured Rocks Cruises	*100 City Park Dr, Munising MI 49862*
MI	Munising	Shipwreck Tours	*1204 Commercial St #1354, Munising MI 49862*
MI	Muskegon	Michigan's Adventure Amusement Park	*4750 Whitehall Rd, Muskegon MI 49445*
MI	Naubinway	Garlyn Zoological Park	*9104 US-2, Naubinway MI 49762*
MI	Naubinway	Top-The Lake Snowmobile Museum	*W11660 US-2, Naubinway MI 49762*
MI	New Baltimore	Cabela's	*45959 Towne Center Blvd, New Baltimore MI 48047*
MI	Newberry	Oswald Bear Ranch	*13814 Co Rd 407, Newberry MI 49868*
MI	Niles	Pizza Transit	*217 E Main St, Niles MI 49120*
MI	Ontonagon	Porcupine mountains outpost	*107th Engineers Memorial Hwy, Ontonagon MI 49953*

MI	Paradise	Great Lakes Shipwreck Museum	*18335 N Whitefish Point Rd, Paradise MI 49768*
MI	Paradise	Tahquamenon Falls Brewery & Pub	*HPHW+HP, Paradise MI 49768*
MI	Pentwater	Cosmic Candy Co	*218 S Hancock St, Pentwater MI 49449*
MI	Petoskey	Grandpa Shorter's Gifts	*301 E Lake St, Petoskey MI 49770*
MI	Pinckney	Screams Ice Cream from Hell - Scream's Souvenirs	*4045 Patterson Lake Rd, Pinckney MI 48169*
MI	Portage	Air Zoo	*Air Zoo - Main Exhibit, Portage MI 49002*
MI	Richardsons Mill	Palms Book State Park	*2J49+GP Richardsons Mill, Richardsons Mill MI 49854*
MI	Saginaw	Cabela's	*5202 Bay Rd, Saginaw MI 48604*
MI	Saginaw	Children's Zoo at Celebration Square	*1716 S Washington Ave, Saginaw MI 48601*
MI	Sault Ste. Marie	Great Lakes Gifts	*315 W Portage Ave, Sault Ste. Marie MI 49783*
MI	South Haven	Oh My Darlings	*508 Phoenix St, South Haven MI 49090*
MI	St. Ignace	Castle Rock	*N2690 Castle Rock Rd, St. Ignace MI 49781*
MI	St. Ignace	Deer Ranch	*1540 US-2, St. Ignace MI 49781*
MI	St. Ignace	Kewadin Casinos - St Ignace	*3015 Mackinac Trail, St. Ignace MI 49781*
MI	St. Ignace	Mystery Spot	*150 Martin Lake Rd, St. Ignace MI 49781*
MI	St. Ignace	Souvenir Barn	*149 S 2nd St, St. Ignace MI 49781*
MI	St. Ignace	Village Inn	*250 S State St, St. Ignace MI 49781*
MI	St. James	Beaver Island	*37970 Michigan Ave, St. James MI 49782*
MI	St. Joseph	Silver Beach Carousel	*333 Broad St, St. Joseph MI 49085*
MI	Stanton	Anderson & Girls Orchards	*2985 N Sheridan Rd, Stanton MI 48888*

MI	Timberlost	Tahquamenon Falls State Park	*JR24+HW Timberlost, Timberlost MI 49768*
MI	Timberlost	Tahquamenon Falls State Park	*JR24+JM Timberlost, Timberlost MI 49768*
MI	Traverse City	Great Wolf Lodge - Traverse City	*3575 US-31, Traverse City MI 49684*
MI	Traverse City	Mr Bill's Shirt Co	*228 E Front St, Traverse City MI 49684*
MI	Trout Creek	Bond Falls Outpost	*GXRM+W2 Trout Creek, Trout Creek MI 49967*
MI	Westland	Nankin Mills Nature Center	*Wayne County Parks, Westland MI 48185*

Minnesota			
MN	Alexandria	Runestone Museum Penny Press	*206 Broadway St, Alexandria MN 56308*
MN	Apple Valley	Minnesota Zoo Gift Shop	*East Entrance, Apple Valley MN 55124*
MN	Austin	SPAM Museum	*1101 Main St N, Austin MN 55912*
MN	Bloomington	Bubba Gump Shrimp Co.	*156 South Avenue, Bloomington MN 55425*
MN	Bloomington	Crayola Experience Minneapolis	*60 E Broadway, Bloomington MN 55425*
MN	Bloomington	I Love Minnesota	*60 E Broadway, Bloomington MN 55425*
MN	Bloomington	Mall of America	*240 West Market, Bloomington MN 55425*
MN	Bloomington	Minnesotaaah	*60 E Broadway, Bloomington MN 55425*
MN	Bloomington	Moose Mountain Adventure Golf	*60 E Broadway, Bloomington MN 55425*
MN	Bloomington	Nickelodeon Universe	*Mall of America®, Bloomington MN 55425*
MN	Bloomington	Rainforest Cafe	*306 South Avenue, Bloomington MN 55425*
MN	Bloomington	SEA LIFE Minnesota Aquarium	*120 E Broadway, Bloomington MN 55425*
MN	Cannon Falls	Phillippo Scout Camp	*30646 32nd Ave Way, Cannon Falls MN 55009*
MN	Castle Danger	Gooseberry Falls State Park	*4GQP+MG Castle Danger, Castle Danger MN 55616*
MN	Chaska	Minnesota Landscape Arboretum	*Snyder Building, Chaska MN 55318*
MN	Duluth	Edgewater Hotel & Waterpark	*2400 London Rd, Duluth MN 55812*
MN	Duluth	Great Lakes Aquarium	*353 Harbor Dr #100, Duluth MN 55802*

MN	Duluth	Lake Superior Zoo	*7210 Fremont St, Duluth MN 55807*
MN	Duluth	Minnesota Gifts of Duluth	*394 S Lake Ave, Duluth MN 55802*
MN	Duluth	Minnesota Gifts of Duluth	*394 S Lake Ave, Duluth MN 55802*
MN	East Grand Forks	Cabela's	*Cabela's, East Grand Forks MN 56721*
MN	Ely	Zupancich Brothers Inc	*303 E Sheridan St, Ely MN 55731*
MN	Falcon Heights	KARE 11 At The Fair	*1260 Nelson St, Falcon Heights MN 55108*
MN	Falcon Heights	Visit Duluth	*1372 Cosgrove St, Falcon Heights MN 55108*
MN	Grand Marais	Joynes Ben Franklin	*105 Wisconsin St, Grand Marais MN 55604*
MN	Grand Rapids	Itasca County Historical Society	*201 N Pokegama Ave, Grand Rapids MN 55744*
MN	Harmony	Niagara Cave	*29842 Co Rd 30, Harmony MN 55939*
MN	International Falls	Border Bob's	*200 2nd Ave, International Falls MN 56649*
MN	Kellogg	Lark Toy Company	*63292 170th Ave, Kellogg MN 55945*
MN	Kellogg	LARK Toys	*63604 170th Ave, Kellogg MN 55945*
MN	Lake George	Itasca State Park	*5RWP+23 Lake George, Lake George MN 56458*
MN	Longville	Kellogg's Northwoods Shop	*1494 1st St N, Longville MN 56655*
MN	Lonsdale	Stillwater Olive Oil Company	*203 Jasper Ave, Lonsdale MN 55046*
MN	Marine on Saint Croix	Camp Kiwanis	*56HP+MR Marine on Saint Croix, Marine on Saint Croix MN 55047*

MN	Minneapolis	Minnesota Artists Penny Press	*1011 Washington Ave S #100, Minneapolis MN 55415*
MN	Minneapolis	Sexworld	*127 N Washington Ave, Minneapolis MN 55401*
MN	Minneapolis	Target Field	*1100 N 3rd Ave, Minneapolis MN 55403*
MN	New Ulm	The Hermann Monument Society	*10 Monument St, New Ulm MN 56073*
MN	Nisswa	Totem Pole	*23930 Smiley Rd, Nisswa MN 56468*
MN	Owatonna	Cabela's	*3900 Cabela Dr NW, Owatonna MN 55060*
MN	Rogers	Cabela's	*20200 Rogers Dr, Rogers MN 55374*
MN	Saint Paul	Como Friends	*1225 Estabrook Dr, Saint Paul MN 55103*
MN	Saint Paul	Como Town	*1268 Kaufman Dr, Saint Paul MN 55103*
MN	Saint Paul	Minnesota Children's Museum	*10 7th St W, Saint Paul MN 55102*
MN	Saint Paul	Minnesota History Center	*345 W Kellogg Blvd, Saint Paul MN 55102*
MN	Saint Paul	Renewal by Anderson	*1430 MN-51, Saint Paul MN 55108*
MN	Saint Paul	Science Museum of Minnesota	*120 W Kellogg Blvd W, Saint Paul MN 55102*
MN	Saint Paul	Union Depot	*Union Depot & Gate A1, Saint Paul MN 55101*
MN	Shakopee	Valleyfair	*1 Valley Fair Dr, Shakopee MN 55379*
MN	Silver Bay	AmericInn Lodge & Suites Silver Bay	*150 Mensing Dr, Silver Bay MN 55614*
MN	Silver Bay	Tettegouche State Park	*5702 MN-61, Silver Bay MN 55614*
MN	St. Cloud	Green Thumb Etc	*701 W St Germain St, St. Cloud MN 56301*

MN	Tower	Lake Vermilion-Soudan Underground Mine State Park	*1313 McKinley Park Rd, Tower MN 55790*
MN	Two Harbors	Lake County Chamber & Information Center	*1330 MN-61, Two Harbors MN 55616*
MN	Two Harbors	Split Rock Lighthouse	*Split Rock Lighthouse Visitor Center, Two Harbors MN 55616*
MN	Two Harbors	Split Rock Lighthouse	*Split Rock Lighthouse Visitor Center, Two Harbors MN 55616*
MN	Vergas	Trowbridge Creek Zoo	*50618 Co Rd 17, Vergas MN 56587*
MN	Walker	Walker General Store	*418 Minnesota Ave W, Walker MN 56484*
MN	Walker	Walker General Store	*516 Minnesota Ave W, Walker MN 56484*
MN	Woodbury	Cabela's	*8400 Hudson Rd, Woodbury MN 55125*
MN	Woodbury	Cabela's	*8400 Hudson Rd, Woodbury MN 55125*

Missouri			
MO	Arrow Rock	Boardwalk Canteen	*302 Main St, Arrow Rock MO 65320*
MO	Bonne Terre	Bonne Terre Mine	*39 N Allen St, Bonne Terre MO 63628*
MO	Bonne Terre	Bonne Terre Mine Dive Shop	*39 N Allen St, Bonne Terre MO 63628*
MO	Branson	Apple Tree Mall	*1830 W 76 Country Blvd, Branson MO 65616*
MO	Branson	Branson Casual Wear	*2843 W 76 Country Blvd, Branson MO 65616*
MO	Branson	Branson Landing	*208 Promenade Way, Branson MO 65616*
MO	Branson	Branson's Promised Land ZOO	*2751 Shepherd of the Hills Expy, Branson MO 65616*
MO	Branson	Branson's Wild World	*Branson's Wild World, Branson MO 65616*
MO	Branson	Cakes & Cream Desserts	*2805 W 76 Country Blvd, Branson MO 65616*
MO	Branson	Dannas BBQ and Burgers	*963 Historic Hwy 165, Branson MO 65616*
MO	Branson	Dick's Oldtime 5 & 10	*103 W Main St, Branson MO 65616*
MO	Branson	Dixie Outfitters	*1819 W 76 Country Blvd # 1, Branson MO 65616*
MO	Branson	Dolly Partons Stampede	*150 Songbird Dr, Branson MO 65616*
MO	Branson	Grand Country Resort	*1945 W 76 Country Blvd F, Branson MO 65616*
MO	Branson	Inspiration Tower - 1	*6165 W 76 Country Blvd, Branson MO 65616*
MO	Branson	Inspiration Tower - 2	*MM9V+VJ Branson, Branson MO 65616*
MO	Branson	Krazy Shirts	*2410 State Hwy 76, Branson MO 65616*

MO	Branson	Mr B's Ice Cream Parlor	*102 S 2nd St, Branson MO 65616*
MO	Branson	Music Road Mall	*3010 W 76 Country Blvd #8, Branson MO 65616*
MO	Branson	Ozarks Discovery Imax Theater	*3562 Shepherd of the Hills Expy, Branson MO 65616*
MO	Branson	Ripley's Believe It or Not	*3326 State Hwy 76, Branson MO 65616*
MO	Branson	Shorty Small's	*2600 W 76 Country Blvd, Branson MO 65616*
MO	Branson	Showboat Branson Belle	*McAdoo's Boatworks, Branson MO 65616*
MO	Branson	Silver Dollar City	*3505 State Hwy 76, Branson MO 65616*
MO	Branson	Silver Dollar City	*399 Silver Dollar City Pkwy, Branson MO 65616*
MO	Branson	Starvin Marvin's	*3400 W 76 Country Blvd, Branson MO 65616*
MO	Branson	The Butterfly Palace & Rainforest Adventure	*4106 W 76 Country Blvd, Branson MO 65616*
MO	Branson	The Shepherd of the Hills	*5583 W 76 Country Blvd, Branson MO 65616*
MO	Branson	The Track Family Fun Parks Track 4	*3388 W 76 Country Blvd, Branson MO 65616*
MO	Branson	Titanic Museum	*3235 W 76 Country Blvd, Branson MO 65616*
MO	Branson	Worlds Largest Toy Museum	*3609 W 76 Country Blvd, Branson MO 65616*
MO	Branson West	Talking Rocks Cavern	*423 Fairy Cave Ln, Branson West MO 65737*
MO	Branson West	Talking Rocks Taverns	*423 Fairy Cave Ln, Branson West MO 65737*
MO	Camdenton	Bridal Cave	*526 Bridal Cave Rd, Camdenton MO 65020*
MO	Camdenton	Bridal Cave	*526 Bridal Cave Rd, Camdenton MO 65020*

MO	Carthage	Carthage, MO Penny Press Machine	*125 S Garrison Ave, Carthage MO 64836*
MO	Carthage	Precious Moments Chapel Center	*4321 S Chapel Rd, Carthage MO 64836*
MO	Carthage	The Precious Moments Chapel	*4321 S Chapel Rd, Carthage MO 64836*
MO	Cassville	Roaring River State Park Store	*24517 State Hwy 112, Cassville MO 65625*
MO	Charleston	Boomtown	*100 Bealsey Park Rd., Charleston MO 63834*
MO	Chesterfield	St Louis Carousel	*St. Louis Carousel, Chesterfield MO 63017*
MO	Chesterfield	St. Louis Carousel at Faust Park	*St. Louis Carousel, Chesterfield MO 63017*
MO	Crossroads	Onondaga Cave State Park	*3Q67+QG Crossroads, Crossroads MO 65535*
MO	Crossroads	Onondaga Cave State Park	*3Q67+QG Crossroads, Crossroads MO 65535*
MO	Cuba	Fanning 66 Outpost Llc	*5957 Old Rte 66, Cuba MO 65453*
MO	Eagle Rock	Roaring River State Park	*H5PJ+F4 Eagle Rock, Eagle Rock MO 65641*
MO	Eureka	Six Flags St. Louis	*4900 Six Flags Rd, Eureka MO 63025*
MO	Excelsior Springs	Watkins Mill State Park	*CP2W+65 Excelsior Springs, Excelsior Springs MO 64024*
MO	Fenton	Wally's	*950 Assembly Pkwy, Fenton MO 63026*
MO	Hannibal	Mark Twain Boyhood Home & Museum	*120 N Main St, Hannibal MO 63401*
MO	Hannibal	Mark Twain Cave Complex	*Mark Twain Cave, Hannibal MO 63401*
MO	Hannibal	Mark Twain Museum and Gallery	*206 Hill St, Hannibal MO 63401*
MO	Hannibal	Mark Twain Riverboat	*100-110 Center St, Hannibal MO 63401*

MO	Hollister	Edwards Mill	*1 Opportunity Ave, Hollister MO 65672*
MO	Independence	Bass Pro Shops	*18001 Bass Pro Dr, Independence MO 64055*
MO	Jamesport	Jamesport Mercantile	*114 E Auberry Grove, Jamesport MO 64648*
MO	Jefferson City	Missouri Veterinary Medical Assn.	*2500 Country Club Dr, Jefferson City MO 65109*
MO	Jefferson City	Missouri Veterinary Museum	*2500 Country Club Dr, Jefferson City MO 65109*
MO	Joplin	Iron Skillet	*4240 State Rte 43, Joplin MO 64804*
MO	Joplin	Joplin Museum	*504 S Schifferdecker Ave, Joplin MO 64801*
MO	Kansas City	Arabia Steamboat Museum	*400 Grand Blvd, Kansas City MO 64106*
MO	Kansas City	Arabia Steamboat Museum	*400 Grand Blvd, Kansas City MO 64106*
MO	Kansas City	Kansas City Union Station	*30 W Pershing Rd Suite 210, Kansas City MO 64108*
MO	Kansas City	Kansas City Zoo & Aquarium	*6800 Zoo Drive, Kansas City MO 64132*
MO	Kansas City	LEGOLAND Discovery Center Kansas City	*2475 Grand Blvd, Kansas City MO 64108*
MO	Kansas City	National World War I Museum and Memorial	*Liberty Memorial, Kansas City MO 64108*
MO	Kansas City	Science City	*Union Station, Kansas City MO 64108*
MO	Kansas City	SEA LIFE Kansas City	*2427 Grand Blvd, Kansas City MO 64108*
MO	Kansas City	The Pressed Penny Tavern	*1509 Westport Rd, Kansas City MO 64111*
MO	Kansas City	Worlds Of Fun	*4545 Worlds of Fun Ave, Kansas City MO 64161*
MO	Kirkwood	The Magic House St. Louis Children's Museum	*516 Old Rte 66, Kirkwood MO 63122*

MO	Lake Ozark	Dogpatch Arcade	*1476 Bagnell Dam Blvd, Lake Ozark MO 65049*
MO	Lake Ozark	Dogpatch Store	*1482 Bagnell Dam Blvd, Lake Ozark MO 65049*
MO	Lake Ozark	Leather Man	*1446 Bagnell Dam Blvd, Lake Ozark MO 65049*
MO	Marceline	Walt Disney Hometown Museum	*120 E Santa Fe Ave, Marceline MO 64658*
MO	Marceline	Walt Disney Hometown Museum	*120 E Santa Fe Ave, Marceline MO 64658*
MO	Ozark	Lamberts	*1800 W State Hwy J, Ozark MO 65721*
MO	Point Lookout	Ralph Foster Museum	*155 Cultural Ct, Point Lookout MO 65726*
MO	Rolla	Mule Trading Post	*11160 Dillon Outer Rd, Rolla MO 65401*
MO	Rolla	The Mule Trading Post & Tobacco Barn	*11132 Dillon Outer Rd, Rolla MO 65401*
MO	Saint Charles	Bass Pro Shops Outdoor World	*1365 S 5th St, Saint Charles MO 63301*
MO	Saint Charles	Louis and Clark Boathouse	*1050 S Riverside Dr, Saint Charles MO 63301*
MO	Saint Joseph	Pony Express National Museum	*914 Penn St, Saint Joseph MO 64503*
MO	Saint Robert	Uranus Fudge Factory	*14400 State Hwy Z, Saint Robert MO 65584*
MO	Saint Robert	Uranus Fudge Factory	*14400 State Hwy Z, Saint Robert MO 65584*
MO	Springfield	American National Fish	*518 W Sunshine St, Springfield MO 65807*
MO	Springfield	Bass Pro Shops	*1935 S Campbell Ave, Springfield MO 65807*
MO	Springfield	Buc-ee's	*3284 N Mulroy Rd, Springfield MO 65803*
MO	Springfield	Buc-ee's	*5207 Buc-ee's Blvd, Springfield MO 65803*

MO	Springfield	Dickerson Park Zoo	*Dickerson Park Zoo Gift Shop, Springfield MO 65803*
MO	Springfield	Wonders of Wildlife	*118122 Park Central Square, Springfield MO 65806*
MO	St. Louis	Busch Stadium	*700 Clark Ave, St. Louis MO 63102*
MO	St. Louis	Busch Stadium / St. Louis Cardinals Baseball	*700 Clark Ave, St. Louis MO 63102*
MO	St. Louis	City Museum	*701 N 15th St, St. Louis MO 63103*
MO	St. Louis	Gateway Arch Riverboat Tours	*38 Washington Ter, St. Louis MO 63112*
MO	St. Louis	Jefferson National Expansion Memorial	*38 Washington Ter, St. Louis MO 63112*
MO	St. Louis	Jefferson National Parks Association	*1 Memorial Dr UNIT 1800, St. Louis MO 63102*
MO	St. Louis	Missouri Civil War Museum	*222 Worth Rd, St. Louis MO 63125*
MO	St. Louis	Missouri History Museum	*Dula Plaza, St. Louis MO 63112*
MO	St. Louis	Museum of Transportation	*2927 Barrett Station Rd, St. Louis MO 63122*
MO	St. Louis	St. Louis Aquarium at Union Station	*201 S 18th St, St. Louis MO 63103*
MO	St. Louis	St. Louis Science Center	*5050 Oakland Ave 2nd floor, St. Louis MO 63110*
MO	St. Louis	St. Louis Zoological Park	*6457 Government Dr, St. Louis MO 63110*
MO	Sullivan	Meramec Caverns	*1135 Hwy W, Sullivan MO 63080*
MO	Valley Park	World Bird Sanctuary	*Visitor Information Center, Valley Park MO 63088*

Mississippi			
MS	Biloxi	Beauvoir	*2244 Beach Blvd, Biloxi MS 39531*
MS	Biloxi	Big Play Family Fun Center	*153 Veterans Ave, Biloxi MS 39531*
MS	Biloxi	Big Play Family Fun Center	*1836 Beach Blvd, Biloxi MS 39531*
MS	Biloxi	Edgewater Mall (indoor, outside Aqua Massage)	*2600 Beach Blvd, Ste. #70, Biloxi MS 39531*
MS	Biloxi	Sharkheads	*1701 Beach Blvd, Biloxi MS 39531*
MS	Biloxi	Slap Ya Momma's BBQ Smokehouse	*1836 Beach Blvd, Biloxi MS 39531*
MS	Biloxi	Souvenir City	*2026 Beach Blvd, Biloxi MS 39531*
MS	Gulfport	Lynn Meadows Discovery Center	*246 Dolan Ave, Gulfport MS 39507*
MS	Natchez	Old South Trading Post	*600 S Canal St, Natchez MS 39120*
MS	Ocean Springs	Aunt Jenny's Catfish Restaurant	*1217 Washington Ave, Ocean Springs MS 39564*
MS	Oxford	University Sporting Goods	*105 Courthouse Square, Oxford MS 38655*
MS	Oxford	University Sporting Goods	*103 Courthouse Square, Oxford MS 38655*
MS	Pearl	Bass Pro Shops	*100 Bass Pro Dr, Pearl MS 39208*
MS	Pearlington	INFINITY Science Center	*1 Discovery Cir, Pearlington MS 39572*
MS	Vicksburg	Biedenharn Coca-Cola Museum	*1107 Washington St, Vicksburg MS 39183*

			Montana
MT	Billings	Cabela's	*4550 King Ave E, Billings MT 59101*
MT	Billings	Zoo Montana	*Yellowstone Arboretum, Billings MT 59106*
MT	Bozeman	Museum of the Rockies	*540 W Kagy Blvd, Bozeman MT 59715*
MT	Cardwell	Lewis & Clark Caverns State Park	*R4MQ+CC Cardwell, Cardwell MT 59759*
MT	Darby	Souvenir Coins	*202 S Main St, Darby MT 59829*
MT	Fort Benton	Jack's Bar & Lanes LLC	*1314 Front St, Fort Benton MT 59442*
MT	Garryowen	Custer Battlefield Museum	*4185 Garryowen Rd, Garryowen MT 59031*
MT	Glendive	Makoshika State Park	*1300 Snyder St, Glendive MT 59330*
MT	Helena	Barnes Jewelry	*357 N Last Chance Gulch, Helena MT 59601*
MT	Helena	ExplorationWorks	*995 Carousel Way, Helena MT 59601*
MT	Hungry Horse	Hungry Horse Dam Visitor Centre	*100 Hungry Horse Dm Rd, Hungry Horse MT 59919*
MT	Kalispell	Cabela's	*125 Treeline Rd, Kalispell MT 59901*
MT	Kalispell	Cabela's	*125 Treeline Rd, Kalispell MT 59901*
MT	Missoula	A Carousel for Missoula	*101 Carousel Dr, Missoula MT 59802*
MT	Missoula	Cabela's	*3650 Brooks St, Missoula MT 59801*
MT	Missoula	Montana Snowbowl	*1700 Snow Bowl Rd, Missoula MT 59808*
MT	Saint Regis	St Regis Travel Center	*1129 10 E, Saint Regis MT 59866*
MT	Virginia City	Nevada City Hotel	*1578 MT-287, Virginia City MT 59755*

MT	West Glacier	Apgar Village Lodge	*258 Apgar Lp Rd, West Glacier MT 59936*
MT	West Glacier	Eddies Cafe & Gifts	*236 Apgar Lp Rd, West Glacier MT 59936*
MT	West Glacier	West Glacier Gifts	*200 Going-to-the-Sun Rd, West Glacier MT 59936*
MT	West Yellowstone	Eagle's Store	*3 N Canyon St, West Yellowstone MT 59758*
MT	West Yellowstone	Forever Young	*8 N Canyon St, West Yellowstone MT 59758*
MT	West Yellowstone	Grizzly & Wolf Discovery Center	*201 S Canyon St, West Yellowstone MT 59758*
MT	West Yellowstone	Grizzly & Wolf Discovery Center	*201 S Canyon St, West Yellowstone MT 59758*
MT	West Yellowstone	Grizzly & Wolf Discovery Center	*201 S Canyon St, West Yellowstone MT 59758*
MT	West Yellowstone	Market Place	*22 Madison Ave, West Yellowstone MT 59758*
MT	West Yellowstone	Yellowstone IMAX Theatre	*101 S Canyon St, West Yellowstone MT 59758*
MT	West Yellowstone	Yellowstone Motorhed	*111 Yellowstone Ave, West Yellowstone MT 59758*
MT	West Yellowstone	Yellowstone Park Village Gift Shop	*8 N Canyon St, West Yellowstone MT 59758*

			North Carolina
NC	Albemarle	Fresh House	*805 W Main St, Albemarle NC 28001*
NC	Asheboro	North Carolina Zoo	*4401 Zoo Pkwy, Asheboro NC 27205*
NC	Asheboro	North Carolina Zoo	*J6CV+XG Asheboro, Asheboro NC 27205*
NC	Asheville	WNC Nature Center	*77 Gashes Crk Rd, Asheville NC 28805*
NC	Atlantic Beach	Fort Macon	*2305 E Fort Macon Rd, Atlantic Beach NC 28512*
NC	Atlantic Beach	Fort Macon State Park	*2305 E Fort Macon Rd, Atlantic Beach NC 28512*
NC	Banner Elk	Wilderness Run Alpine Coaster	*3265 Tynecastle Hwy, Banner Elk NC 28604*
NC	Beaufort	North Carolina Maritime Museum	*315 Front St, Beaufort NC 28516*
NC	Blowing Rock	Mystery Hill	*129 Mystery Hill Ln, Blowing Rock NC 28605*
NC	Blowing Rock	Sunset Tee's & Hattery	*1117 Main St, Blowing Rock NC 28605*
NC	Blowing Rock	The Blowing Rock	*432 The Rock Rd, Blowing Rock NC 28605*
NC	Blowing Rock	Tweetsie Railroad	*288 Tweetsie Railroad Ln, Blowing Rock NC 28605*
NC	Blowing Rock	Tweetsie Railroad	*100 Tweetsie Railroad Ln, Blowing Rock NC 28605*
NC	Boone	Dan I Boone Inn	*130 Hardin St, Boone NC 28607*
NC	Brevard	Celestial Mountain Music	*15 W Main St, Brevard NC 28712*
NC	Brevard	Southern Comfort Records	*28 W Main St, Brevard NC 28712*
NC	Bryson City	Fort Tomahawk	*8A Franklin St, Bryson City NC 28713*

NC	Bryson City	Smoky Mountain Trains	*100 Greenlee St, Bryson City NC 28713*
NC	Bryson City	Smoky Mountain Trains	*100 Greenlee St, Bryson City NC 28713*
NC	Charlotte	Discovery Place	*308 N Tryon St, Charlotte NC 28202*
NC	Charlotte	Discovery Place Science	*168 W 6th St, Charlotte NC 28202*
NC	Charlotte	Pinkys Westside Grill	*1600 W Morehead St, Charlotte NC 28208*
NC	Cherokee	B&S Gifts	*1084 Tsalagi Rd, Cherokee NC 28719*
NC	Cherokee	Gift Mart	*1093 Tsalagi Rd, Cherokee NC 28719*
NC	Cherokee	Great Smokies Gifts	*1928 Big Cove Rd, Cherokee NC 28719*
NC	Cherokee	Great Smokies Gifts	*1928 Big Cove Rd, Cherokee NC 28719*
NC	Cherokee	Museum of the Cherokee Indian	*589 Tsali Blvd, Cherokee NC 28719*
NC	Cherokee	Museum of the Cherokee Indian	*589 Tsali Blvd, Cherokee NC 28719*
NC	Cherokee	Ravenhawk Gifts & Collectibles	*686 Tsali Blvd, Cherokee NC 28719*
NC	Cherokee	Ravenhawk Gifts & Collectibles	*686 Tsali Blvd, Cherokee NC 28719*
NC	Cherokee	Smoky Mountain Gold-Ruby Mine	*971 Tsali Blvd, Cherokee NC 28719*
NC	Cherokee	Smoky Mountain Gold-Ruby Mine	*971 Tsali Blvd, Cherokee NC 28719*
NC	Cherokee	Smoky Mountain Trader	*845 Tsali Blvd, Cherokee NC 28719*
NC	Concord	Bass Pro Shops Tracker Boat Center	*8181 Concord Mills Boulevard, Concord NC 28027*
NC	Concord	Charlotte Motor Speedway	*5555 Concord Pkwy S, Concord NC 28027*

NC	Concord	Great Wolf Lodge Concord	*10175 Weddington Rd, Concord NC 28027*
NC	Concord	Roush Fenway Racing	*4606 Roush Pl, Concord NC 28027*
NC	Concord	Roush Racing Inc	*4600 Roush Pl, Concord NC 28027*
NC	Concord	SEA LIFE	*8111 Concord Mills Boulevard Ste 743, Concord NC 28027*
NC	Concord	SEA LIFE Charlotte-Concord Aquarium	*8111 Concord Mills Boulevard Ste 743, Concord NC 28027*
NC	Corolla	Flying Smiles Kites	*1159 Austin St, Corolla NC 27927*
NC	Crumpler	Shatley Springs Inn	*446 Shatley Springs Rd, Crumpler NC 28617*
NC	Crumpler	Shatley Springs Inn	*407 Shatley Springs Rd, Crumpler NC 28617*
NC	Duck	Outside "Dazzles" at the Water Front Shops	*1232 Duck Rd, Duck NC 27949*
NC	Durham	Museum of Life and Science	*433 W Murray Ave, Durham NC 27704*
NC	Fayetteville	Airborne & Special Operations Museum Foundation	*100 Bragg Blvd, Fayetteville NC 28301*
NC	Garner	Bass Pro Shops	*201 Cabela Dr, Garner NC 27529*
NC	Garner	Cabela's	*201 Cabela Dr, Garner NC 27529*
NC	Gastonia	Schiele Museum-Natural History	*1500 E Garrison Blvd, Gastonia NC 28054*
NC	Gastonia	The Schiele Museum of Natural History & Planetariu	*1500 E Garrison Blvd, Gastonia NC 28054*
NC	Granite Falls	PC PARAMEDIX	*12 Dudley Ave, Granite Falls NC 28630*
NC	Granite Falls	PC PARAMEDIX	*12 Dudley Ave, Granite Falls NC 28630*

NC	Greensboro	Greensboro Science Center	*4301 Lawndale Dr, Greensboro NC 27455*
NC	Greensboro	Wet n Wild Emerald Pointe Water Park	*3910 S Holden Rd, Greensboro NC 27406*
NC	Greensboro	Wet n Wild Emerald Pointe Water Park	*3910 S Holden Rd, Greensboro NC 27406*
NC	Hatteras	Hatteras Landing	*58848 Marina Way, Hatteras NC 27943*
NC	Holden Beach	Beach Mart	*3368 Holden Beach Rd SW, Holden Beach NC 28462*
NC	Holden Beach	Beach Mart	*3368 Holden Beach Rd SW, Holden Beach NC 28462*
NC	Hothouse	Fields of the Wood	*4PCX+6W Hothouse, Hothouse NC 28906*
NC	Huntersville	Joe Gibbs Racing	*13415 Reese Blvd W, Huntersville NC 28078*
NC	Jacksonville	New River Bowling Center	*AS205, Jacksonville NC 28540*
NC	Kure Beach	Fort Fisher Historic Museum	*1610 Fort Fisher Blvd S, Kure Beach NC 28449*
NC	Kure Beach	Fort Fisher State Historic Site	*1610 Fort Fisher Blvd S, Kure Beach NC 28449*
NC	Kure Beach	North Carolina Aquarium At Fort Fisher	*900 Loggerhead Rd, Kure Beach NC 28449*
NC	Lake Lure	Chimney Rock at Chimney Rock State Park	*1638 Chimney Rock Park Rd, Lake Lure NC 28746*
NC	Lake Lure	Cliff Dwellers Gift Shop	*1638 Chimney Rock Park Rd, Lake Lure NC 28746*
NC	Lexington	425 Industrial Dr	*425 Industrial Dr, Lexington NC 27295*
NC	Lexington	Lexington Style Trimmings	*1513 E Center St Ext, Lexington NC 27292*
NC	Lexington	Speedy's Barbecue Inc	*1317 Winston Rd, Lexington NC 27295*
NC	Lexington	Speedy's BBQ INC	*1317 Winston Rd, Lexington NC 27295*

NC	Linville	Grandfather Mountain	*2050 Blowing Rock Hwy, Linville NC 28646*
NC	Linville	Grandfather Mountain	*2050 Blowing Rock Hwy, Linville NC 28646*
NC	Linville	Mile High Swinging Bridge	*2050 Blowing Rock Hwy, Linville NC 28646*
NC	Locust	Fresh House	*809 W Main St, Locust NC 28097*
NC	Maggie Valley	Engineerkate	*1080 Ski Lodge Rd, Maggie Valley NC 28751*
NC	Maggie Valley	Maggie Mountaineer Crafts	*2394 Soco Rd, Maggie Valley NC 28751*
NC	Maggie Valley	Maggie Mountaineer Crafts	*2394 Soco Rd, Maggie Valley NC 28751*
NC	Manteo	Friends of Elizabeth II	*603 Harriot St Room 9, Manteo NC 27954*
NC	Manteo	North Carolina Aquarium on Roanoke Island	*374 Airport Rd, Manteo NC 27954*
NC	Manteo	North Carolina Aquarium on Roanoke Island	*374 Airport Rd, Manteo NC 27954*
NC	Manteo	Roanoke Island Festival Park	*1 Festival Park, Manteo NC 27954*
NC	Marion	Linville Caverns	*19929 US-221, Marion NC 28752*
NC	Marion	Linville Caverns, Inc.	*19929 US-221, Marion NC 28752*
NC	Moncure	US Army Corps of Engineers	*2082 Jordan Dam Rd, Moncure NC 27559*
NC	Mooresville	Dale Earnhardt Inc	*1675 Coddle Creek Hwy, Mooresville NC 28115*
NC	Mooresville	Dale Earnhardt Inc	*1675 Coddle Creek Hwy, Mooresville NC 28115*
NC	Mooresville	JR Motorsports	*349 Cayuga Dr, Mooresville NC 28117*
NC	Mooresville	North Carolina Auto Racing Hall of Fame	*119 Knob Hill Rd, Mooresville NC 28117*

NC	Mooresville	North Carolina Auto Racing Hall of Fame	*119 Knob Hill Rd, Mooresville NC 28117*
NC	Mooresville	Team Penske	*200 Penske Way, Mooresville NC 28115*
NC	Mount Airy	BEAR CREEK GIFTS and FUDGE FACTORY	*165 N Main St, Mount Airy NC 27030*
NC	Mount Airy	BEAR CREEK GIFTS and FUDGE FACTORY LLC	*165 N Main St, Mount Airy NC 27030*
NC	Mount Airy	Mayberry Market and Souvenirs	*182 N Main St, Mount Airy NC 27030*
NC	Mount Airy	Memories on Main Antiques	*140 N Main St, Mount Airy NC 27030*
NC	Nags Head	Jennette's Pier	*7223 S Virginia Dare Trail, Nags Head NC 27959*
NC	Nags Head	Jennette's Pier	*7223 S Virginia Dare Trail, Nags Head NC 27959*
NC	Nags Head	kitty hawk	*3933 S Croatan Hwy, Nags Head NC 27959*
NC	Nags Head	Kitty Hawk Kites Hang Gliding School	*302 W Carolista Dr, Nags Head NC 27959*
NC	New Bern	Birthplace of Pepsi Cola	*256 Middle St, New Bern NC 28560*
NC	New Bern	Birthplace of Pepsi Cola	*252 Middle St, New Bern NC 28560*
NC	New Bern	North Carolina History Center at Tryon Palace	*529 S Front St, New Bern NC 28562*
NC	New Bern	North Carolina History Center at Tryon Palace	*529 S Front St, New Bern NC 28562*
NC	Ocracoke	Teach's Hole	*935 Irvin Garrish Hwy, Ocracoke NC 27960*
NC	Pine Knoll Shores	North Carolina Aquarium at Pine Knoll Shores	*1 Roosevelt Blvd, Pine Knoll Shores NC 28512*
NC	Poplar Branch	Diggers Dungeon	*5658 Caratoke Hwy, Poplar Branch NC 27965*
NC	Raleigh	Lyons General Store	*4325 Glenwood Ave Suite 1070, Raleigh NC 27612*

NC	Raleigh	Marbles Kids Museum	*215 E Hargett St, Raleigh NC 27601*
NC	Raleigh	North Carolina Museum of History	*5 E Edenton St, Raleigh NC 27601*
NC	Raleigh	North Carolina Museum of Natural Sciences	*100 N Salisbury St, Raleigh NC 27601*
NC	Raleigh	North Carolina: Museum of Natural Sciences	*100 N Salisbury St, Raleigh NC 27601*
NC	Raleigh	Pullen Park	*Pullen Park, Raleigh NC 27606*
NC	Raleigh	Pullen Park	*440 Park Ave, Raleigh NC 27606*
NC	Raleigh	Raleigh Union Station	*510 W Martin St, Raleigh NC 27603*
NC	Randleman	Richard Petty Museum	*309 Branson Mill Rd, Randleman NC 27317*
NC	Robbinsville	Deal's Gap Motorcycle Resort	*17548 Tapoco Rd, Robbinsville NC 28771*
NC	Robbinsville	Deals Gap Motorcycle Resort	*17548 Tapoco Rd, Robbinsville NC 28771*
NC	Robbinsville	Tail of the Dragon	*17555 Tapoco Rd, Robbinsville NC 28771*
NC	Robbinsville	Tail of the Dragon / Deals Gap	*17555 Tapoco Rd, Robbinsville NC 28771*
NC	Scotland Neck	Sylvan Heights Bird Park	*220 Lees Meadow Rd, Scotland Neck NC 27874*
NC	Spencer	N.C. Transportation Museum	*1 Samuel Spencer Dr, Spencer NC 28159*
NC	Spindale	KidSenses Children's INTERACTIVE Museum	*172 W Main St, Spindale NC 28160*
NC	Spindale	KidSenses Children's INTERACTIVE Museum	*172 W Main St, Spindale NC 28160*
NC	Sunset Beach	Sunset Beach Trading Co.	*423 State Rd 1172, Sunset Beach NC 28468*
NC	Surf City	Topsail Island Trading Co	*201 N New River Dr, Surf City NC 28445*

NC	Surf City	Topsail Island Trading Co	*201 N New River Dr, Surf City NC 28445*
NC	Thomasville	City Of Thomasville	*10 Salem St, Thomasville NC 27360*
NC	Troutman	Zootastic Park	*448 Pilch Rd, Troutman NC 28166*
NC	Welcome	Richard Childress Racing Museum	*236 Industrial Dr, Welcome NC 27374*
NC	West Jefferson	Ashe County Cheese Inc	*106 E Main St, West Jefferson NC 28694*
NC	West Jefferson	Ashe County Cheese Inc	*106 E Main St, West Jefferson NC 28694*
NC	Whittier	Santa's Land Fun Park & Zoo	*571 Wolfetown Rd, Whittier NC 28789*
NC	Wilmington	Battleship North Carolina	*1 Battleship Rd NE, Wilmington NC 28401*
NC	Wilmington	Museum of the Bizarre	*201 S Water St, Wilmington NC 28401*
NC	Wilmington	U.S.S. North Carolina	*1 Battleship Rd NE, Wilmington NC 28401*
NC	Wilmington	Village Market	*101 Market St, Wilmington NC 28401*
NC	Winston-Salem	Old Salem Visitor Center	*900 Old Salem Rd, Winston-Salem NC 27101*
NC	Woodworth	Buchanan's Store	*6547 Drewry-Virginia Line Rd, Woodworth NC 27553*
NC	Woodworth	Buchanan's Store	*6547 Drewry-Virginia Line Rd, Woodworth NC 27553*
NC	Wrightsville Beach	Redix Southern Lifestyle Outfitters	*120 Causeway Dr, Wrightsville Beach NC 28480*

			North Dakota
ND	Bismarck	Dakota Zoo	*604 Riverside Park Rd, Bismarck ND 58504*
ND	Bismarck	Dakota Zoo	*602 Riverside Park Rd, Bismarck ND 58504*
ND	Bismarck	North Dakota Heritage Center	*604 E Boulevard Ave, Bismarck ND 58505*
ND	Bismarck	North Dakota Heritage Center & State Museum	*612 E Boulevard Ave, Bismarck ND 58505*
ND	Fargo	Fargo-Moorhead Red Hawks	*1515 15th Ave N, Fargo ND 58102*
ND	Fargo	Red River Zoo	*4255 23rd Ave S, Fargo ND 58104*
ND	Jamestown	National Buffalo Museum	*500 17th St SE, Jamestown ND 58401*
ND	Jamestown	National Buffalo Museum	*500 17th St SE, Jamestown ND 58401*
ND	Medora	Dacotah Territories Gift Shop	*272 Pacific Ave, Medora ND 58645*
ND	Medora	Dacotah Territory Gifts 2	*275 Pacific Ave, Medora ND 58645*
ND	Medora	Hitching Post	*440 3rd St, Medora ND 58645*
ND	Medora	Hitching Post	*440 3rd St, Medora ND 58645*
ND	Minot	Roosevelt Park Zoo	*25 10th St SE, Minot ND 58701*
ND	Wahpeton	Chahinkapa Zoo	*Wahpeton Parks & Rec Wahpeton Parks & Rec, Wahpeton ND 58075*
ND	Wahpeton	Chahinkapa Zoo	*1006 Rj Hughes Dr, Wahpeton ND 58075*

Nebraska			
NE	Alliance	Alliance Knight Museum	*908 Yellowstone Ave, Alliance NE 69301*
NE	Alliance	Carhenge	*2151 Co Rd 59, Alliance NE 69301*
NE	Ashland	Simmons wildlife safari park	*16406 292nd St, Ashland NE 68003*
NE	Ashland	Strategic Air Command & Aerospace Museum	*28210 W Park Hwy, Ashland NE 68003*
NE	Aurora	Edgerton Explorit center	*208 16th St, Aurora NE 68818*
NE	Gothenburg	Pony express station museum	*Ehmen Park, Gothenburg NE 69138*
NE	Grand Island	Stuhr Museum	*3670 E Airport Rd, Grand Island NE 68801*
NE	Gretna	Valas Pumpkin Patch	*12102 S 180th St, Gretna NE 68028*
NE	Hastings	Hastings Museum of Natural and Cultural History	*Hastings Museum, Hastings NE 68901*
NE	Kearney	Cabela's	*3600 US-30, Kearney NE 68847*
NE	Kearney	Great Platte River Road Archway	*3060 E 1st St, Kearney NE 68847*
NE	La Vista	Cabela's	*12703 Westport Pkwy, La Vista NE 68138*
NE	Lincoln	Lincoln Children's Museum	*1420 P St, Lincoln NE 68508*
NE	Lincoln	University of NE State Museum	*645 N 14th St, Lincoln NE 68588*
NE	Minden	Pioneer Village	*138 North St, Minden NE 68959*
NE	North Platte	Ft. Cody Trading Post	*3246 W Eugene Ave, North Platte NE 69101*
NE	North Platte	Golden Spike Tower	*1249 N Homestead Rd, North Platte NE 69101*
NE	Omaha	Henry Doorly Zoo	*3701 S 10th St, Omaha NE 68107*
NE	Royal	Ashfall Fossil Beds	*86798 Ashfall State Historical Park Recreation Rd, Royal NE 68773*

NE	Sidney	Cabela's	*115 Cabela Dr, Sidney NE 69162*
NE	Sidney	Cabela's	*115 Cabela Dr, Sidney NE 69162*
NE	Valentine	Shell	*101 US-20, Valentine NE 69201*

New Hampshire

NH	Concord	McAuliffe-Shepard Discovery Center	*2 Institute Dr, Concord NH 03301*
NH	Conway	Conway Scenic Railroad	*38 Norcross Cir, Conway NH 03860*
NH	Conway	The Rugged Mill	*2633 White Mountain Hwy, Conway NH 03860*
NH	Franconia	Cannon Mountain Aerial Tramway	*260 Tramway Dr, Franconia NH 03580*
NH	Gorham	Great Glen Trails Outdoor Center	*62 Main St, Gorham NH 03581*
NH	Hampton	Hampton Beach Casino	*169 Ocean Blvd, Hampton NH 03842*
NH	Holderness	Clark's Bears - White Mtn Railroad	*110 US-3, Holderness NH 03245*
NH	Hooksett	Common Man Roadside	*25 Springer Rd, Hooksett NH 03106*
NH	Hooksett	New Hampshire Welcome Center (Common Man Roadside North)	*530 W River Rd, Hooksett NH 03106*
NH	Jackson	Mount Washington Summit	*Summit Station, Jackson NH 03846*
NH	Jefferson	Santa's Village	*528 Presidential Hwy, Jefferson NH 03583*
NH	Lincoln	Clark's Trading Post - gift shop	*110 Daniel Webster Hwy, Lincoln NH 03251*
NH	Lincoln	Flume Gorge	*482V+C4 Lincoln, Lincoln NH 03251*
NH	Mason	Parker's Maple Barn	*1316 Brookline Rd, Mason NH 03048*
NH	Moultonborough	The Old Country Store and Museum	*1847 Whittier Hwy, Moultonborough NH 03254*
NH	Mount WASHINGTON	Mt Washington State Park	*Mt. Washington State Park, Mount WASHINGTON NH 03589*

NH	New Hampton	Yogi Bear's Jellystone Park Campground - Ashland	*62 Jellystone Park, New Hampton NH 03256*
NH	Pittsfield	Suncook Valley Rotary Hot Air Balloon Rally	*41 Main St, Pittsfield NH 03263*
NH	Rumney	Polar Caves Park	*Polar Caves Park, Rumney NH 03266*
NH	Salem	Canobie Lake Park	*86 N Policy St, Salem NH 03079*
NH	Wolfeboro	Black's Paper Store & Gift Shop	*8 S Main St, Wolfeboro NH 03894*
NH	Woodstock	Lost River Gorge & Boulder Caves	*Lost River Reservation, Woodstock NH 03262*

New Jersey			
NJ	Atlantic City	Absecon Lighthouse	*301 Pacific Ave, Atlantic City NJ 08401*
NJ	Atlantic City	Bass Pro Shops	*30 Christopher Columbus Blvd, Atlantic City NJ 08401*
NJ	Atlantic City	IT SUGAR	*1 Atlantic Ocean Suite 1110, Atlantic City NJ 08401*
NJ	Atlantic City	Mall on pier on boardwalk across from ceasers.	*The Pier Shops at Caesars 1 Atlantic Ocean, Atlantic City NJ 08401*
NJ	Atlantic City	Rainforest Cafe	*2218-2200, Atlantic City NJ 08401*
NJ	Atlantic City	Steel Pier	*Steeplechase Pier Heliport, Atlantic City NJ 08401*
NJ	Beach Haven	Silver Mall	*210 N Bay Ave, Beach Haven NJ 08008*
NJ	Blairstown	Land of Make Believe & Pirate's Cove	*354 Great Meadows Rd, Blairstown NJ 07825*
NJ	Bridgewater	Somerset Patriots Baseball	*1 Patriots Park, Bridgewater NJ 08807*
NJ	Camden	Adventure Aquarium	*1 Riverside Dr, Camden NJ 08103*
NJ	Camden	Battleship New Jersey	*100 Clinton St, Camden NJ 08103*
NJ	Camden	Camden Children's Garden	*3 Riverside Dr, Camden NJ 08103*
NJ	Cape May	Grand Hotel	*1039 Beach Ave, Cape May NJ 08204*
NJ	Cape May Point	Cape May Lighthouse	*215 Lighthouse Rd, Cape May Point NJ 08212*
NJ	Cape May Point	Cape May Lighthouse	*215 Lighthouse Rd, Cape May Point NJ 08212*
NJ	East Rutherford	Sea Life New Jersey	*1 American Dream Way, East Rutherford NJ 07073*
NJ	Edison	Rainforest Cafe	*520 Menlo Park Dr, Edison NJ 08837*
NJ	Egg Harbor Township	Storybook Land	*6415 Black Horse Pike, Egg Harbor Township NJ 08234*

NJ	Jackson Township	Six Flags Great Adventure	*4HP6+H4, Jackson Township NJ 08514*
NJ	Jersey City	Ellis Island	*Psychopathic Ward, Jersey City NJ 07305*
NJ	Jersey City	Statue of Liberty National Monument	*1 Communipaw Ave, Jersey City NJ 07304*
NJ	Knowlton Township	Camp Taylor	*85 Mt Pleasant Rd, Knowlton Township NJ 07832*
NJ	Lower Township	Cape May Ferry Terminal	*1200 Lincoln Blvd, Lower Township NJ 08204*
NJ	Margate City	Lucy the Elephant	*9200 Atlantic Ave, Margate City NJ 08402*
NJ	Middle Township	Cape May County Park & Zoo	*707 US-9, Middle Township NJ 08210*
NJ	Montvale	Montvale Service Area	*Milemarker 172, Montvale NJ 07645*
NJ	Ocean City	Jilly's Arcade	*1168 Boardwalk, Ocean City NJ 08226*
NJ	Ocean City	Playland's Castaway Cove	*1020 Boardwalk, Ocean City NJ 08226*
NJ	Ocean Township	Prehistoric Fossils	*101 Veterans Blvd, Ocean Township NJ 08758*
NJ	Paramus	Bergen County Zoo	*216 Forest Ave, Paramus NJ 07652*
NJ	Point Pleasant Beach	Jenkinson's Aquarium	*300 Ocean Ave, Point Pleasant Beach NJ 08742*
NJ	Point Pleasant Beach	Jenkinson's Ice Cream & Sweet	*300 Ocean Ave, Point Pleasant Beach NJ 08742*
NJ	Seaside Heights	Casino Pier and Breakwater Beach Waterpark	*62 Grant Ave, Seaside Heights NJ 08751*
NJ	Secaucus	Alexander Hamilton Service Area	*111.6 NJ Tpke, Secaucus NJ 07094*
NJ	Toms River	Insectropolis	*1761 US-9, Toms River NJ 08755*
NJ	Trenton	Richard Stockton Travel Plaza	*200 Uncle Pete's Rd, Trenton NJ 08691*

NJ	West Orange	Turtle Back Zoo	*560 Northfield Ave, West Orange NJ 07052*
NJ	Wildwood	Penny Press	*3409 Boardwalk, Wildwood NJ 08260*

			New Mexico
NM	Alamogordo	McGinn's PistachioLand - Pistachio Tree Ranch	*7320 US-54, Alamogordo NM 88310*
NM	Alamogordo	New Mexico Museum of Space History	*3198 State Rte 2001, Alamogordo NM 88310*
NM	Alamogordo	White Sands National Park - White Sands Trading Company Gift	*19955 US-70, Alamogordo NM 88310*
NM	Albuquerque	ABQ BioPark - Zoo	*Band Shell, Albuquerque NM 87102*
NM	Albuquerque	Albuquerque Aquarium & Rio Grande Botanical Garden	*38W7+PQ Albuquerque, Albuquerque NM 87104*
NM	Albuquerque	Albuquerque Botanical Garden	*38W7+9V Albuquerque, Albuquerque NM 87104*
NM	Albuquerque	Anderson Abruzzo Albuquerque International Balloon	*9201 Balloon Museum Dr NE, Albuquerque NM 87113*
NM	Albuquerque	Coverd Wagon	*2034 S Plaza St NW, Albuquerque NM 87104*
NM	Albuquerque	Explora Science Center	*1701 Mountain Rd. NW, Albuquerque NM 87104*
NM	Albuquerque	Hotel Albuquerque at Old Town	*800 Rio Grande Blvd NW, Albuquerque NM 87104*
NM	Albuquerque	Indian Pueblo Cultural Center	*2401 12th St NW, Albuquerque NM 87104*
NM	Albuquerque	New Mexico Museum of Natural History	*1801 Mountain Rd NW, Albuquerque NM 87104*
NM	Albuquerque	New Mexico Museum of Natural History and Science	*1801 Mountain Rd NW, Albuquerque NM 87104*
NM	Albuquerque	Old Town - Wild West T's & Gifts	*401 San Felipe Street Northwest (Old Town), Albuquerque NM 87104*
NM	Albuquerque	Old Town T-Shirt Co	*323 Romero St NW #14, Albuquerque NM 87104*

NM	Albuquerque	Rattlesnake Museum	*202 San Felipe St NW, Albuquerque NM 87104*
NM	Albuquerque	Sandia Peak Ski & Tram	*20 Tramway Rd NE, Albuquerque NM 87122*
NM	Albuquerque	Sawmill Market	*1909 Bellamah Ave NW, Albuquerque NM 87104*
NM	Albuquerque	The Breaking Bad Store ABQ	*2047 S Plaza St NW, Albuquerque NM 87104*
NM	Capitan	Smokey Bear Museum	*Smokey Bear Historical Park, Capitan NM 88316*
NM	Carlsbad	Carlsbad Caverns National Park	*854Q4CXV+48, Carlsbad NM 88220*
NM	Carlsbad	Carlsbad Caverns National Park	*727 Carlsbad Cavern Hwy, Carlsbad NM 88220*
NM	Carlsbad	Living Desert Zoo & Gardens State Park	*CPRF+XH Carlsbad, Carlsbad NM 88220*
NM	Carlsbad	New Mexico Living Desert State Park (Zoo and Gardens)	*1504 Miehls Dr, Carlsbad NM 88220*
NM	Cedar Crest	Tinkertown Museum	*7556 Sandia Crest Rd, Cedar Crest NM 87008*
NM	Chama	Cumbres Mall	*493 Highway 17, Chama NM 87520*
NM	Chama	Iron Rail Inn - Restaurant & Bar	*501 Terrace Ave, Chama NM 87520*
NM	Chama	Mountainview Mall Cumbres Mall	*503 Terrace Ave, Chama NM 87520*
NM	Cimarron	Philmont Scout Ranch	*47 Sombra Rd, Cimarron NM 87714*
NM	Clines Corners	Clines Corner	*1 Yacht Club Dr, Clines Corners NM 87070*
NM	Cloudcroft	Cloudcroft Hotel and Gift Shop	*306 Burro Ave, Cloudcroft NM 88317*
NM	Farmington	HMS Host at the Delaware Welcome Center	*799 Sandstone Ave, Farmington NM 87401*

NM	Fort Sumner	Billy The Kid Museum	*1435 Sumner Ave, Fort Sumner NM 88119*
NM	Gallup	Hotel El Rancho	*1011 E Hwy 66, Gallup NM 87301*
NM	Gallup	Manuelito Visitor Center	*Hadden Park, Gallup NM 87301*
NM	Glenrio	Glenrio VIC Tourism	*37315-C I-40, Glenrio NM 88434*
NM	Grants	New Mexico Mining Museum	*100 Iron Ave, Grants NM 87020*
NM	La Luz	PistachioLand	*15 Griffin Rd, La Luz NM 88337*
NM	Las Cruces	Hotel Encanto de Las Cruces	*705 S Telshor Blvd, Las Cruces NM 88011*
NM	Las Cruces	Mesilla Valley Maze	*3855 W Picacho Ave, Las Cruces NM 88007*
NM	Lordsburg	Lordsburg Visitor Center	*191 Stagecoach Rd, Lordsburg NM 88045*
NM	Los Alamos	Aspen Copies & Office supplies Penny Pincher Souvenir Coins	*1907 Central Ave, Los Alamos NM 87544*
NM	Mesilla	Billy the Kid Gift Shop	*2385 Calle De Guadalupe, Mesilla NM 88046*
NM	Ranchos de Taos	Chimayo Trading Del Norte	*70 Ranchos Plz, Ranchos de Taos NM 87557*
NM	Roswell	International UFO Museum And Research Center	*114 N Main St, Roswell NM 88203*
NM	Roswell	Roswell visitor center	*Pioneer Plaza, Roswell NM 88201*
NM	Ruidoso	Four Seasons Mall	*2500 Sudderth Dr Ste. 6, Ruidoso NM 88345*
NM	Ruidoso Downs	Billy the Kid Scenic Byway Visitor Center	*791 US-70, Ruidoso Downs NM 88346*
NM	San Jon	Russell's truck and travel center	*1383 Frontage Rd, San Jon NM 88411*
NM	Santa Fe	Loretto Chapel	*207 Old Santa Fe Trail, Santa Fe NM 87501*
NM	Santa Fe	Santa Fe Visitors Center	*491 Old Santa Fe Trail, Santa Fe NM 87501*

NM	Santa Fe	Sunwest on the Plaza	*56-58 Lincoln Ave, Santa Fe NM 87501*
NM	Taos	Kit Carson Home and Museum	*113 Kit Carson Rd, Taos NM 87571*
NM	Taos	Taos Mercantile Co	*102 Cam De Santa Fe, Taos NM 87571*
NM	Tucumcari	Del's Restaurant & Gifts	*1202 U.S. Rte 66, Tucumcari NM 88401*
NM	Tucumcari	Mesalands Dinosaur Museum and Natural Sciences Lab	*222 E Laughlin Ave, Tucumcari NM 88401*
NM	Tucumcari	Tee Pee Curios	*924 E Rte 66 Blvd, Tucumcari NM 88401*
NM	Tularosa	White Sands National Monument	*854MQMPF+VP, Tularosa NM 88352*

			Nevada
NV	Baker	Great Basin NP Lehman Cave Visitor Center Cafe	*85C7WPQW+W2, Baker NV 89311*
NV	Boulder City	Grandma Daisy's	*530 Nevada Way, Boulder City NV 89005*
NV	Boulder City	Grandma Daisy's Candy Store and Ice Cream Parlor	*530 Nevada Way, Boulder City NV 89005*
NV	Boulder City	High Scaler Cafe	*2785+G7, Boulder City NV 89005*
NV	Boulder City	Hoover Dam Outlook Gift shop	*75 Hoover Dam Access Rd, Boulder City NV 89005*
NV	Boulder City	Las Vegas Boat Harbor	*26HH+P5 Boulder City, Boulder City NV 89005*
NV	Boulder City	Papillon Grand Canyon Helicopters	*1265 Airport Rd, Boulder City NV 89005*
NV	Carson City	Nevada State Museum	*700 N Carson St, Carson City NV 89701*
NV	Carson City	Nevada State Railroad Museum	*2180 S Carson St, Carson City NV 89701*
NV	Carson City	The Children's Museum of Northern Nevada	*813 N Carson St, Carson City NV 89701*
NV	Denio	Royal Peacock Mine	*110 Juniper Dr, Denio NV 89404*
NV	Genoa	Pony Express in Genoa, Nevada	*182 Nixon St, Genoa NV 89411*
NV	Goodsprings	Goodsprings General Store	*175 NV-161, Goodsprings NV 89019*
NV	Hawthorne	Hawthorne Ordnance Museum	*501 E St, Hawthorne NV 89415*
NV	Incline Village	Village TOYS	*899 Tahoe Blvd, Incline Village NV 89451*
NV	Jackpot	Barton's Club 93	*1002 US-93, Jackpot NV 89825*
NV	Las Vegas	Area 15 / Meow Wolf	*3215 S Rancho Dr Suite 190, Las Vegas NV 89102*
NV	Las Vegas	Bass Pro Shops Outdoor World (At Silverton Hotel & Casino)	*8200 Dean Martin Dr, Las Vegas NV 89139*

NV	Las Vegas	Bonanza Gift Shop	*2440 S Las Vegas Blvd, Las Vegas NV 89104*
NV	Las Vegas	Bubba Gump Shrimp Co.	*3717 S Las Vegas Blvd, Las Vegas NV 89109*
NV	Las Vegas	Circus Circus	*2880 S Las Vegas Blvd, Las Vegas NV 89109*
NV	Las Vegas	CSI: The Experience	*3339 S Las Vegas Blvd, Las Vegas NV 89109*
NV	Las Vegas	Downtown Container Park	*707 E Fremont St, Las Vegas NV 89101*
NV	Las Vegas	Downtown Las Vegas - Container Park	*707 E E Fremont St, Las Vegas NV 89101*
NV	Las Vegas	Excalibur Food Court	*Excalibur Hotel & Casino, Las Vegas NV 89109*
NV	Las Vegas	Fabulous Las Vegas Jewelry and Gifts LLC	*310 Fremont St, Las Vegas NV 89104*
NV	Las Vegas	Golden Nugget Hotel & Casino	*124 S 1st St, Las Vegas NV 89101*
NV	Las Vegas	Gotta Have It	*New York New York Casino, Las Vegas NV 89109*
NV	Las Vegas	Harley-Davidson Cafe	*3725 S Las Vegas Blvd, Las Vegas NV 89109*
NV	Las Vegas	Hawaiian Marketplace	*3745 Las Vegas Blvd S, Las Vegas NV 89109*
NV	Las Vegas	Hershey Chocolate World Las Vegas	*New York New York Casino, Las Vegas NV 89109*
NV	Las Vegas	High Roller	*3953 Audrie St, Las Vegas NV 89109*
NV	Las Vegas	Las Vegas Harley-Davidson	*5191 S Las Vegas Blvd, Las Vegas NV 89119*
NV	Las Vegas	Las Vegas Natural History Museum	*900 Las Vegas Blvd N, Las Vegas NV 89101*
NV	Las Vegas	LINQ Hotel & Casino Auto Collection?The Auto Colle	*3545 S Las Vegas Blvd, Las Vegas NV 89109*
NV	Las Vegas	M & M	*3785 Las Vegas Blvd S, Las Vegas NV 89109*

NV	Las Vegas	Madame Tussauds Las Vegas	*3377 S Las Vegas Blvd, Las Vegas NV 89109*
NV	Las Vegas	Neon Museum	*770 Las Vegas Blvd N, Las Vegas NV 89101*
NV	Las Vegas	Nevada State Museum Las Vegas	*309 S Valley View Blvd, Las Vegas NV 89107*
NV	Las Vegas	Pinball Hall of Fame	*1610 E Tropicana Ave, Las Vegas NV 89119*
NV	Las Vegas	Pioneer Gift Shop	*25 Fremont St, Las Vegas NV 89101*
NV	Las Vegas	Rainforest Cafe	*3717 S Las Vegas Blvd, Las Vegas NV 89109*
NV	Las Vegas	Seaquest	*3506 S Maryland Pkwy, Las Vegas NV 89109*
NV	Las Vegas	Shark Reef Aquarium at Mandalay Bay	*3940 S Las Vegas Blvd, Las Vegas NV 89119*
NV	Las Vegas	Speedway World Gift Shop	*Parking lot, Las Vegas NV 89115*
NV	Las Vegas	Springs Preserve	*333 S Valley View Blvd, Las Vegas NV 89107*
NV	Las Vegas	Stratosphere Casino Hotel & Tower	*2020 S Las Vegas Blvd, Las Vegas NV 89701*
NV	Las Vegas	Studio 21 Tattoo Gallery	*6020 W Flamingo Rd, Las Vegas NV 89103*
NV	Las Vegas	Stupidiotic	*New York New York Casino, Las Vegas NV 89109*
NV	Las Vegas	The Mob Museum	*300 Stewart Ave, Las Vegas NV 89101*
NV	Las Vegas	The Roller Coaster	*New York New York Casino, Las Vegas NV 89109*
NV	Las Vegas	Titanic: The Artifact Exhibition	*3960 S Las Vegas Blvd, Las Vegas NV 89119*
NV	Las Vegas	Toy Shack	*450 Fremont St, Las Vegas NV 89101*
NV	Laughlin	Avi Resort & Casino	*10000 Aha Macav Pkwy, Laughlin NV 89029*

NV	Laughlin	Golden Nugget Casino Hotel Laughlin	*2300 S Casino Dr, Laughlin NV 89029*
NV	Laughlin	Regency Casino Gift Shop	*1950 S Casino Dr, Laughlin NV 89029*
NV	Laughlin	Tropicana Laughlin Hotel and Casino	*2121 S Casino Dr, Laughlin NV 89029*
NV	Moapa Valley	Lost City Museum	*721 S Moapa Valley Blvd, Moapa Valley NV 89040*
NV	Primm	Buffalo Bill's Casino & Hotel	*31700 S Las Vegas Blvd, Primm NV 89019*
NV	Primm	Buffalo Bills Casino at Bonnie and Clyde exhibt	*100 W Primm Blvd, Primm NV 89019*
NV	Reno	Boomtown Reno	*2100 Garson Rd, Reno NV 89523*
NV	Reno	Cabela's	*8650 Garson Rd, Reno NV 89523*
NV	Reno	Circus Circus Reno Hotel & Casino	*500 N Sierra St, Reno NV 89501*
NV	Reno	Lucky 7	*231 N Virginia St, Reno NV 89501*
NV	Reno	National Automobile Museum	*10 Lake St, Reno NV 89501*
NV	Stateline	Harrah's Arcade	*Harrah's Lake Tahoe - A Caesars Rewards Destination, Stateline NV 89449*
NV	Virginia City	Fourth Ward School Museum	*537 S C St, Virginia City NV 89440*
NV	Virginia City	Historic Fourth Ward School Museum	*537 S C St, Virginia City NV 89440*
NV	Virginia City	Old Time Photo	*98 C St, Virginia City NV 89440*
NV	Virginia City	Pops Country Collectables	*178 S C St, Virginia City NV 89440*
NV	Virginia City	Sawdust Trails	*164 South C St B, Virginia City NV 89440*
NV	Virginia City	Sundance Saloon & Shop	*208 N C Street, Virginia City NV 89440*
NV	Virginia City	Virginia City Visitor Center	*86 S C St, Virginia City NV 89440*
NV	Virginia City	Zepha's Cove	*145 S C St #D, Virginia City NV 89440*

			New York
NY	Albany	Crossgates Mall	*1 Crossgates Mall Rd, Albany NY 12203*
NY	Albany	Crossgates Mall - Finish Line store	*1 Crossgates Mall Rd, Albany NY 12203*
NY	Albany	New York State Museum	*222 Madison Ave, Albany NY 12202*
NY	Albany	USS SLATER	*141 Broadway, Albany NY 12202*
NY	Alexandria Bay	The Ship Gift Shop	*22 James St, Alexandria Bay NY 13607*
NY	Apalachin	Big Dipper Ice Cream	*6935 NY-434, Apalachin NY 13732*
NY	Auburn	Bass Pro Shops	*1579 Clark Street Rd, Auburn NY 13021*
NY	Auburn	Bass Pro Shops Sportsman's Center	*1579 Clark Street Rd, Auburn NY 13021*
NY	Binghamton	Binghamton Zoo at Ross Park	*60 Morgan Rd, Binghamton NY 13903*
NY	Buffalo	Buffalo History Museum (formerly the Buffalo & Eri	*1 Museum Ct, Buffalo NY 14216*
NY	Buffalo	Buffalo Museum of Science	*1 Martin Luther King Park, Buffalo NY 14211*
NY	Buffalo	The Buffalo History Museum	*1 Museum Ct, Buffalo NY 14216*
NY	Buffalo	The Buffalo Zoo	*300 Parkside Ave, Buffalo NY 14214*
NY	Castile	Letchworth State Park	*6514 Park Rd, Castile NY 14427*
NY	Clayton	Karla's Christmas Shoppe	*506 Riverside Dr, Clayton NY 13624*
NY	Cooperstown	Pioneer Sports Cards	*106 Main St, Cooperstown NY 13326*
NY	Cooperstown	Yastrzemski Sports	*83 Main St, Cooperstown NY 13326*

NY	Corfu	Darien Lake Amusement Park	*9993 Alleghany Rd, Corfu NY 14036*
NY	Corfu	Pembroke Travel Plaza	*8319 Indian Falls Rd, Corfu NY 14036*
NY	Elmira	Eldridge Park	*200 N Main St, Elmira NY 14901*
NY	Elmira	Harris Hill	*557 Harris Hill Rd, Elmira NY 14903*
NY	Fairport	Lollypop Farm Humane Society of Greater Rochester	*99 Victor Rd, Fairport NY 14450*
NY	Garden City	Cradle of Aviation Museum	*141 Charles Lindbergh Blvd, Garden City NY 11530*
NY	Glens Falls North	Six Flags Great Escape Lodge & Indoor Water park	*1213 US-9, Glens Falls North NY 12804*
NY	Glens Falls North	Six Flags Great Escape Lodge & Indoor Water park	*1213 US-9, Glens Falls North NY 12804*
NY	Gloversville	Adirondack Animal Land	*3549 NY-30, Gloversville NY 12078*
NY	Hamburg	Erie County Fair	*5600 McKinley Pkwy, Hamburg NY 14075*
NY	Highland Falls	Overlook Lodge at Bear Mountain	*3020 Seven Lakes Drive, Highland Falls NY 10986*
NY	Highland Falls	US Military Academy Visitors Center	*2107 New South Post Rd, Highland Falls NY 10928*
NY	Howes Cave	Howe Caverns	*255 Discovery Dr, Howes Cave NY 12092*
NY	Irondequoit	Seneca Park Zoo	*105 Winona Blvd, Irondequoit NY 14617*
NY	Irondequoit	Seneca Park Zoo Machine 2	*105 Winona Blvd, Irondequoit NY 14617*
NY	Ithaca	Cayuga Nature Center	*1420 Taughannock Blvd, Ithaca NY 14850*
NY	Ithaca	Museum of the Earth	*1259 Trumansburg Rd, Ithaca NY 14850*

NY	Ithaca	Sunny Days Of Ithaca	*215 E State St # 200, Ithaca NY 14850*
NY	Jamestown	Lucille Ball Desi Arnaz Museum	*6 W 3rd St, Jamestown NY 14701*
NY	Jamestown	Lucy Desi Museum & Center for Comedy	*6 W 3rd St, Jamestown NY 14701*
NY	Jamestown	National Comedy Center	*211 W 2nd St, Jamestown NY 14701*
NY	Keeseville	Ausable Chasm	*2144 US-9, Keeseville NY 12911*
NY	Lake George	Beef Jerky Outlet	*1424 US-9, Lake George NY 12845*
NY	Lake George	Lake George Expedition Park	*Route 9 & Bloody Pond Rd(Expedition Pk), Lake George NY 12845*
NY	Lake George	Riley's Famous $2 T-Shirts	*1839 US-9, Lake George NY 12845*
NY	Lake George	Rileys Lake George	*9 Lochlea Ln, Lake George NY 12845*
NY	Maple Springs	Midway State Park	*6H2G+PR Maple Springs, Maple Springs NY 14712*
NY	Mumford	Genesee Country Village & Museum	*1410 Flint Hill Rd, Mumford NY 14511*
NY	Naples	RMSC Cumming Nature Center	*6472 Gulick Rd, Naples NY 14512*
NY	New Rochelle	New Roc City	*37 Lecount Pl, New Rochelle NY 10801*
NY	New York	American Museum of Natural History	*200 Central Prk W, New York NY 10024*
NY	New York	Ben & Jerrys Ice Cream Shop	*200 W 44th St, New York NY 10036*
NY	New York	Central Park Zoo	*The Arsenal, New York NY 10065*
NY	New York	Citi Field	*41 Seaver Wy, New York NY 11368*
NY	New York	Daredevil Tattoo	*MING TOWER, New York NY 10002*

NY	New York	Ellen's Stardust Diner	*1650 Broadway, New York NY 10019*
NY	New York	Hard Rock Cafe	*3103 Broadway, New York NY 10027*
NY	New York	Hard Rock Cafe Times Square	*1501 Broadway, New York NY 10036*
NY	New York	Jewish Children's Museum - JCM	*792 Eastern Pkwy, New York NY 11213*
NY	New York	M&M's World	*1600 Broadway, New York NY 10019*
NY	New York	New York Aquarium	*602 Surf Ave, New York NY 11224*
NY	New York	New York Hall Of Science	*47-01 111th St, New York NY 11368*
NY	New York	NY Loves us	*30 Vesey St Floor 14, New York NY 10007*
NY	New York	One World Trade Center - One World Observatory	*185 Greenwich St, New York NY 10007*
NY	New York	Prospect Park Zoo	*450 Flatbush Ave, New York NY 11238*
NY	New York	Queens Zoo	*Discovery Center, New York NY 11368*
NY	New York	Staten Island Zoo	*614 Broadway, New York NY 10310*
NY	New York	USS Intrepid Sea Air & Space Museum	*1 Intrepid Square, New York NY 10036*
NY	New York	Wildlife Conservation Society	*2300 Southern Blvd Trail, New York NY 10460*
NY	New York	Yankee Stadium	*33 River Ave, New York NY 10452*
NY	Niagara Falls	Hard Rock Cafe Niagara Falls	*333 Prospect St, Niagara Falls NY 14303*
NY	Niagara Falls	Haunted House of Wax	*222 Rainbow Blvd, Niagara Falls NY 14303*
NY	Niagara Falls	Niagara Aerospace Museum	*9990 Porter Rd, Niagara Falls NY 14304*

NY	Niagara Falls	Niagara Wax Museum of History	*303 Prospect St, Niagara Falls NY 14303*
NY	Niagara Falls	prospect point gift shop #1	*316 Prospect St, Niagara Falls NY 14303*
NY	Niagara Falls	Quality Hotel & Suites At The Falls	*240 1st St, Niagara Falls NY 14303*
NY	Niagara Falls	Rainforest Cafe Niagara	*300 3rd St, Niagara Falls NY 14303*
NY	Niagara Falls	Top of The Falls Gift Shop	*41 Goat Island Rd, Niagara Falls NY 14303*
NY	Niagara Falls	Wax Museum Souvenir Shop	*303 Prospect St, Niagara Falls NY 14303*
NY	Olcott	Olcott Beach	*Olcott Beach Carousel Park, Olcott NY 14126*
NY	Old Bethpage	Old Bethpage Village Restoration	*Old Bethpage Dog Run Park, Old Bethpage NY 11804*
NY	Old Forge	Enchanted Forest Water Safari	*3183 NY-28, Old Forge NY 13420*
NY	Old Forge	Wilderness Interiors	*139 Main St, Old Forge NY 13420*
NY	Phoenicia	Phoenicia Diner	*5681 NY-28, Phoenicia NY 12464*
NY	Port Jefferson	Sea Creations	*134 Main St #8, Port Jefferson NY 11777*
NY	Port Jefferson Station	Port Jeff Bowl Inc	*31 Chereb Ln, Port Jefferson Station NY 11776*
NY	Pottersville	Natural Stone Bridge & Caves	*535 Stone Bridge Rd, Pottersville NY 12860*
NY	Riverhead	Long Island Aquarium & Exhibition Center	*467 E Main St, Riverhead NY 11901*
NY	Rochester	Rochester Museum & Science Center	*10 S Goodman St, Rochester NY 14607*
NY	Rochester	The Strong Museum	*One Manhattan Square Dr, Rochester NY 14607*
NY	Rome	Oneida Travel Plaza	*5365 NY State Thruway, Rome NY 13490*

NY	Salamanca	Allegany State Park	*2398 King's Row, Salamanca NY 14779*
NY	Saratoga Springs	Impressions of Saratoga	*368 Broadway Studio 10, Saratoga Springs NY 12866*
NY	Schenectady	Guilderland Travel Plaza	*1 Guilderland Service Plz, Schenectady NY 12303*
NY	Seneca Falls	Seneca Falls Visitor Center	*89 Fall St, Seneca Falls NY 13148*
NY	Sloatsburg	NY State Thruway, Sloatsburg Service Area - Northbound	*54 Orange Turnpike, Sloatsburg NY 10974*
NY	Sloatsburg	Ramapo Travel Plaza	*15 New York State Trwy S, Sloatsburg NY 10974*
NY	Syracuse	MOST Syracuse (Museum of Science & Technology)	*500 S Franklin St, Syracuse NY 13202*
NY	Syracuse	Syracuse Zoo (Rosamond Gifford Zoo)	*Rosamond Gifford Zoo, Syracuse NY 13204*
NY	Tomkins Cove	Bear Mountain Inn	*965 US-9W, Tomkins Cove NY 10986*
NY	Utica	Utica Zoo	*1 Utica Zoo Way, Utica NY 13501*
NY	Wallkill	Modena Travel Plaza	*6603 I-87, Wallkill NY 12589*
NY	Watkins Glen	Famous Brands Outlet	*408 N Franklin St, Watkins Glen NY 14891*
NY	Yonkers	LEGOLAND Discovery Center Westchester	*59 Fitzgerald Street, Yonkers NY 10710*

			Ohio
OH	Akron	Akron Zoo	*500 Edgewood Ave, Akron OH 44307*
OH	Akron	Stan Hywet Hall and Gardens - Carriage House	*714 N Portage Path, Akron OH 44303*
OH	Amherst	Ohio Turnpike Middle Ridge	*46402 Ohio Tpke, Amherst OH 44001*
OH	Ashland	Grandpas Cheesebarn Inc.	*668 US-250, Ashland OH 44805*
OH	Avon	Cabela's	*35685 Chester Rd, Avon OH*
OH	Bedford Heights	Southeast Harley Davidson	*23105 Aurora Rd, Bedford Heights OH 44146*
OH	Bogart	Kalahari Resorts and Conventions	*99M5+H8 Bogart, Bogart OH 44870*
OH	Broadview Heights	Great Lakes Service Plaza	*2000 E Edgerton Rd, Broadview Heights OH 44147*
OH	Broadview Heights	Towpath Service Plaza	*10037 Broadview Rd, Broadview Heights OH 44147*
OH	Canton	McKinley Presidential Library & Museum	*898 Mc Kinley Monument Dr NW, Canton OH 44708*
OH	Canton	Pro Football Hall of Fame	*2121 George Halas Dr NW, Canton OH 44708*
OH	Cincinnati	Cincinnati Zoo & Botanical Garden Outside of Gift Shop	*Vine St & Erkenbrecher Ave, Cincinnati OH 45220*
OH	Cincinnati	Cincinnati Zoo At Night Hunters Building Entrance	*3400 Vine St, Cincinnati OH 45220*
OH	Cincinnati	Cincinnati Zoo Inside Manatee Springs Building	*4FWR+H5 Cincinnati, Cincinnati OH 45220*
OH	Cincinnati	Cincinnati Zoo Main Entrance	*3400 Vine St, Cincinnati OH 45220*
OH	Cincinnati	Cincinnati Zoo Near Train Station Ticket Booth	*3400 Vine St, Cincinnati OH 45220*
OH	Cincinnati	Cincinnati Zoo Outside of LaRosa's Pizza	*116 Forest Ave, Cincinnati OH 45220*

OH	Circleville	140 W Main St	*140 W Main St, Circleville OH 43113*
OH	Circleville	The Rustic Harvest ForEVer Rowdy Farms	*10363 Tarlton Rd, Circleville OH 43113*
OH	Cleveland	Christmas Story House and Museum	*3159 W 11th St, Cleveland OH 44109*
OH	Cleveland	cleveland aquarium	*2000 Sycamore St, Cleveland OH 44113*
OH	Cleveland	Cleveland Metroparks Zoo	*3889 Wildlife Way, Cleveland OH 44109*
OH	Cleveland	Cleveland Museum of Natural History	*1 Wade Oval Dr, Cleveland OH 44106*
OH	Cleveland	Great Lakes Science Center	*601 Erieside Ave, Cleveland OH 44114*
OH	Cleveland	Greater Cleveland Aquarium	*2000 Sycamore St, Cleveland OH 44113*
OH	Cleveland	The Christmas Story House	*3159 W 11th St, Cleveland OH 44109*
OH	Clyde	Commodore Perry Service Plaza	*888 N County Rd 260, Clyde OH 43410*
OH	Clyde	Commodore Perry Travel Plaza	*845 E Maple St, Clyde OH 43410*
OH	Columbus	COSI	*75 Washington Blvd, Columbus OH 43215*
OH	Columbus	Statehouse Museum Shop	*1 Capitol Sq, Columbus OH 43215*
OH	Cumberland	The Wilds	*14000 International Rd, Cumberland OH 43732*
OH	Dalton	Lehman's	*4757 Kidron Rd, Dalton OH 44618*
OH	Dayton	Boonshoft Museum of Discovery	*Boonshoft Museum of Discovery, Dayton OH 45414*
OH	Dayton	Hasty Tasty Pancake House	*3509 Linden Ave, Dayton OH 45410*
OH	Delaware	Olentangy Indian Caverns	*1779 Home Rd, Delaware OH 43015*

OH	Dennison	Dennison Railroad Depot Museum	*400 Center St, Dennison OH 44621*
OH	Fairfield	Jungle Jims International Market Fairfield	*Jungle Jim's Plaza, Fairfield OH 45014*
OH	Geneva	Sports Center	*5440 Lake Rd E, Geneva OH 44041*
OH	Genoa	Blue Heron Service Plaza	*6164 Creek 165, Genoa OH 43430*
OH	Genoa	Wyandot Service Plaza	*6410 County Rd 165, Genoa OH 43430*
OH	Granville	Lazy River At Granville Campground	*2759 Dry Creek Rd NE, Granville OH 43023*
OH	Greenville	Garst Museum	*205 N Broadway St, Greenville OH 45331*
OH	Hartville	Hartville Kitchen Restaurant & Bakery	*1015 Edison St NW, Hartville OH 44632*
OH	Hartville	Hartville Mercantile	*649 Sunnyside St SW, Hartville OH 44632*
OH	Kelleys Island	Kelleys Island General Store	*118 Division St, Kelleys Island OH 43438*
OH	Kettering	Carillon Historical Park	*2039 S Patterson Blvd, Kettering OH 45409*
OH	Lakeside Marblehead	Marblehead Lighthouse Historical Society	*Marblehead Lighthouse, Lakeside Marblehead OH 43440*
OH	Logan	Fox's High Rock Farm	*14977 OH-664, Logan OH 43138*
OH	Logan	Lake Logan Marina	*30443 Lake Logan Rd, Logan OH 43138*
OH	Loveland	The Works Pizza	*20 Grear Millitzer Pl, Loveland OH 45140*
OH	Lucas	Malabar Farm State Park	*4050 Bromfield Rd, Lucas OH 44843*
OH	Maineville	Great Wolf Lodge	*2501 Great Wolf Dr, Maineville OH 45039*

OH	Mansfield	Ohio Bird Sanctuary	*3774 Orweiler Rd, Mansfield OH 44903*
OH	Mansfield	Ohio State Reformatory	*100 Reformatory Rd, Mansfield OH 44905*
OH	Mansfield	Ohio State Reformatory	*100 Reformatory Rd, Mansfield OH 44905*
OH	Mansfield	Richland Carrousel Park Inc.	*101 S Main St, Mansfield OH 44902*
OH	Mantua	Bradys Leap Service Plaza	*9250 Limeridge Rd, Mantua OH 44255*
OH	Mantua	Portage Service Plaza	*9270 Limeridge Rd, Mantua OH 44255*
OH	Mesopotamia	End of the Commons General Store	*8719 State Rte 534, Mesopotamia OH 44439*
OH	Middlefield	Great Lakes Outdoor Supply	*14855 N State Ave, Middlefield OH 44062*
OH	Middletown	Central House of Brews	*2205 Central Ave, Middletown OH 45044*
OH	Millersburg	Amish Country	*4826 E Main St, Millersburg OH 44654*
OH	Millersburg	Keim Lumber Company	*4441 Co Rd 70, Millersburg OH 44654*
OH	Millersburg	Sols In Berlin	*4902 W Main St, Millersburg OH 44654*
OH	New Bremen	The Bicycle Museum of America	*7 W Monroe St, New Bremen OH 45869*
OH	New Springfield	Glacier Hills Service Plaza/ Eastbound	*3600 Glacier Rd, New Springfield OH 44443*
OH	New Springfield	Mahoning Valley Service Plaza	*WCR7+6J, New Springfield OH 44443*
OH	Newark	The Works	*55 S 1st St, Newark OH 43055*
OH	Oberlin	Watson's Hardware	*26 S Main St, Oberlin OH 44074*
OH	Ontario	Showcase Coins & Bullion	*2152 Walker Lake Rd, Ontario OH 44903*

OH	Perrysburg	Bass Pro Outdoor World Shop	*9278 Bass Pro Blvd, Perrysburg OH 43551*
OH	Perrysville	Mohican Lodge and Conference Center	*4700 Goon Rd, Perrysville OH 44864*
OH	Port Clinton	African Safari Wildlife Park	*267 S Lightner Rd, Port Clinton OH 43452*
OH	Port Clinton	Rainbow Acres Educational	*2267 E Harbor Rd, Port Clinton OH 43452*
OH	Powell	Columbus Zoo and Aquarium	*10121 Riverside Dr, Powell OH 43065*
OH	Put-in-Bay	Adventure Bay	*2001 Put-In-Bay Rd, Put-in-Bay OH 43456*
OH	Put-in-Bay	Put-in-Bay Chamber of Commerce & Visitors Bureau	*104 Delaware Ave, Put-in-Bay OH 43456*
OH	Put-in-Bay	Stoiber Carriage House	*160 Delaware Ave, Put-in-Bay OH 43456*
OH	Riverside	National Museum of the U.S.A.F.	*1100 Spaatz St, Riverside OH 45431*
OH	Sandusky	Cedar Point	*1 Cedar Point Dr, Sandusky OH 44870*
OH	Sandusky	Great Wolf Lodge Sandusky	*4600 Milan Rd, Sandusky OH 44870*
OH	Sandusky	Merry-Go-Round Museum	*301 Jackson St, Sandusky OH 44870*
OH	Shiloh	Planktown Hardware	*14 E Main St, Shiloh OH 44878*
OH	Smithville	The Barn Restaurant	*877 W Main St, Smithville OH 44677*
OH	Springfield	Clark County Historical Society	*117 S Fountain Ave, Springfield OH 45502*
OH	Toledo	Imagination Station	*1 Discovery Way, Toledo OH 43604*
OH	Toledo	Toledo Zoo Parking Lot	*Toledo Zoo, Toledo OH 43609*
OH	Wapakoneta	Armstrong Air & Space Museum	*500 Apollo Dr, Wapakoneta OH 45895*

OH	West Liberty	Ohio Caverns	*R OH-245, West Liberty OH 43357*
OH	West Liberty	Piatt Castles	*10051 Co Rd 47, West Liberty OH 43357*
OH	West Unity	Tiffin River Service Plaza	*21747 Co Rd M, West Unity OH 43570*
OH	Wetherington	Cabela's	*7240 Cabela Priv Dr, Wetherington OH 45069*
OH	Wetherington	The Cone	*6855 Tylersville Rd, Wetherington OH 45069*
OH	Yellow Springs	Young's Jersey Dairy	*Parking lot, Yellow Springs OH 45387*

			Oklahoma
OK	Afton	Afton Station	*12 S 1st St, Afton OK 74331*
OK	Arcadia	Pops 66 Soda Ranch	*660 E 2nd St, Arcadia OK 73007*
OK	Ardmore	Tucker Tower	*18407 Scenic Highway 77, Ardmore OK 73401*
OK	Atoka	Reba's Place	*301 E Court St, Atoka OK 74525*
OK	Bartlesville	Woolaroc Museum & Wildlife Preserve	*MV7Q+CJ, Bartlesville OK 74003*
OK	Broken Arrow	Bass Pro Shops	*101 Bass Pro Drive, Broken Arrow OK 74012*
OK	Broken Bow	Beavers Bend State Resort Park	*48J5+FP Broken Bow, Broken Bow OK 74728*
OK	Broken Bow	Cornbread Trading Co.	*10251 N US Hwy 259, Broken Bow OK 74728*
OK	Calumet	Cherokee Trading Post	*301 S Walbaum Rd, Calumet OK 73014*
OK	Catoosa	Blue Whale of Catoosa	*2600 OK-66, Catoosa OK 74015*
OK	Claremore	J.M. Davis Arms & Historical Museum	*330 N J M Davis Blvd, Claremore OK 74017*
OK	Claremore	Will Rogers Memorial Museums	*1720 W Will Rogers Blvd, Claremore OK 74017*
OK	Davis	Arbickle Wilderness	*6132 Kay Starr Trail, Davis OK 73030*
OK	Davis	Chickasaw Nation Welcome Center	*35 N Colbert Dr, Davis OK 73030*
OK	Davis	Turner Falls	*6250 US-77, Davis OK 73030*
OK	Hochatown	Beaver's Bend Mining Company	*9231 US-259, Hochatown OK 74728*
OK	Hulbert	Sequoyah State Park - Oklahoma	*19808 Park 10, Hulbert OK 74441*
OK	Idabel	Museum of the red river	*812 E Lincoln Rd, Idabel OK 74745*
OK	Jenks	Oklahoma Aquarium	*300 Aquarium Dr, Jenks OK 74037*
OK	Jenks	Oklahoma Aquarium	*300 Aquarium Dr, Jenks OK 74037*

OK	Norman	Sam Noble Oklahoma Museum of Natural History	*2401 Chautauqua Ave, Norman OK 73072*
OK	Okemah	Pamela's Flowers & Custom Designs	*115 W Broadway St, Okemah OK 74859*
OK	Oklahoma City	American Banjo Museum	*9 E Sheridan Ave, Oklahoma City OK 73104*
OK	Oklahoma City	Bass Pro Shops	*200 Bass Pro Dr, Oklahoma City OK 73104*
OK	Oklahoma City	Cabela's	*1200 W Memorial Rd, Oklahoma City OK 73114*
OK	Oklahoma City	Frontier City	*11501 N I- 35 Service Rd, Oklahoma City OK 73131*
OK	Oklahoma City	Museum of Osteology	*10301 S Sunnylane Rd, Oklahoma City OK 73160*
OK	Oklahoma City	National Cowboy & Western Heritage Museum	*1700 NE 63rd St, Oklahoma City OK 73111*
OK	Oklahoma City	Oklahoma City Zoo	*2101 NE 50th St, Oklahoma City OK 73111*
OK	Oklahoma City	Oklahoma History Center	*800 Nazih Zuhdi Dr, Oklahoma City OK 73105*
OK	Oklahoma City	Science Museum Oklahoma	*2100 NE 52nd St, Oklahoma City OK 73111*
OK	Sulphur	Chickasaw Cultural Center	*Charles F, Sulphur OK 73086*
OK	Sulphur	Chickasaw Visitor Center	*901 W 1st St, Sulphur OK 73086*
OK	Tahlequah	Cherokee Heritage Center	*21192 S Keeler Dr, Tahlequah OK 74464*
OK	Tulsa	Tulsa Zoo	*6421 E 36th St N, Tulsa OK 74115*
OK	Vinita	McDonald's	*767 Will Rogers Turnpike, Vinita OK 74301*
OK	Vinita	Will Rogers Archway	*767 Will Rogers Turnpike, Vinita OK 74301*
OK	Weatherford	Stafford Air & Space Museum	*3000 Logan Rd, Weatherford OK 73096*

OK	Whippoorwill	Copper World	*WWRQ+GP Whippoorwill, Whippoorwill OK 74056*

Oregon			
OR	Albany	Historic Carousel & Museum	*250 Broadalbin St SW, Albany OR 97321*
OR	Albany	Historic Carousel & Museum	*250 Broadalbin St SW, Albany OR 97321*
OR	Ashland	Science Works	*1500 E Main St, Ashland OR 97520*
OR	Ashland	ScienceWorks Hands-on Museum	*1500 E Main St, Ashland OR 97520*
OR	Astoria	Astoria Column	*1 Coxcomb Dr, Astoria OR 97103*
OR	Astoria	Flavel House Museum	*441 8th St, Astoria OR 97103*
OR	Astoria	Vintage Hardware	*1343 Commercial St, Astoria OR 97103*
OR	Baker City	Oregon Trail Interpretive Center	*22267 OR-86, Baker City OR 97814*
OR	Bandon	Big Wheel General Store	*130 Baltimore Ave SE, Bandon OR 97411*
OR	Bend	High Desert Museum	*59800 US-97, Bend OR 97702*
OR	Bend	Lava Lanes Bend	*1555 NE Forbes Rd, Bend OR 97701*
OR	Bonneville	Bradford Island Visitor Center (Bonneville Dam Vis	*J2QX+9F Bonneville, Bonneville OR 97014*
OR	Cannon Beach	Bruces candy shop. 256 N Hemlock St, Cannon Beach, OR 97110	*256 N Hemlock St, Cannon Beach OR 97110*
OR	Cannon Beach	Mo's Restaurant	*195 W Warren Way, Cannon Beach OR 97145*
OR	Cascade Locks	Bonneville Fish Hatchery	*70543 NE Herman Loop, Cascade Locks OR 97014*
OR	Cascade Locks	Marine Park (Columbia Gorge Sternwheeler Visitors'	*Cascade Locks Marine Park, Cascade Locks OR 97014*
OR	Cave Junction	Chateau at the Oregon Caves	*21000 Caves Hwy, Cave Junction OR 97523*

OR	Chiloquin	Train Mountain Railroad Museum	*Umatilla Marina rv park, Chiloquin OR 97624*
OR	Coos Bay	Shore Acres State Park	*89526 Cape Arago Hwy, Coos Bay OR 97420*
OR	Corbett	Multnomah Falls Lodge Restaurant	*48314 Historic Columbia River Hwy, Corbett OR 97019*
OR	CRATER LAKE	Rim Village Cafe and Gift Shop	*84JVWV63+C7, CRATER LAKE OR 97604*
OR	Depoe Bay	Paradise Gifts	*N.E 4, Depoe Bay OR 97341*
OR	Eugene	Coburg Pizza Company & Nana's Caffe	*90999 S Willamette St, Eugene OR 97408*
OR	Eugene	Roaring Rapids Pizza Company	*206 N Concord Ave, Eugene OR 97403*
OR	Florence	Mo's	*1436 Bay St, Florence OR 97439*
OR	Florence	Sea Lion Caves	*91560 US-101, Florence OR 97439*
OR	Florence	Wind Drift Gallery	*129 Maple St, Florence OR 97439*
OR	Gearhart	Seaside Carousel Mall	*318 Broadway St, Gearhart OR 97138*
OR	Gold Hill	The Oregon Vortex	*4303 Sardine Creek L Fork Rd, Gold Hill OR 97525*
OR	Government Camp	Timberline Lodge and Ski Area	*27500 Timberline Hwy, Government Camp OR 97028*
OR	Grand Ronde	Spirit Mountain Casino	*27100 Salmon River Hwy, Grand Ronde OR 97347*
OR	Grand Ronde	Spirit Mountain Casino	*27100 Salmon River Hwy, Grand Ronde OR 97347*
OR	Grants Pass	Hellsgate Excursions	*934 SE 6th St, Grants Pass OR 97526*
OR	Grants Pass	Wildlife Images	*11705 Lower River Rd, Grants Pass OR 97526*
OR	Joseph	Heidis Gift Shoppe	*59974 Mount Howard Ln, Joseph OR 97846*
OR	Lincoln City	MO's Restaurant	*860 Southwest 51st Street, Lincoln City OR 97367*

OR	Lincoln City	The Chocolate Frog	*3521 SE Hwy 101, Lincoln City OR 97367*
OR	Madras	Madras Municipal Airport Erickson Aircraft Collect	*MR8R+J6 Madras, Madras OR 97741*
OR	McMinnville	Evergreen Aviation & Space Museum	*500 NE Captain Michael King Smith Way, McMinnville OR 97128*
OR	Newport	Hatfield Marine Science Center Oregon State	*Reasearch Support Facility(RSF) Building #951, Newport OR 97366*
OR	Newport	Oregon Coast Aquarium	*2820 SE Ferry Slip Rd, Newport OR 97365*
OR	Newport	Ripley's Believe It or Not!	*250 SW Bay Blvd., Newport OR 97365*
OR	Pendleton	Arrowhead Travel Plaza	*72489 OR-331, Pendleton OR 97801*
OR	Pendleton	Pendleton Chamber of Commerce	*501 S Main St, Pendleton OR 97801*
OR	Portland	Moda Center	*1 N Center Ct St, Portland OR 97227*
OR	Portland	OMSI	*1945 SE Water Ave, Portland OR 97214*
OR	Portland	Oregon Zoo	*4001 SW Canyon Rd, Portland OR 97221*
OR	Portland	Portland Children's Museum	*4015 SW Canyon Rd, Portland OR 97221*
OR	Portland	Portlander Inn & Marketplace	*10350 N Vancouver Way, Portland OR 97217*
OR	Portland	Rocket Fizz	*609 SW Alder St, Portland OR 97205*
OR	Portland	The Freakybuttrue Peculiarium and Museum	*2234 NW Thurman St, Portland OR 97210*
OR	Rockaway Beach	Flamingo Jim's Gifts & Clothing	*234 South US-101, Rockaway Beach OR 97136*
OR	Salem	B-17 Alliance Museum	*B-17 Alliance Museum & Restoration Hangar, Salem OR 97302*

OR	Salem	Oregon Lottery	*500 Airport Rd SE, Salem OR 97301*
OR	Salem	Oregon State Capitol	*900 Court St NE, Salem OR 97301*
OR	Salem	Salem's Riverfront Carousel	*101 Front St NE, Salem OR 97301*
OR	Sandy	Sandy Historical Society	*39345 Pioneer Blvd, Sandy OR 97055*
OR	Santiam Junction	Hoodoo Ski Area	*C44G+Q3 Santiam Junction, Santiam Junction OR 97759*
OR	Seaside	Promenade Inn & Suites	*30 N Prom, Seaside OR 97138*
OR	Seaside	Seaside Aquarium	*200 N Prom, Seaside OR 97138*
OR	Seaside	Seaside Candyman	*21 N Columbia St # 101, Seaside OR 97138*
OR	Silverton	Oregon Garden Visitor Center	*879 W Main St, Silverton OR 97381*
OR	Springfield	Cabela's	*2800 Gateway St, Springfield OR 97477*
OR	St. Helens	Spilt Ink Souvenir Penny Press	*291 S 1st St, St. Helens OR 97051*
OR	Sumpter	Sumpter Valley Railroad	*211 Austin St, Sumpter OR 97877*
OR	Tillamook	Tillamook Air Museum	*6030 Hangar Rd, Tillamook OR 97141*
OR	Tillamook	Tillamook Cheese Factory Visitor's Center	*4165 N Hwy 101, Tillamook OR 97141*
OR	Turner	Enchanted Forest	*8462 Enchanted Way SE, Turner OR 97392*
OR	Warrenton	Astoria / Warrenton / Seaside KOA Resort	*1100 NW Ridge Rd, Warrenton OR 97121*
OR	Warrenton	Fort Stevens	*1675 Peter Iredale Rd, Warrenton OR 97121*
OR	White City	Annie Creek Restaurant & Gift Shop	*1023 Ave C, White City OR 97503*
OR	Winston	Wildlife Safari	*1790 Safari Rd, Winston OR 97496*

Pennsylvania			
PA	Allentown	Da Vinci Science Center	*361 S Cedar Crest Blvd, Allentown PA 18103*
PA	Altoona	Horseshoe Curve National Historic Landmark CLOSED	*2417 Pittsburgh Trak, Altoona PA 16601*
PA	Altoona	Railroaders Memorial Museum	*1300 9th Ave, Altoona PA 16602*
PA	Ashland	Pioneer Tunnel Coal Mine	*1900 Oak St, Ashland PA 17921*
PA	Austin	Wildlife Center at Sinnemahoning State Park	*4843 Park Dr, Austin PA 16720*
PA	Benezette	Elk Country Visitor Center	*134 Homestead Dr, Benezette PA 15821*
PA	Benezette	Elk Country Visitor Center	*134 Homestead Dr, Benezette PA 15821*
PA	Bethlehem	Pressed Penny Souvenir	*550 Main St, Bethlehem PA 18018*
PA	Bird in Hand	Smokehouse BBQ & Brews at Plain & Fancy Farm	*3121 Old Philadelphia Pike, Bird in Hand PA 17505*
PA	Bloomsburg	Bloomsburg Fair Grounds	*620 W 3rd St, Bloomsburg PA 17815*
PA	Brookville	Frosty Freeze	*864 PA-36, Brookville PA 15825*
PA	Bushkill	Bushkill Falls	*138 Bushkill Falls Trail, Bushkill PA 18324*
PA	Carlisle	Carlisle Events	*1000 Bryn Mawr Rd, Carlisle PA 17013*
PA	Carlisle	U.S. Army Heritage and Education Center	*95 Soldiers Dr, Carlisle PA 17013*
PA	Catawissa	Lake Glory Campground	*88 Eisenhower Rd, Catawissa PA 17820*
PA	Centre Hall	Grange Fairgrounds	*132 Sharer Ave, Centre Hall PA 16828*
PA	Columbia	Turkey Hill Experience	*301 Linden St, Columbia PA 17512*
PA	Coopersburg	The Inside Scoop	*301 N 3rd St, Coopersburg PA 18036*

PA	Corry	Corry Area Historical Society, Inc. Museum	*945 Mead Ave, Corry PA 16407*
PA	Coudersport	Pennsylvania Lumber Museum	*5660 US-6, Coudersport PA 16915*
PA	Cresco	Callie's Pretzel Factory	*6281 PA-191, Cresco PA 18326*
PA	Dorneyville	Dorney Park & Wildwater Kingdom Amusement Park	*HFH9+59 Dorneyville, Dorneyville PA 18104*
PA	Doylestown	Bucks County Free Library	*150 S Pine St, Doylestown PA 18901*
PA	Doylestown	Bucks County Free Library	*150 S Pine St, Doylestown PA 18901*
PA	East Earl	Shady Maple Smorgasbord	*129 Toddy Dr, East Earl PA 17519*
PA	East Stroudsburg	Odd Lot Outlet	*765 Seven Bridge Rd, East Stroudsburg PA 18301*
PA	Easton	Crayola Experience	*30 Centre Sq Cir, Easton PA 18042*
PA	Easton	National Canal Museum	*2750 Hugh Moore Park Rd, Easton PA 18042*
PA	Easton	National Canal Museum	*2750 Hugh Moore Park Rd, Easton PA 18042*
PA	Elysburg	Knoebels Amusement Resort	*391 Knoebels Boulevard, Elysburg PA 17824*
PA	Emerald Lakes	Spa Kalahari	*250 Kalahari Blvd, Emerald Lakes PA 18349*
PA	Erie	Erie Zoo	*423 W 38th St, Erie PA 16508*
PA	Erie	Erie Zoo	*423 W 38th St, Erie PA 16508*
PA	Erie	Sara's Restaurant	*25 Peninsula Dr, Erie PA 16505*
PA	Erie	Splash Lagoon	*8091 Peach St, Erie PA 16509*
PA	Erie	Tom Ridge Environmental Center	*301 Peninsula Dr, Erie PA 16505*
PA	Fort Littleton	Camp Sinoquipe Lake Dam	*32WM+2C Fort Littleton, Fort Littleton PA 17223*
PA	Gettysburg	Artifact at 777	*777 Baltimore St # 104, Gettysburg PA 17325*

PA	Gettysburg	Drummer Boy Camping Resort	*1335 Hanover Rd, Gettysburg PA 17325*
PA	Gettysburg	Drummer Boy Camping Resort	*1 Rocky Grove Rd, Gettysburg PA 17325*
PA	Gettysburg	Gettysburg Diorama	*241 Steinwehr Ave, Gettysburg PA 17325*
PA	Gettysburg	Gettysburg Diorama	*217 Steinwehr Ave, Gettysburg PA 17325*
PA	Gettysburg	Gettysburg Ghost Tours	*47 Steinwehr Ave, Gettysburg PA 17325*
PA	Gettysburg	Gettysburg Heritage Center	*297 Steinwehr Ave, Gettysburg PA 17325*
PA	Gettysburg	Gettysburg Heritage Center	*297 Steinwehr Ave, Gettysburg PA 17325*
PA	Gettysburg	Gettysburg National Military Park	*National Park Service Museum and Visitor Center, Gettysburg PA 17325*
PA	Gettysburg	Gettysburg National Military Park Museum and Visit	*National Park Service Museum and Visitor Center, Gettysburg PA 17325*
PA	Gettysburg	Gettysburg Souvenirs & Gifts	*217 Steinwehr Ave, Gettysburg PA 17325*
PA	Gettysburg	Gettysburg Souvineer/ Haunted Ghost Tour	*27 Steinwehr Ave, Gettysburg PA 17325*
PA	Gettysburg	Gettysburg Tour Center	*778 Baltimore St, Gettysburg PA 17325*
PA	Gettysburg	Hall of Presidents	*789 Baltimore St #200, Gettysburg PA 17325*
PA	Gettysburg	Jenni's Funhouse	*11 US-15 BUS, Gettysburg PA 17325*
PA	Gettysburg	Jennie Wade House	*548 Baltimore St, Gettysburg PA 17325*
PA	Gettysburg	Lincoln Train Museum	*425 Steinwehr Ave, Gettysburg PA 17325*
PA	Gettysburg	Old Gettysburg Village	*777 Baltimore St # 104, Gettysburg PA 17325*

PA	Gettysburg	The Antique Center of Gettysburg	*28 Baltimore St, Gettysburg PA 17325*
PA	Gettysburg	The Antique Center of Gettysburg	*30 Baltimore St, Gettysburg PA 17325*
PA	Grove City	Keystone Safari	*2264 Mercer Butler Pike, Grove City PA 16127*
PA	Halifax	Lake Tobias Wildlife Park	*G423+RJ, Halifax PA 17032*
PA	Hamburg	Cabela's	*100 Cabela Dr, Hamburg PA 19526*
PA	Harrisburg	Bass Pro Shops	*3501 Paxton St, Harrisburg PA 17111*
PA	Harrisburg	PA Farm Show Complex and Expo Center	*2300 N Cameron St, Harrisburg PA 17110*
PA	Harrisburg	Pennsylvania State Capitol Complex	*501 N 3rd St, Harrisburg PA 17120*
PA	Harrisburg	The National Civil War Museum	*2411 Lincoln Cir #240, Harrisburg PA 17103*
PA	Harrisburg	Whitaker Center for Science and the Arts	*218 Market St, Harrisburg PA 17101*
PA	Hershey	Hershey's Chocolate World	*101 Chocolate World Wy, Hershey PA 17033*
PA	Hershey	Hershey's Chocolate World	*101 Chocolate World Wy, Hershey PA 17033*
PA	Hershey	Hershey's Chocolate World	*101 Chocolate World Wy, Hershey PA 17033*
PA	Hershey	Hersheypark	*100 Hersheypark Dr, Hershey PA 17033*
PA	Hershey	Troegs Brewing Company	*200E Hersheypark Dr, Hershey PA 17033*
PA	Hershey	ZooAmerica North American Wildlife Park	*201 Park Ave, Hershey PA 17033*
PA	Hesston	Raystown Lake Visitor Center	*6993 Seven Points Rd, Hesston PA 16647*
PA	Hughesville	Lycoming County Fair Association	*510 Broadway St, Hughesville PA 17737*

PA	Hummelstown	Hersheypark Camping Resort	*1200 Matlack Rd, Hummelstown PA 17036*
PA	Hummelstown	Indian Echo Caverns	*368 Middletown Rd, Hummelstown PA 17036*
PA	Hummelstown	Indian Echo Caverns	*368 Middletown Rd, Hummelstown PA 17036*
PA	Hummelstown	The Antique Automobile Club of America Museum	*161 Museum Dr, Hummelstown PA 17036*
PA	Huntingdon	Lincoln Caverns	*7761 William Penn Hwy, Huntingdon PA 16652*
PA	Johnstown	The Johnstown Inclined Plane	*711 Edgehill Dr, Johnstown PA 15905*
PA	Jones Mills	Living Treasures Animal Park	*300 PA-711, Jones Mills PA 15646*
PA	Kane	Kinzua Bridge State Park	*296 Viaduct Rd, Kane PA 16735*
PA	King of Prussia	United Artists King of Prussia 16 IMAX & RPX	*300 Goddard Blvd, King of Prussia PA 19406*
PA	King of Prussia	Visitor Center At Valley Forge	*1100 N Outer Line Dr, King of Prussia PA 19406*
PA	Kutztown	Crystal Cave Road	*874 Crystal Cave Rd, Kutztown PA 19530*
PA	Lancaster	Dutch Wonderland	*2249 Lincoln Hwy E, Lancaster PA 17602*
PA	Langhorne	Sesame Place	*28 Sesame Rd, Langhorne PA 19047*
PA	Lehighton	Country Junction	*6565 Interchange Rd, Lehighton PA 18235*
PA	Ligonier	Idlewild and SoakZone	*2554 US-30, Ligonier PA 15658*
PA	Linesville	The Spillway	*21261 Hartstown Rd, Linesville PA 16424*
PA	Mars	Jimmy's Strip District Grille	*220 SR 3015, Mars PA 16046*
PA	Meadville	Market House	*910 Market St, Meadville PA 16335*
PA	Meadville	Market House	*910 Market St, Meadville PA 16335*

PA	Meyersdale	Meyersdale Train Station	*527 Main St, Meyersdale PA 15552*
PA	Middletown	Perfectly Pennsylvania	*1 Terminal Dr, Middletown PA 17057*
PA	Middletown	Perfectly Pennsylvania	*1 Terminal Dr, Middletown PA 17057*
PA	Mill Run	Scarlett Knob Campground Inc	*133 Scarlett Knob Rd, Mill Run PA 15464*
PA	Mount Gretna	The Jigger Shop	*202 Gettysburg Ave, Mount Gretna PA 17064*
PA	Mount Gretna	The Jigger Shop	*202 Gettysburg Ave, Mount Gretna PA 17064*
PA	Mount Jewett	Kinzua Bridge Visitor's Center	*QC66+8H Mount Jewett, Mount Jewett PA 16735*
PA	New Castle	Living Treasures Animal Park	*628 Fox Rd, New Castle PA 16101*
PA	Northampton	Science Central	*2418 Cherryville Rd, Northampton PA 18067*
PA	Nottingham	Herr Foods Visitor Center	*508 E Christine Rd, Nottingham PA 19362*
PA	Nottingham	Herr's Factory Tours	*20 Herr Dr, Nottingham PA 19362*
PA	Nottingham	Herrs Snack Factory Tour	*271 Old Baltimore Pike, Nottingham PA 19362*
PA	Ohiopyle	Ohiopyle Old Mill General Store	*2 Negley St, Ohiopyle PA 15470*
PA	Orrtanna	Mr.Ed's Elephant Emporium and candy	*6019 Chambersburg Rd, Orrtanna PA 17353*
PA	Philadelphia	1650 Market St	*Liberty Place, Philadelphia PA 19103*
PA	Philadelphia	Betsy Ross House	*239 Arch St, Philadelphia PA 19106*
PA	Philadelphia	Betsy Ross House	*239 Arch St, Philadelphia PA 19106*
PA	Philadelphia	Eastern State Penitentiary	*2027 Fairmount Ave, Philadelphia PA 19130*

PA	Philadelphia	Independence Gift Shop	*599 Market St 2nd Floor, Philadelphia PA 19106*
PA	Philadelphia	Independence Seaport Museum	*211 S Christopher Columbus Blvd, Philadelphia PA 19106*
PA	Philadelphia	Independence Visitor Center	*525 Market St, Philadelphia PA 19106*
PA	Philadelphia	Museum of the American Revolution	*306 Market St, Philadelphia PA 19106*
PA	Philadelphia	National Constitution Center	*525 Arch St, Philadelphia PA 19106*
PA	Philadelphia	National Liberty Museum	*325 Chestnut St Unit 800, Philadelphia PA 19106*
PA	Philadelphia	One Liberty Place	*1650 Market St 42nd Fl, Philadelphia PA 19103*
PA	Philadelphia	Philadelphia Zoo	*3400 W Girard Ave, Philadelphia PA 19104*
PA	Philadelphia	Please Touch Museum	*4231 Avenue of the Republic, Philadelphia PA 19131*
PA	Philadelphia	The Academy of Natural Sciences of Drexel Universi	*1 Logan Square, Philadelphia PA 19103*
PA	Philadelphia	The Franklin Institute	*222 N 20th St, Philadelphia PA 19103*
PA	Philadelphia	United States Mint	*151 S Independence Mall E, Philadelphia PA 19106*
PA	Pittsburgh	125 W Station Square Dr	*125 W Station Square Dr, Pittsburgh PA 15219*
PA	Pittsburgh	Carnegie Museum of Natural History	*4400 Forbes Ave, Pittsburgh PA 15213*
PA	Pittsburgh	Carnegie Science Center	*1 Allegheny Ave, Pittsburgh PA 15212*
PA	Pittsburgh	Children's Museum of Pittsburgh	*10 Children's Way, Pittsburgh PA 15212*
PA	Pittsburgh	National Aviary	*700 Arch St, Pittsburgh PA 15212*
PA	Pittsburgh	Pittsburgh Zoo & PPG Aquarium	*7370 Baker St, Pittsburgh PA 15206*

PA	Pittsburgh	Pittsburgh Zoo & PPG Aquarium	*1 One Wild Pl, Pittsburgh PA 15206*
PA	Pittsburgh	Senator John Heinz History Center	*1212 Smallman St, Pittsburgh PA 15222*
PA	Pittsburgh	The Duquesne Incline	*The Duquesne Incline, Pittsburgh PA 15211*
PA	Pittsburgh	The Society for the Preservation of the Duquesne H	*Duquesne Incline, Pittsburgh PA 15211*
PA	Pittsburgh	The Terminal	*2020 Smallman St, Pittsburgh PA 15222*
PA	Plymouth Meeting	LEGOLAND Discovery Center Philadelphia	*500 W Germantown Pike Suite 1510, Plymouth Meeting PA 19462*
PA	Pocono Township	Great Wolf Lodge Pocono Mountains	*1 Great Wolf Dr, Pocono Township PA 18355*
PA	Punxsutawney	Official Groundhog Souvenirs	*102 W Mahoning St, Punxsutawney PA 15767*
PA	Punxsutawney	Punxsutawney Area Chamber of Commerce	*110 W Mahoning St, Punxsutawney PA 15767*
PA	Rankin	Rivers of Steel: Carrie Blast Furnaces National Historic Lan	*801 Carrie Furnace Blvd, Rankin PA 15104*
PA	Reading	FirstEnergy Stadium	*1950 Centre Avenue, Reading PA 19605*
PA	Reading	Reading City Hall	*815 Washington St., Reading PA 19601*
PA	Reading	The Pagoda	*98 Duryea Dr, Reading PA 19602*
PA	Reading	The Pagoda	*98 Duryea Dr, Reading PA 19602*
PA	Ronks	Cherry Crest Adventure Farm	*147 Cherry Hill Rd, Ronks PA 17572*
PA	Ronks	Strasburg Rail Road	*321 Gap Rd, Ronks PA 17572*
PA	Ronks	Strasburg Rail Road	*321 Gap Rd, Ronks PA 17572*

PA	Ronks	The Red Caboose Motel	*312 Paradise Ln, Ronks PA 17572*
PA	Ronks	The Red Caboose Motel & Restaurant	*312 Paradise Ln, Ronks PA 17572*
PA	Roulette	Allegheny River Campground	*1737 US-6, Roulette PA 16746*
PA	Schnecksville	Lehigh Valley Zoo	*5150 Game Preserve Rd, Schnecksville PA 18078*
PA	Scranton	Electric City Aquarium & Reptile Den	*300 Lackawanna Ave Floor 2, Scranton PA 18503*
PA	Scranton	Electric City Trolley Museum	*300 Cliff St, Scranton PA 18503*
PA	Scranton	Lackawanna Coal Mine Tour	*22 Bald Mountain Rd, Scranton PA 18504*
PA	Scranton	McDade Park	*C78Q+RG Scranton, Scranton PA 18504*
PA	Soudersburg	Miller's Smorgasbord Restaurant	*2811 Lincoln Hwy E, Soudersburg PA 17572*
PA	Spring Mills	Penn's Cave & Wildlife Park	*222 Penns Cave Rd, Spring Mills PA 16875*
PA	Strasburg	Railroad Museum of Pennsylvania	*300 Gap Rd, Strasburg PA 17579*
PA	Strasburg	Strasburg Railroad Gift Shop	*301 Gap Rd, Strasburg PA 17579*
PA	Tannersville	Camelback Mountain Adventures	*243 Resort Dr, Tannersville PA 18372*
PA	Tannersville	Camelback Mountain Resort	*Camelbeach Headquarters, Tannersville PA 18372*
PA	Tipton	DelGrosso's Park	*118 T-789, Tipton PA 16684*
PA	Titusville	Oil Creek & Titusville Railroad	*221 S Perry St, Titusville PA 16354*
PA	Titusville	Oil Creek & Titusville Railroad	*221 S Perry St, Titusville PA 16354*
PA	West Hamburg	Cabela's	*Cabelas, West Hamburg PA 19526*

PA	West Mifflin	Kennywood	*4800 Kennywood Blvd, West Mifflin PA 15122*
PA	York	Cones & Clubs	*5745 Lincoln Hwy, York PA 17406*
PA	York	Cones & Clubs	*5745 Lincoln Hwy, York PA 17406*
PA	York	Harley-Davidson Vehicle Operations	*1425 Eden Road, York PA 17402*

Rhode Island

RI	Burrillville	Wright's Chicken Farm Restaurant	*84 Inman Rd, Burrillville RI 02830*
RI	Burrillville	Wright's Farm Restaurant	*84 Inman Rd, Burrillville RI 02830*
RI	Newport	House of Scrimshaw	*132 Thames St, Newport RI 02840*
RI	Newport	House of Scrimshaw & Gifts	*132 Thames St, Newport RI 02840*
RI	Providence	Roger Williams Park Zoo	*1000 Elmwood Ave, Providence RI 02907*
RI	Westerly	Beach Store	*162 Atlantic Ave, Westerly RI 02891*
RI	Westerly	The Beach Store	*156 Atlantic Ave, Westerly RI 02891*

			South Carolina
SC	Beaufort	Kazoobie Kazoo Factory	*12 John Galt Rd, Beaufort SC 29906*
SC	Beaufort	Marine Corps Recruit Depot, Parris Island	*202 Boulevard De France, Beaufort SC 29902*
SC	Charleston	Charles Towne Landing State Historic Site	*Charles Towne Landing State Historic Site, Charleston SC 29407*
SC	Charleston	South Carolina Aquarium	*100 Aquarium Wharf, Charleston SC 29401*
SC	Clarks Hill	Thurmond Lake & Visitor Center	*510 Clarks Hill Hwy, Clarks Hill SC 29821*
SC	Cleveland	Caesars Head State Park	*24 Cliff Ridge Dr, Cleveland SC 29635*
SC	Columbia	EdVenture Children's Museum	*211 Gervais St, Columbia SC 29201*
SC	Columbia	Riverbanks Zoo and garden	*500 Wildlife Pkwy, Columbia SC 29210*
SC	Columbia	South Carolina State Museum	*514 Williams St, Columbia SC 29201*
SC	Florence	Buc-ee's	*3390 N Williston Rd, Florence SC 29506*
SC	Fort Mill	Cabela's	*3700 Avenue of the Carolinas, Fort Mill SC 29708*
SC	Fort Mill	Carowinds	*14523 Carowinds Blvd, Fort Mill SC 29708*
SC	Fort Mill	Carowinds	*14523 Carowinds Blvd, Fort Mill SC 29708*
SC	Fripp Island	Hunting Island State Park	*9G5X+C5 Fripp Island, Fripp Island SC 29920*
SC	Greenville	Bass Pro Shops	*29607, Greenville SC 29607*
SC	Greenville	The Childrens Museum of the Upstate	*300 College St, Greenville SC 29601*
SC	Hamer	South of the Border Restaurant	*3346 US-301, Hamer SC 29547*

SC	Hilton Head Island	Harbour Town Lighthouse	*160 Lighthouse Rd, Hilton Head Island SC 29928*
SC	Hilton Head Island	Pirate's Island Hilton Head SC	*8 Marina Side Dr, Hilton Head Island SC 29928*
SC	Johns Island	Islands Mercantile	*544 Freshfields Dr, Johns Island SC 29455*
SC	Johns Island	Kiawah Shop	*1 Kiawah Beach Dr, Johns Island SC 29455*
SC	Moncks Corner	Cypress Gardens	*3030 Cypress Gardens Rd, Moncks Corner SC 29461*
SC	Myrtle Beach	2nd Ave Pier	*2nd Ave Ocen Blvd. North, Myrtle Beach SC 29577*
SC	Myrtle Beach	Bass Pro Shops	*10177 North Kings Highway, Myrtle Beach SC 29572*
SC	Myrtle Beach	Broadway at the Beach	*1325 Celebrity Cir, Myrtle Beach SC 29577*
SC	Myrtle Beach	Broadway at the Beach	*1325 Celebrity Cir, Myrtle Beach SC 29577*
SC	Myrtle Beach	Broadway Magic	*1197 Celebrity Cir, Myrtle Beach SC 29577*
SC	Myrtle Beach	Captain Hooks Adventure Golf	*2205 US-17 BUS, Myrtle Beach SC 29577*
SC	Myrtle Beach	Gay Dolphin Gift Cove	*916 N Ocean Blvd, Myrtle Beach SC 29577*
SC	Myrtle Beach	Klig’s Kites (Broadway at the Beach)	*1215 Celebrity Cir, Myrtle Beach SC 29577*
SC	Myrtle Beach	Ocean Lakes Family Campground	*6001 Ocean Lakes Dr, Myrtle Beach SC 29575*
SC	Myrtle Beach	Pier 14 Restaurant & Lounge	*1306 N Ocean Blvd, Myrtle Beach SC 29577*
SC	Myrtle Beach	Pirates Voyage	*8907 N Kings Hwy, Myrtle Beach SC 29572*
SC	Myrtle Beach	River Street Sweets	*1171 Celebrity Circle, Myrtle Beach SC 29577*
SC	Myrtle Beach	River Street Sweets	*4912a White Pt Lp, Myrtle Beach SC 29572*

SC	Myrtle Beach	Tervis Store	*1315 Celebrity Cir, Myrtle Beach SC 29577*
SC	Myrtle Beach	The Bowery	*110 9th Ave N, Myrtle Beach SC 29577*
SC	Myrtle Beach	The Original Benjamin's Calabash Seafood	*9593 N Kings Hwy, Myrtle Beach SC 29572*
SC	Myrtle Beach	Waccatee Zoological Farm	*8500 Enterprise Rd, Myrtle Beach SC 29588*
SC	Myrtle Beach	WonderWorks Myrtle Beach	*1313 Celebrity Cir, Myrtle Beach SC 29577*
SC	North Charleston	Clemson Conservation center	*1250 Supply St, North Charleston SC 29405*
SC	North Myrtle Beach	Alligator Adventure	*902 White Point Rd, North Myrtle Beach SC 29582*
SC	North Myrtle Beach	Black Market Minerals	*4892 US-17, North Myrtle Beach SC 29582*
SC	North Myrtle Beach	House of Blues Myrtle Beach	*4640 Hwy 17 S, North Myrtle Beach SC 29582*
SC	Port Royal	MCRD Parris Island	*283 Blvd De France, Port Royal SC 29905*
SC	Pumpkintown	Table Rock State Park	*27MW+V9 Pumpkintown, Pumpkintown SC 29671*
SC	Williston	Floral Mark-It	*12910 W Main St, Williston SC 29853*

South Dakota			
SD	Aberdeen	Storybook Land Wylie Park	*421 24th Ave NW, Aberdeen SD 57401*
SD	Aberdeen	Wylie Park	*FFRJ+W3 Aberdeen, Aberdeen SD 57401*
SD	Belle Fourche	Tri-State Museum	*415 5th Ave, Belle Fourche SD 57717*
SD	Beresford	Truck Towne Plaza	*47016 SD-46, Beresford SD 57004*
SD	Box Elder	South Dakota Air and Space Museum	*2890 Davis Dr, Box Elder SD 57706*
SD	Creighton	Badlands National Park	*85MVVM46+54, Creighton SD 57790*
SD	Custer	Coolidge General Store	*13201 US-16A, Custer SD 57730*
SD	Custer	Creekside Lodge	*13389 US Hwy 16A, Custer SD 57730*
SD	Custer	Jewel Cave National Monument	*11149 US-16, Custer SD 57730*
SD	Custer	Wild Bill's Antiques Mall & Rock	*RC35+MX Custer, Custer SD 57730*
SD	Deadwood	Deadwood Gift Shoppe	*664 Main St, Deadwood SD 57732*
SD	Deadwood	Gold Nugget Trading Post/Chinatown	*673 675 Main St, Deadwood SD 57732*
SD	Deadwood	Pams Purple Door Discount Outlet	*637 Main St, Deadwood SD 57732*
SD	Hill City	Broken Arrow Trading Co	*249 Main St, Hill City SD 57745*
SD	Hill City	Broken Arrow Trading Co	*249 Main St, Hill City SD 57745*
SD	Hill City	Mountain Treats	*269 Main St, Hill City SD 57745*
SD	Hill City	Palmer Gulch	*12620 SD-244, Hill City SD 57745*
SD	Hot Springs	Evans Plunge Mineral Springs	*Evans Plunge Grounds, Hot Springs SD 57747*
SD	Hot Springs	The Mammoth Site of Hot Springs SD	*1800 US-18 BYP, Hot Springs SD 57747*

SD	Keystone	1880 Train	*Keystone Station, Keystone SD 57751*
SD	Keystone	Big Thunder Gold mine	*604 Blair St, Keystone SD 57751*
SD	Keystone	Broken Arrow Trading Co	*220 Winter St # B, Keystone SD 57751*
SD	Keystone	Goodtime Photo	*804 US-16A, Keystone SD 57751*
SD	Keystone	Mount Rushmore National Memorial	*13000 SD-244, Keystone SD 57751*
SD	Keystone	Rushmore Cave	*13622 SD-40, Keystone SD 57751*
SD	Keystone	The Keystone Mall	*804 US-16A, Keystone SD 57751*
SD	Mitchell	Cabela's	*601 Cabela Dr, Mitchell SD 57301*
SD	Mitchell	Corn Palace Gift Shop	*613 N Main St, Mitchell SD 57301*
SD	Murdo	Star Family Restaurant	*103 5th St, Murdo SD 57559*
SD	Oacoma	Al's Oasis Inc	*1000 E South Dakota, Oacoma SD 57365*
SD	Philip	Badlands Trading Post	*21290 SD-240, Philip SD 57567*
SD	Rapid City	Bear Country USA	*XPG2+C8P, Rapid City SD 57702*
SD	Rapid City	Black Hills Caverns	*2600 Cavern Rd, Rapid City SD 57702*
SD	Rapid City	Black Hills National Forest	*8221 Mt Rushmore Rd, Rapid City SD 57702*
SD	Rapid City	Cabela's	*3231 E Mall Dr, Rapid City SD 57701*
SD	Rapid City	Cosmos Mystery Area	*24032 Cosmos Rd, Rapid City SD 57702*
SD	Rapid City	Dinosaur Park	*940 Skyline Dr, Rapid City SD 57701*
SD	Rapid City	Ft. Hays Chuckwagon Supper & Show	*2255 Fort Hayes Dr, Rapid City SD 57702*
SD	Rapid City	Old MacDonald's Farm	*23691 Busted Five Ln, Rapid City SD 57702*
SD	Rapid City	Reptile Gardens	*8955 US-16, Rapid City SD 57702*

SD	Rapid City	Rushmore Mall Penny Machine	*2200 N Maple Ave ste 500, Rapid City SD 57701*
SD	Rapid City	Storybook Island	*1301 Sheridan Lake Rd, Rapid City SD 57702*
SD	Sioux Falls	Butterfly House & Marine Cove	*Butterfly House & Aquarium, Sioux Falls SD 57106*
SD	Sioux Falls	Giftport News Concourse	*2801 N Jaycee Ln, Sioux Falls SD 57104*
SD	Sioux Falls	Great Plains Zoo & Delbridge Museum of Natural His	*805 S Kiwanis Ave, Sioux Falls SD 57104*
SD	Sioux Falls	Old Courthouse Museum	*Old Courthouse Museum, Sioux Falls SD 57104*
SD	Spearfish	High Moutain Outfitters	*313 W Jackson Blvd, Spearfish SD 57783*
SD	Sturgis	Park Bench Apparel Penny Machine	*1012 Main St #11, Sturgis SD 57785*
SD	Wall	Wall Drug Store	*510 Main St, Wall SD 57790*
SD	Watertown	Bramble Park Zoo	*Terry Redlin Environmental Center / Discovery Center, Watertown SD 57201*

			Tennessee
TN	Athens	Mayfield Dairy Farms	*4 Mayfield Ln, Athens TN 37303*
TN	Bristol	Bristol Motor Speedway	*151 Speedway Blvd, Bristol TN 37620*
TN	Buchanan	Paris Landing KOA Campgrond	*6290 E Antioch Rd, Buchanan TN 38222*
TN	Chattanooga	AT&T Field	*215 Chestnut St, Chattanooga TN 37402*
TN	Chattanooga	Chattanooga Zoo	*301 N Holtzclaw Ave, Chattanooga TN 37404*
TN	Chattanooga	Creative Discovery Museum	*321 Chestnut St, Chattanooga TN 37402*
TN	Chattanooga	Raccoon Mountain	*283 W Hills Dr, Chattanooga TN 37419*
TN	Chattanooga	Ruby Falls	*Ruby Falls, Chattanooga TN 37409*
TN	Chattanooga	Southern Belle Riverboat	*151 Riverfront Pkwy, Chattanooga TN 37402*
TN	Chattanooga	Tennessee Aquarium	*1 Broad St, Chattanooga TN 37402*
TN	Christiana	Miller's Grocery-Christiana	*7011 Main St, Christiana TN 37037*
TN	Crossville	Buc-ee's	*2055 Genesis Rd, Crossville TN 38555*
TN	Dandridge	Bush's Beans Visitor Center	*3901 US-411, Dandridge TN 37725*
TN	Gatlinburg	Arcadia Arcade & Gatlinburg Space Needle	*115 Airport Rd, Gatlinburg TN 37738*
TN	Gatlinburg	Beef Jerky Outlet - Gatlinburg	*636 Parkway, Gatlinburg TN 37738*
TN	Gatlinburg	Bubba Gump Shrimp Co.	*902 Parkway, Gatlinburg TN 37738*
TN	Gatlinburg	Buckboard Too	*616 Parkway, Gatlinburg TN 37738*

TN	Gatlinburg	Dick's Last Resort - Gatlinburg	*903 Parkway, Gatlinburg TN 37738*
TN	Gatlinburg	Ely's Mill	*393 Roaring Fork Rd, Gatlinburg TN 37738*
TN	Gatlinburg	Gatlinburg Shopping Strip	*520 TN-71, Gatlinburg TN 37738*
TN	Gatlinburg	Gatlinburg Sky Lift	*765 Parkway, Gatlinburg TN 37738*
TN	Gatlinburg	Gatlinburg SkyShop	*765 Parkway, Gatlinburg TN 37738*
TN	Gatlinburg	Gatlinburg Welcome Center	*1011 Banner Rd, Gatlinburg TN 37738*
TN	Gatlinburg	Great Smoky Mountains Collectable Pennies at All American So	*730 Parkway, Gatlinburg TN 37738*
TN	Gatlinburg	Jonathan's "The Bear Necessities"	*733 Parkway, Gatlinburg TN 37738*
TN	Gatlinburg	Maples Tree	*639 Parkway, Gatlinburg TN 37738*
TN	Gatlinburg	Mountain Mall	*611 Parkway # B7, Gatlinburg TN 37738*
TN	Gatlinburg	New pennies	*88 River Rd, Gatlinburg TN 37738*
TN	Gatlinburg	Ober Gatlinburg Amusement Park & Ski Area	*1904 Maris Drive Ober Gatlinburg, Gatlinburg TN 37738*
TN	Gatlinburg	Parkway Boutique	*917 Parkway, Gatlinburg TN 37738*
TN	Gatlinburg	Ripley's Believe It or Not	*812 Parkway #102, Gatlinburg TN 37738*
TN	Gatlinburg	Ripley's Davy Crockett Mini-Golf	*188 Parkway, Gatlinburg TN 37738*
TN	Gatlinburg	Ripley's Marvelous Mirror Maze	*623 Parkway, Gatlinburg TN 37738*
TN	Gatlinburg	Ripley's Moving Theater	*904 Parkway, Gatlinburg TN 37738*

TN	Gatlinburg	SkyPark	*765 Parkway, Gatlinburg TN 37738*
TN	Gatlinburg	Sweet!	*756 Parkway, Gatlinburg TN 37738*
TN	Gatlinburg	The Silver Galleon	*1904 Maris Drive Ober Gatlinburg, Gatlinburg TN 37738*
TN	Gray	Hands On! Discovery Center	*1212 Suncrest Dr, Gray TN 37615*
TN	Hurricane Mills	Loretta Lynn's Kitchen	*15366 TN-13, Hurricane Mills TN 37078*
TN	Jackson	Casey Jones Home & Railroad Museum	*30 Casey Jones Ln, Jackson TN 38305*
TN	Knoxville	Zoo Knoxville	*1009 N Mary St, Knoxville TN 37914*
TN	Limestone	Bright's Zoo	*3425 US-11E, Limestone TN 37681*
TN	Lookout Mountain	Incline Railway	*Lookout Mountain, Lookout Mountain TN 37350*
TN	Lynchburg	Courthouse Square	*117 Main St, Lynchburg TN 37352*
TN	Lynchburg	Lynchburg Hardware & General Store	*52 Mechanic St S, Lynchburg TN 37352*
TN	McMinnville	Cumberland Caverns	*1437 Cumberland Caverns Rd, McMinnville TN 37110*
TN	Memphis	Bass Pro Shops	*Memphis Pyramid, Memphis TN 38105*
TN	Memphis	Beale Street Blues Gift Shop	*Handy Park, Memphis TN 38103*
TN	Memphis	Boulevard Souvenirs (moved to 676 Marshall Ave Suite 103 Mem	*3706 Elvis Presley Blvd, Memphis TN 38116*
TN	Memphis	Elvis Presley Automobile Museum Gift Store.	*3727 Elvis Presley Blvd, Memphis TN 38116*
TN	Memphis	Graceland	*3717 Elvis Presley Blvd, Memphis TN 38116*

TN	Memphis	Memphis Outlets	*3855 Elvis Presley Blvd, Memphis TN 38116*
TN	Memphis	Memphis Riverboats	*251 Riverside Dr, Memphis TN 38103*
TN	Memphis	Memphis Zoo	*2000 Prentiss Pl, Memphis TN 38112*
TN	Memphis	Pink Palace Family of Museums	*3050 Central Ave, Memphis TN 38111*
TN	Memphis	Tater Red's Lucky Mojos and Voodoo Healing	*153 Beale St, Memphis TN 38103*
TN	Nashville	Adventure Science Center	*800 Fort Negley Blvd, Nashville TN 37203*
TN	Nashville	Andrew Jackson's Hermitage	*The Hermitage, Nashville TN 37076*
TN	Nashville	Aquarium Restaurant	*516 Opry Mills Dr, Nashville TN 37214*
TN	Nashville	Bass Pro Shops	*323 Opry Mills Dr, Nashville TN 37214*
TN	Nashville	Belle Meade Plantation	*511 Parmer Ave, Nashville TN 37205*
TN	Nashville	Cooter's Place in Nashville	*2613B McGavock Pk, Nashville TN 37214*
TN	Nashville	Hatch Show Print	*224 Rep. John Lewis Way S, Nashville TN 37203*
TN	Nashville	Legends Gifts	*428 Rep. John Lewis Way N, Nashville TN 37203*
TN	Nashville	Madame Tussauds Nashville	*Opry Mills, Nashville TN 37214*
TN	Nashville	Nashville Zoo at Grassmere	*Nashville Zoo Station Inbound, Nashville TN 37211*
TN	Nashville	Opryland Hotel	*2800 Opryland Dr, Nashville TN 37214*
TN	Nashville	Patsy Cline Museum	*119 3rd Ave S, Nashville TN 37201*
TN	Nashville	Rainforest Cafe	*353 Opry Mills Dr, Nashville TN 37214*

TN	Nashville	The Johnny Cash Museum & Cafe	*119 3rd Ave S, Nashville TN 37201*
TN	Nashville	The Parthenon	*2500 West End Ave, Nashville TN 37203*
TN	Nashville	Wildhorse Saloon	*118 2nd Ave N, Nashville TN 37201*
TN	Nashville	Willie Nelson and Friends Museum and General Store	*2613B McGavock Pk, Nashville TN 37214*
TN	Paris	Trolinger's	*2305 E Wood St, Paris TN 38242*
TN	Pigeon Forge	Alcatraz East Museum	*2757 Parkway, Pigeon Forge TN 37863*
TN	Pigeon Forge	Beef Jerky Outlet	*131 The Island Dr, Pigeon Forge TN 37863*
TN	Pigeon Forge	Big Rock Candy Kitchen	*131 The Island Dr, Pigeon Forge TN 37863*
TN	Pigeon Forge	Christmas Place	*2470 Parkway, Pigeon Forge TN 37863*
TN	Pigeon Forge	Country Barn Gift Shop Inc	*2869 Parkway, Pigeon Forge TN 37863*
TN	Pigeon Forge	Dollywood	*2700 Dollywood Parks Blvd, Pigeon Forge TN 37863*
TN	Pigeon Forge	Fast Tracks	*2879 US-441 Scenic, Pigeon Forge TN 37863*
TN	Pigeon Forge	Fast Tracks Arcade	*2879 Parkway, Pigeon Forge TN 37863*
TN	Pigeon Forge	Flyaway Indoor Skydiving	*3068 Parkway, Pigeon Forge TN 37863*
TN	Pigeon Forge	Goats on the Roof	*1341 Wears Valley Rd, Pigeon Forge TN 37863*
TN	Pigeon Forge	Haywood Turquoise Jewelry	*Wynns Mountain Village Scooter Rentals, Pigeon Forge TN 37863*
TN	Pigeon Forge	Patriot Peddler	*131 The Island Dr #9138, Pigeon Forge TN 37863*

TN	Pigeon Forge	Pigeon Forge Gem Mine	*2865 Parkway, Pigeon Forge TN 37863*
TN	Pigeon Forge	Sweet!	*5120 The Island Dr, Pigeon Forge TN 37863*
TN	Pigeon Forge	The Comedy Barn Theater	*2775 Parkway, Pigeon Forge TN 37863*
TN	Pigeon Forge	The Old Mill General Store	*175 Old Mill Ave, Pigeon Forge TN 37863*
TN	Pigeon Forge	Titanic Museum	*2134 Parkway, Pigeon Forge TN 37863*
TN	Pigeon Forge	WonderWorks - Pigeon Forge	*100 Music Rd, Pigeon Forge TN 37863*
TN	Sevierville	Bass Pro Shops	*3629 Outdoor Sportsman Pl, Sevierville TN 37764*
TN	Sevierville	Buc-ee's	*170 Buc-ee's Blvd, Sevierville TN 37764*
TN	Sevierville	NASCAR SpeedPark	*1545 Parkway, Sevierville TN 37862*
TN	Sevierville	Parrot Mountain & Garden of Eden	*1288 McCarter Hollow Rd, Sevierville TN 37862*
TN	Sevierville	RainForest Adventures Discovery Zoo	*109 Nascar Dr, Sevierville TN 37862*
TN	Sevierville	Ripley's Old MacDonald's Farm Mini Golf	*1639 Parkway, Sevierville TN 37862*
TN	Sevierville	Wilderness At the Smokies	*1425 Old Knoxville Hwy, Sevierville TN 37876*
TN	Spencer	Fall Creek Falls State Park Inn and Conference Cen	*2536 Lakeside Rd, Spencer TN 38585*
TN	Sweetwater	The Lost Sea Adventure	*140 Lost Sea Rd, Sweetwater TN 37874*
TN	Tellico Plains	Charles Hall Museum	*229 Cherohala Skyway A, Tellico Plains TN 37385*
TN	Townsend	Townsend / Great Smokies KOA Holiday	*8533 TN-73, Townsend TN 37882*

			Texas
TX	Abilene	Abilene Zoo	*C8R5+68 Abilene, Abilene TX 79602*
TX	Abilene	Abilene Zoological Gardens	*C8R4+G9 Abilene, Abilene TX 79602*
TX	Abilene	The Grace Museum	*102 Cypress St, Abilene TX 79601*
TX	Allen	Cabela's	*201 Cabela Dr, Allen TX 75013*
TX	Alpine	Alpine Visitor Center	*106 N 3rd St, Alpine TX 79830*
TX	Alpine	Gumslinger's	*108 N 5th St, Alpine TX 79830*
TX	Amarillo	Big Texan Gift Shop	*7701 Interstate 40 Access Rd, Amarillo TX 79118*
TX	Amarillo	Buc-ee's	*9900 E Interstate 40 Hwy, Amarillo TX 79118*
TX	Amarillo	Golden Corral	*7220 I-40, Amarillo TX 79106*
TX	Amarillo	Texas Rt 66 Visitor Center	*1900 SW 6th Ave, Amarillo TX 79106*
TX	Arlington	Six Flags Over Texas	*2201 E Road to Six Flags St, Arlington TX 76011*
TX	Athens	Texas Freshwater Fisheries Center	*5550 FM2495, Athens TX 75752*
TX	Austin	Austin Aquarium	*13530 US-183, Austin TX 78750*
TX	Austin	Austin Visitor Center	*103 E 5th St, Austin TX 78701*
TX	Austin	Austin Zoo	*10807 Rawhide Trail, Austin TX 78736*
TX	Austin	Beerland	*711 Red River St, Austin TX 78701*
TX	Austin	Susanna Dickinson Museum	*411 E 5th St., Austin TX 78701*

TX	Austin	Terra Toys Penny Machine	*2438 W Anderson Ln., Austin TX 78757*
TX	Austin	Texas Capitol Visitors Center	*112 E 11th St, Austin TX 78701*
TX	Austin	Thinkery	*1830 Simond Ave, Austin TX 78723*
TX	Balmorhea	Balmorhea State Park	*9207 TX-17, Balmorhea TX 79718*
TX	Balmorhea	Balmorhea State Park	*9207 TX-17, Balmorhea TX 79718*
TX	Bastrop	Buc-ee's	*601 Jackson St, Bastrop TX 78602*
TX	Baytown	Buc-ee's	*4084 East Fwy, Baytown TX 77521*
TX	Beaumont	Crossroads Bowling Center Inc	*4370 Dowlen Rd, Beaumont TX 77706*
TX	Beaumont	Laugh it Up! Gifts & Novelties	*4414 Dowlen Rd Suite 106B, Beaumont TX 77706*
TX	Belton	Bell County Museum	*201a N Main St, Belton TX 76513*
TX	Boerne	Cascade Caverns	*226 Cascade Cavern, Boerne TX 78015*
TX	Boerne	Pearl Antler Boutique - Boerne	*322 S Main St, Boerne TX 78006*
TX	Bonham	Bonham Visitor Center	*327 N Main St, Bonham TX 75418*
TX	Brownsville	Children's Museum of Brownsville	*501 E Ringgold St Unit 5, Brownsville TX 78520*
TX	Brownsville	Gladys Porter Zoo	*1445 E 6th St, Brownsville TX 78520*
TX	Buda	Cabela's	*15570 I-35, Buda TX 78610*
TX	Burnet	Inks Lake State Park	*3630 Park Rd 4 W, Burnet TX 78611*

TX	Comfort	Chevron	*42 US-87, Comfort TX 78013*
TX	Commerce	Northeast Texas Children's Msm	*2501 TX-24, Commerce TX 75428*
TX	Concan	Garner State Park	*396 Garner State Pk Rd, Concan TX 78838*
TX	Corpus Christi	Corpus Christi Museum of Science & History	*1900 N Chaparral St, Corpus Christi TX 78401*
TX	Corpus Christi	Ocean Treasures	*14049 S Padre Island Dr, Corpus Christi TX 78418*
TX	Corpus Christi	Sea Treasures	*1315-Surfside @Breakwater, Corpus Christi TX 78402*
TX	Corpus Christi	Texas State Aquarium	*2710 N Shoreline Blvd, Corpus Christi TX 78402*
TX	Corpus Christi	Treasures On the Beach	*2818 Surfside Blvd, Corpus Christi TX 78402*
TX	Corpus Christi	USS Lexington	*2914 N Shoreline Blvd, Corpus Christi TX 78402*
TX	Dallas	Dallas Heritage Village	*2814 Main St, Dallas TX 75215*
TX	Dallas	Dallas Zoo	*318 S Lancaster Ave, Dallas TX 75203*
TX	Dallas	Reunion Tower	*Reunion Tower, Dallas TX 75207*
TX	Dallas	The Dallas World Aquarium (2 machines)	*1801 N Griffin St, Dallas TX 75202*
TX	Dallas	The Sixth Floor Museum at Dealey Plaza	*401 Elm St, Dallas TX 75202*
TX	Denton	Buc-ee's	*2800 Stemmons Fwy, Denton TX 76210*
TX	El Paso	El Paso Zoo	*4001 E Paisano Dr, El Paso TX 79905*
TX	El Paso	Wyler Aerial Tramway	*1700 McKinley Ave, El Paso TX 79930*

TX	Ennis	Ennis Buc-ee's	*Address: 1402 I-45, Ennis, TX 75119, Ennis TX 75119*
TX	Fort Davis	Indian Lodge	*16453 Park Rd 3, Fort Davis TX 79734*
TX	Fort Worth	Buc-ee's	*15901 Outlet Blvd, Fort Worth TX 76177*
TX	Fort Worth	C R Smith Museum	*4601 Hwy 360 Skyview Dr 3, Fort Worth TX 76155*
TX	Fort Worth	Cabela's	*12901 Cabela Dr, Fort Worth TX 76177*
TX	Fort Worth	Fort Worth Museum of Science and History	*1600 Gendy St, Fort Worth TX 76107*
TX	fort worth	Fort Worth Stockyards National Historic District	*131 E Exchange Ave, fort worth TX 76164*
TX	Fort Worth	Fort Worth Zoo	*2325 Mistletoe Dr, Fort Worth TX 76110*
TX	Fort Worth	La Gran Plaza	*La Gran Plaza de 4200, Fort Worth TX 76110*
TX	Fort Worth	Longhorn General Store	*131 E Exchange Ave, Fort Worth TX 76164*
TX	Fort Worth	Texas Motor Speedway	*3545 Lone Star Cir, Fort Worth TX 76177*
TX	Fredericksburg	Clear River	*138 E Main St, Fredericksburg TX 78624*
TX	Fredericksburg	Enchanted Rock State Natural Area	*16710 Ranch Rd 965, Fredericksburg TX 78624*
TX	Fredericksburg	Luckenbach Texas	*412 Luckenbach Town Loop, Fredericksburg TX 78624*
TX	Fredericksburg	National Museum of the Pacific War	*311 E Austin St, Fredericksburg TX 78624*
TX	Gainesville	Frank Buck Zoo	*1000 W California St, Gainesville TX 76240*
TX	Galveston	61st Street Pier	*6101 Seawall Blvd Suite 3, Galveston TX 77551*

TX	Galveston	Ben & Jerry's	*4408 Seawall Blvd, Galveston TX 77550*
TX	Galveston	Bubba Gump Shrimp Co.	*2501 Seawall Blvd, Galveston TX 77550*
TX	Galveston	Fish Tales	*2502 Seawall Blvd, Galveston TX 77550*
TX	Galveston	Galveston Fishing Pier	*9001 Seawall Blvd, Galveston TX 77554*
TX	Galveston	Galveston Railroad Museum	*2602 Santa Fe Pl, Galveston TX 77550*
TX	Galveston	La King's Confectionery	*2323 The Strand, Galveston TX 77550*
TX	Galveston	Lone Star Flight Museum	*2002 Terminal Dr, Galveston TX 77554*
TX	Galveston	Moody Gardens	*1 Hope Blvd, Galveston TX 77554*
TX	Galveston	Murdochs	*2227 Seawall Blvd, Galveston TX 77550*
TX	Galveston	Ocean Star Off Shore Drilling Rig Museum	*1900 Wharf Rd, Galveston TX 77550*
TX	Galveston	Pier 21 Theater	*8 Pier 21, Galveston TX 77550*
TX	Galveston	Rainforest Cafe	*5310 Seawall Blvd, Galveston TX 77551*
TX	Galveston	Texas Seaport Museum	*2102 Harborside Dr, Galveston TX 77550*
TX	Galveston	Texas Seaport Museum Elissa	*Pier 22 Suite #8, Galveston TX 77550*
TX	Garland	Bass Pro Shops	*1800 Interstate 30 Service Rd, Garland TX 75043*
TX	Georgetown	Inner Space Caverns	*4200 I 35 N Frontage Rd, Georgetown TX 78626*
TX	Glass	Fossil Rim Wildlife Center	*56H2+W3 Glass, Glass TX 76043*

TX	Glen Rose	Dinosaur Valley State Park Store	*1629 Park Rd 59, Glen Rose TX 76043*
TX	Glen Rose	Dinosaur World	*1058 Park Rd 59, Glen Rose TX 76043*
TX	Goldthwaite	Legacy Plaza	*Legacy Plaza, Goldthwaite TX 76844*
TX	Gonzales	Gonzales Memorial Museum	*414 Smith St, Gonzales TX 78629*
TX	Grand Prairie	Ripley's Believe It or Not - Grand Prairie	*601 E Palace Pkwy, Grand Prairie TX 75050*
TX	Grapevine	Bass Pro Shops	*2501 Bass Pro Dr, Grapevine TX 76051*
TX	Grapevine	LEGOLAND Discovery Center Dallas Fort Worth	*3000 Grapevine Mills Pkwy, Grapevine TX 76051*
TX	Grapevine	Rainforest Cafe (2 machines)	*3000 Grapevine Mills Pkwy, Grapevine TX 76051*
TX	Grapevine	SEA LIFE Grapevine Aquarium	*Grapevine Mills, Grapevine TX 76051*
TX	Haltom City	Haltom City Public Library (Formerly at Clown Hamburger)	*4809 Haltom Rd, Haltom City TX 76117*
TX	Helotes	John T. Floore's Country Store	*14492 Old Bandera Rd, Helotes TX 78023*
TX	Houston	Children's Museum of Houston	*1500 Binz St, Houston TX 77004*
TX	Houston	Downtown Aquarium	*410 Bagby St, Houston TX 77002*
TX	Houston	Houston Rodeo (Only February - March each year)	*1 NRG Pkwy, Houston TX 77054*
TX	Houston	Johnson Space Center	*110 Second St, Houston TX 77058*
TX	Houston	lone star flight museum	*11551 Aerospace Ave, Houston TX 77034*
TX	Houston	Rainforest Cafe	*5015 Westheimer Rd #2315, Houston TX 77056*

TX	Houston	The Houston Museum of Natural Science	*1400 Hermann Loop Dr, Houston TX 77004*
TX	Houston	The Houston Zoo	*6200 Hermann Park Dr, Houston TX 77030*
TX	Irving	National Scouting Museum	*1329 W Walnut Hill Ln Ste 102, Irving TX 75038*
TX	Katy	Bass Pro Shops	*5000 Katy Mills Cir #415, Katy TX 77494*
TX	Katy	Rainforest Cafe	*5000 Katy Mills Cir, Katy TX 77494*
TX	Kemah	Aquarium Restaurant	*215 Kipp Ave Boardwalk #11, Kemah TX 77565*
TX	Kemah	Bubba Gump Shrimp Co.	*5 Waterfront Dr, Kemah TX 77565*
TX	La Porte	Battleship Texas State Historic Site	*3529 Battleground Rd, La Porte TX 77571*
TX	La Porte	The San Jacinto Monument	*1 Monument Cir, La Porte TX 77571*
TX	Leon Valley	San Antonio Aquarium	*6320 Bandera Rd, Leon Valley TX 78238*
TX	Lewisville	Lewisville, Texas Penny Press	*247 W Main St, Lewisville TX 75057*
TX	Longview	Texas Best Smokehouse	*3302 S Eastman Rd, Longview TX 75602*
TX	Los Fresnos	Bobz World	*36451 TX-100, Los Fresnos TX 78566*
TX	Los Fresnos	Laguna Atascosa National Wildlife Refuge	*24514 Buena Vista Blvd, Los Fresnos TX 78566*
TX	Lubbock	Cabela's	*3030 W Loop 289 Acc Rd, Lubbock TX 79407*
TX	Lubbock	Science Spectrum & OMNI Theater	*2579 S Loop 289 #250, Lubbock TX 79423*
TX	Lufkin	Ellen Trout Zoo	*402 Zoo Cir, Lufkin TX 75904*
TX	Luling	Buc-ee's	*10070 I-10, Luling TX 78648*

TX	Madisonville	Buc-ee's	*101 I-45, Madisonville TX 77864*
TX	Magnolia	Magnolia Landmark Building	*18230 FM 1488 Ste 200, Magnolia TX 77354*
TX	Marble Falls	Longhorn Cavern State Park	*6211 Park Rd 4 W, Marble Falls TX 78654*
TX	Midland	Permian Basin Petroleum Museum	*1500 I-20, Midland TX 79701*
TX	Nacogdoches	Oldest Town in Texas	*200 E Main St, Nacogdoches TX 75961*
TX	Nederland	Novrozskys Hamburgers, Etc.	*3016 FM 365, Nederland TX 77627*
TX	New Braunfels	Buc-ee's	*2760 I 35 N Frontage Rd, New Braunfels TX 78130*
TX	New Braunfels	Buc-ee's	*2760 I 35 N Frontage Rd, New Braunfels TX 78130*
TX	New Braunfels	Gruene General Store	*1610 Hunter Rd, New Braunfels TX 78130*
TX	New Braunfels	Schlitterbahn Waterparks & Resorts	*300 W Austin St, New Braunfels TX 78130*
TX	New Braunfels	Snake Farm	*5640 I-35, New Braunfels TX 78132*
TX	Odessa	Meteor Crater	*5599 Meteor Crater Rd, Odessa TX 79763*
TX	Palestine	Texas State Railroad Palestine Depot	*789 Park Rd 70, Palestine TX 75801*
TX	Palestine	Texas State Railroad State Historical Park	*Park Rd 70, Palestine TX 75801*
TX	Rio Frio	Garner State Park	*H7V6+5G Rio Frio, Rio Frio TX 78879*
TX	Rusk	Texas State Railroad Rusk Depot	*2907 W Sixth St, Rusk TX 75785*
TX	San Antonio	Alamo Plaza Shirts	*325 Alamo Plaza #1, San Antonio TX 78205*
TX	San Antonio	AT&T Center	*One Frost Bank Center Dr, San Antonio TX 78219*

TX	San Antonio	Bass Pro Shops	*17907 I-10, San Antonio TX 78257*
TX	San Antonio	Buckhorn Museum	*318 E Houston St, San Antonio TX 78205*
TX	San Antonio	Five & Dime General Store	*520 River Walk, San Antonio TX 78205*
TX	San Antonio	Five & Dime General Store	*520 River Walk, San Antonio TX 78205*
TX	San antonio	Hard Rock Cafe - San Antonio	*111 W Crockett St, San antonio TX 78205*
TX	San Antonio	Hard Rock Cafe- Denver	*111 W Crockett St, San Antonio TX 78205*
TX	San Antonio	Lackland AFB	*216 Galaxy Rd, San Antonio TX 78236*
TX	San Antonio	Louis Tussaud's Waxworks	*301 Alamo Plaza, San Antonio TX 78205*
TX	San Antonio	Mission San jose	*701 E Pyron Ave, San Antonio TX 78214*
TX	San Antonio	Natural Bridge Caverns	*26495 Natural Bridge Caverns Rd, San Antonio TX 78266*
TX	San Antonio	Natural Bridge Wildlife Ranch	*26515 FM3009, San Antonio TX 78266*
TX	San Antonio	Rainforest Cafe	*207 Losoya St, San Antonio TX 78205*
TX	San Antonio	Ripley's Believe It or Not - San Antonio	*301 Alamo Plaza, San Antonio TX 78205*
TX	San Antonio	San Antonio Official Visitor Information Center	*319 Alamo Plaza, San Antonio TX 78205*
TX	San Antonio	San Antonio Zoo	*3903 N St Mary's St, San Antonio TX 78212*
TX	San Antonio	SeaWorld San Antonio Adventure Camps	*10500 SeaWorld Dr, San Antonio TX 78251*
TX	San Antonio	Six Flags Fiesta Texas	*17000 I-10, San Antonio TX 78257*

TX	San Antonio	Splashtown San Antonio	*3600 I-35, San Antonio TX 78219*
TX	San Antonio	The Alamo	*300 Alamo Plaza, San Antonio TX 78205*
TX	San Antonio	The Aztec Theatre	*201 E Commerce St, San Antonio TX 78205*
TX	San Antonio	Tower of the Americas	*801 E César E. Chávez Blvd, San Antonio TX 78205*
TX	San Antonio	Witte Museum	*3805 Broadway, San Antonio TX 78209*
TX	San Marcos	The Meadows Center for Water and the Environment	*Spring Lake Hall, San Marcos TX 78666*
TX	San Marcos	Wonder World Park	*1000 Prospect St, San Marcos TX 78666*
TX	Shiner	Spoetzl Brewery	*603 State Hwy 95, Shiner TX 77984*
TX	Sonora	Caverns of Sonora	*1711 Private Rd 4468, Sonora TX 76950*
TX	South Padre Island	Sea Turtle Inc	*6642 State Park Rd 100, South Padre Island TX 78597*
TX	South Padre Island	South Padre Island Birding And Nature Center	*6801 Padre Blvd, South Padre Island TX 78597*
TX	Sterling City	The National Wallace Monument	*RX83+3V Sterling City, Sterling City TX 76951*
TX	Stonewall	Lyndon B. Johnson State Park & Historic Site	*69PC+X8 Stonewall, Stonewall TX 78671*
TX	Temple	Buc-ee's	*4135 N General Bruce Dr, Temple TX 76501*
TX	Temple	Clem Mikeska's Bar-B-Q	*1217 S 57th St, Temple TX 76504*
TX	Terrell	Buc-ee's	*1281 FM148, Terrell TX 75160*
TX	Texas City	Buc-ee"s	*6201 Gulf Fwy, Texas City TX 77591*

TX	Todd Mission	Texas Renaissance Festival	*7536+W3P, Todd Mission TX 77363*
TX	Tyler	Caldwell Zoo	*2203 W Martin Luther King Jr Blvd, Tyler TX 75702*
TX	Tyler	Texas Best Smokehouse III	*16251 US-271, Tyler TX 75708*
TX	Tyler	The Discovery Science Place	*314 N Broadway Ave, Tyler TX 75702*
TX	Tyler	Tiger Creek Wildlife Refuge	*17552 FM 14, Tyler TX 75706*
TX	Universal City	Polly's Pet Shop - Penny Press	*940 Pat Booker Rd, Universal City TX 78148*
TX	Waco	Cameron Park Zoo	*1701 N 4th St, Waco TX 76707*
TX	Waco	Dr. Pepper Museum & Free Enterprise Institute	*300 S 5th St, Waco TX 76701*
TX	Waco	Mayborn Museum Complex	*1300 S University Parks Dr, Waco TX 76706*
TX	Waco	Mayborn Museum Store	*1300 S University Parks Dr, Waco TX 76706*
TX	Waller	Buc-ee's	*40900 US-290, Waller TX 77484*
TX	Washington	Washington-On-The-Brazos	*23200 Park Rd 12, Washington TX 77880*
TX	Wharton	Buc-ee's	*10484 US-59, Wharton TX 77488*

Utah			
UT	Beaver	beaver chevron gas station	*650 W 1800 S, Beaver UT 84713*
UT	Boulder	Anasazi State Park Museum	*UT-12, Boulder UT 84716*
UT	Bryce Canyon City	Bryce Canyon National Park Visitor Center	*Bryce Canyon Visitor Center (SB), Bryce Canyon City UT 84764*
UT	Bryce Canyon City	Ruby's Inn General Store	*26 S Main St, Bryce Canyon City UT 84764*
UT	Cannonville	Kodachrome Basin State Park	*G294+4C Cannonville, Cannonville UT 84736*
UT	Cedar City	the death place	*4401 Sagebrush Dr, Cedar City UT 84721*
UT	Cisco	Buzzard's Belly	*Cisco Pump House Rd, Cisco UT 84540*
UT	Corinne	Golden Spike Utah	*6450 6400 N Rd, Corinne UT 84307*
UT	Draper	Loveland Living Planet Aquarium	*12033 Lone Peak Pkwy, Draper UT 84020*
UT	Draper	The Living Planet Aquarium	*12033 Lone Peak Pkwy, Draper UT 84020*
UT	Farmington	Lagoon Amusement Park	*375 Lagoon Dr, Farmington UT 84025*
UT	Fillmore	The Jeep Guy Museum	*860 Airway Dr, Fillmore UT 84631*
UT	Fillmore	Utah Territorial Statehouse State Park	*50 W Capitol St, Fillmore UT 84631*
UT	Green River	Goblin Valley State Park	*Goblin Valley Rd, Green River UT 84525*
UT	Heber City	Heber Valley Historic Railroad	*450 S 6th W, Heber City UT 84032*
UT	Heber City	Heber Valley Railroad	*450 S 6th W, Heber City UT 84032*
UT	Herriman	Bingham Canyon Copper	*GVC2+V6 Herriman, Herriman UT 84096*

UT	Hill Air Force Base	Hill Aerospace Museum	*7961 Cottonwood St, Hill Air Force Base UT 84056*
UT	Ivins	Tuacahn Center for the Arts	*1100 Tuacahn Dr, Ivins UT 84738*
UT	Layton	SeaQuest Aquarium Utah	*1201 N Hill Field Rd, Layton UT 84041*
UT	Lehi	Cabela's - Lehi, Utah	*2502 West Grand Terrace Pkwy, Lehi UT 84043*
UT	Lehi	Museum of Ancient Life at Thanksgiving Point	*2929 Thanksgiving Wy, Lehi UT 84043*
UT	Lehi	Thanksgiving Point - Ashton Gardens	*Ashton Gardens at Thanksgiving Point, Lehi UT 84043*
UT	Lehi	Thanksgiving Point - Butterfly Biosphere	*3003 Thanksgiving Wy, Lehi UT 84043*
UT	Lehi	Thanksgiving Point - Farm Country	*3300 W Clubhouse Dr, Lehi UT 84043*
UT	Lehi	Thanksgiving Point - The Natural Curiosity Museum	*3605 Garden Dr, Lehi UT 84043*
UT	Lindon	Airborne Trampoline Park	*635 N 1700 W, Lindon UT 84042*
UT	Magna	Great Salt Lake State Park	*13312 Western Dr, Magna UT 84044*
UT	Manila	Flaming Gorge Market and Mercantile	*75 UT-43, Manila UT 84046*
UT	Moab	Arches National Park Visitor Center	*41 E Center St, Moab UT 84532*
UT	Moab	Dead Horse Point State Park	*85CGF7F5+WQ, Moab UT 84532*
UT	Moab	Desert Dreams	*71 N Main St, Moab UT 84532*
UT	Moab	Island in the Sky Visitor Center	*Grand View Point Rd, Moab UT 84532*
UT	Moab	Kayenta Campground	*85CGF7P5+8H, Moab UT 84532*
UT	Moab	Simply Moab (was Dirt Shirts and Images of Moab)	*78 S Main St, Moab UT 84532*
UT	Moab	The T-Shirt Shop	*50 N Main St, Moab UT 84532*
UT	Monticello	Hole N the Rock	*11037 S Hwy 191, Monticello UT 84535*

UT	Monticello	Hole N" The Rock	*11037 S Hwy 191, Monticello UT 84535*
UT	Murray	Wheeler Historic Farm	*6351 S 900 E, Murray UT 84121*
UT	Murray	Wheeler Historic Farm	*6351 S 900 E, Murray UT 84121*
UT	Ogden	Union Station	*2501 Wall Ave suite a, Ogden UT 84401*
UT	Ogden	Weber State University	*Swenson Building, Ogden UT 84403*
UT	Orderville	Shell	*4490 State St, Orderville UT 84758*
UT	Orderville	Shell Gas Station	*4490 State St, Orderville UT 84758*
UT	Orderville	White Mountain Trading Post	*4490 State St, Orderville UT 84758*
UT	Orem	Utah Valley University Campus Store	*800 West University Parkway, Orem UT 84058*
UT	Park City	Utah Olympic Park	*3419 Olympic Pkwy, Park City UT 84098*
UT	Park City	Utah Olympic Park	*3419 Olympic Pkwy, Park City UT 84098*
UT	Price	The Prehistoric Museum, USU - Eastern	*155 E Main St, Price UT 84501*
UT	Price	USU Eastern Prehistoric Museum	*159 E Main St, Price UT 84501*
UT	Promontory	Transcontinental Railroad	*JF93+W7 Promontory, Promontory UT 84307*
UT	Riverdale	Golden Spike Harley-Davidson	*5152 1500 W, Riverdale UT 84405*
UT	Salt Lake City	Ground floor	*Capitol Park, Salt Lake City UT 84103*
UT	Salt Lake City	National History Museum of Utah	*301 Wakara Way, Salt Lake City UT 84108*
UT	Salt Lake City	The Church of Jesus Christ of Latter-Day Saints History Muse	*45 N W Temple St, Salt Lake City UT 84150*

UT	Salt Lake City	This is the place	*2601 E Sunnyside Ave, Salt Lake City UT 84108*
UT	Salt Lake City	This Is The Place Heritage Park	*2601 E Sunnyside Ave, Salt Lake City UT 84108*
UT	Springdale	Bumbleberry Gifts / Wildcat Willies	*897 Zion Park Blvd, Springdale UT 84767*
UT	Springdale	Springdale Candy Company / Zion Sweet Shop	*865 Zion Park Blvd, Springdale UT 84767*
UT	Springdale	Trailhead Gifts	*865 Zion Park Blvd, Springdale UT 84767*
UT	Springdale	Trailhead Gifts and Gear	*145 Zion Park Blvd, Springdale UT 84767*
UT	Springdale	Zion Canyon Clothing & Gift	*445 Zion – Mount Carmel Hwy, Springdale UT 84767*
UT	Springdale	Zion National park	*7XXF+7F Springdale, Springdale UT 84737*
UT	Springdale	Zion Park Gift & Deli	*866 Zion Park Blvd, Springdale UT 84767*
UT	Sterling	Palisade State Park	*2200 Palisade Rd, Sterling UT 84665*
UT	Syracuse	Antelope Island State Park Visitors Center	*4528 W 1700 S, Syracuse UT 84075*
UT	Vernal	Field House of Natural History / State Park Museum	*496 E Main St, Vernal UT 84078*
UT	Vernal	Utah Field House of Natural History State Park Museum	*496 E Main St, Vernal UT 84078*
UT	Vineyard	Vineyard Chubby's Penny Squasher	*554 N Mill Rd, Vineyard UT 84059*
UT	Virgin	Fort Zion	*1000 W. Hwy 9, Virgin UT 84779*
UT	Washington	Zion Harley Davidson	*2345 N Coral Canyon Blvd, Washington UT 84780*
UT	Washington	Zion Harley-Davidson	*2345 N Coral Canyon Blvd, Washington UT 84780*

Virginia			
VA	Alexandria	George Washington's Mount Vernon	*The Mansion, Alexandria VA 22309*
VA	Ashland	Bass Pro Shops	*11550 VA-782, Ashland VA 23005*
VA	Ashland	Bass Pro Shops	*11550 VA-782, Ashland VA 23005*
VA	Boydton	John H Kerr Dam and Reservoir	*523 Madison St, Boydton VA 23917*
VA	Chantilly	Steven F. Udvar-Hazy Center	*Udvar-Hazy Air & Space Museum, Chantilly VA 20151*
VA	Charlottesville	Michie Tavern	*683 Thomas Jefferson Pkwy, Charlottesville VA 22902*
VA	Charlottesville	Michie Tavern ca. 1784	*683 Thomas Jefferson Pkwy, Charlottesville VA 22902*
VA	Charlottesville	Monticello	*931 Thomas Jefferson Pkwy, Charlottesville VA 22902*
VA	Chincoteague	Pony Tails Taffy	*7011 Maddox Blvd, Chincoteague VA 23336*
VA	Clear Brook	ATM (Flying J Travel Plaza)	*1530 State Rte 669, Clear Brook VA 22624*
VA	Culpeper	Museum of Culpeper History	*113 Commerce St, Culpeper VA 22701*
VA	Doswell	Kings Dominion	*16000 Theme Park Way, Doswell VA 23047*
VA	Entrance Road	Big Meadows Wayside	*130 Big Meadows Entrance Rd, Entrance Road VA 22727*
VA	Fredericksburg	Virginia Welcome Center - Machine is Gone	*Interstate 95 South Mile Marker 132, Fredericksburg VA 22401*
VA	Front Royal	Front Royal Town Tourism Office	*414 E Main St, Front Royal VA 22630*
VA	Front Royal	Front Royal/Warren County Visitor Center	*414 E Main St, Front Royal VA 22630*
VA	Front Royal	Skyline Caverns	*10334 Stonewall Jackson Hwy, Front Royal VA 22630*
VA	Hampton	Virginia Air & Space Center	*600 Settlers Landing Rd, Hampton VA 23669*

VA	Henrico	Cabela's	*5000 Cabela Dr, Henrico VA 23233*
VA	Henrico	Lewis Ginter Botanical Garden	*1800 Lakeside Ave, Henrico VA 23228*
VA	Henrico	Virginia Department of Game and Inland Fisheries	*7896 Villa Park Dr, Henrico VA 23228*
VA	Henrico	Virginia Department of Game and Inland Fisheries	*7896 Villa Park Dr, Henrico VA 23228*
VA	Lexington	Virginia Horse Center	*487 Maury River Rd, Lexington VA 24450*
VA	Luray	Car and Carriage Caravan Museum	*105 Cave Hill Rd, Luray VA 22835*
VA	Luray	Jellystone Park Campground	*2250 US-211, Luray VA 22835*
VA	Luray	Luray Caverns	*970 US HWY 211 W, Luray VA 22835*
VA	Martinsville	Virginia Museum of Natural History	*21 Starling Ave, Martinsville VA 24112*
VA	Martinsville	Virginia Museum of Natural History	*21 Starling Ave, Martinsville VA 24112*
VA	Meadows of Dan	Mabry Mill Restaurant & Gift Shop	*266 Mabry Mill Rd SE, Meadows of Dan VA 24120*
VA	Meadows of Dan	Mabry Mill Restaurant and Gift Shop	*266 Mabry Mill Rd SE, Meadows of Dan VA 24120*
VA	Moseley	Metro Richmond Zoo	*8310 Beaver Bridge Rd, Moseley VA 23120*
VA	Moseley	Metro Richmond Zoo	*8301 Beaver Bridge Rd, Moseley VA 23120*
VA	Mount Crawford	Buc-ee's Rockingham County	*6500 Buc-Ees Blvd, Mount Crawford VA 22841*
VA	Natural Bridge	Caverns at Natural Bridge	*6313 S Lee Hwy, Natural Bridge VA 24578*
VA	Natural Bridge	Dinosaur Kingdom II	*5781 S Lee Hwy, Natural Bridge VA 24578*

VA	Natural Bridge	Natural Bridge Caverns	*6313 S Lee Hwy, Natural Bridge VA 24578*
VA	Natural Bridge	Natural Bridge State Park	*45 Bell Tower Ln, Natural Bridge VA 24578*
VA	Natural Bridge	Natural Bridge State Park Visitor Center	*6477 S Lee Hwy, Natural Bridge VA 24578*
VA	Natural Bridge	Natural Bridge Zoo	*133 State Rte 812, Natural Bridge VA 24578*
VA	Natural Bridge	Natural Bridge Zoo	*5784 S Lee Hwy, Natural Bridge VA 24578*
VA	Natural Bridge	Virginia Safari Park	*229 Safari Ln, Natural Bridge VA 24578*
VA	New Market	Hall of Valor	*8895 George Collins Pkwy, New Market VA 22844*
VA	New Market	New Market Battlefield State Historical Park	*8895 George Collins Pkwy, New Market VA 22844*
VA	Newport News	Virginia Living Museum	*524 VA-312, Newport News VA 23601*
VA	Newport News	Virginia Living Museum	*524 J Clyde Morris Blvd, Newport News VA 23601*
VA	Norfolk	Nauticus	*64 Main St, Norfolk VA 23510*
VA	Norfolk	Nauticus	*1 Waterside Dr Suite 248, Norfolk VA 23510*
VA	Norfolk	Virginia Zoological Park	*3500 Granby St, Norfolk VA 23504*
VA	Norfolk	Virginia Zoological Park	*3000 Church St, Norfolk VA 23504*
VA	Orange	James Madison Museum of Orange County Heritage	*129 Caroline St, Orange VA 22960*
VA	Petersburg	Pamplin Historical Park	*6410 Duncan Rd, Petersburg VA 23803*
VA	Petersburg	Pamplin Historical Park & The National Museum Of T	*6125 Boydton Plank Rd, Petersburg VA 23803*

VA	Richmond	Maymont Nature Center	*The Robins Nature Center at Maymont, Richmond VA 23220*
VA	Richmond	Science Museum of Virginia	*2320 W Broad St, Richmond VA 23269*
VA	Roanoke	Mill Mountain Zoo	*2404 Prospect Rd SE, Roanoke VA 24014*
VA	Roanoke	Mill Mountain Zoo	*2413 Prospect Rd SE, Roanoke VA 24014*
VA	Roanoke	Taubman Museum of Art	*108 Salem Ave SE, Roanoke VA 24011*
VA	Roanoke	Virginia Museum of Transportation	*303 Norfolk Ave SW, Roanoke VA 24016*
VA	Roanoke	Virginia Museum Of Transportation Inc	*303 Norfolk Ave SW, Roanoke VA 24016*
VA	Salem	Dixie Caverns	*5753 Lee Hwy, Salem VA 24153*
VA	SHENDOAH CVRN	Shenandoah Caverns	*57 Caverns Rd, SHENDOAH CVRN VA 22847*
VA	SHENDOAH CVRN	The Yellow Barn	*470 Caverns Rd, SHENDOAH CVRN VA 22847*
VA	SHENDOAH CVRN	The Yellow Barn	*57 Caverns Rd, SHENDOAH CVRN VA 22847*
VA	Smithfield	Isle of Wight County Museum	*103 Main St, Smithfield VA 23430*
VA	Sperryville	Headmasters Pub	*12018 Lee Hwy, Sperryville VA 22740*
VA	Triangle	National Museum of the Marine Corps	*1775 Semper Fidelis Wy, Triangle VA 22172*
VA	Virginia Beach	Cape Henry Lighthouse	*583 Atlantic Ave, Virginia Beach VA 23459*
VA	Virginia Beach	Chesapeake Bay Bridge Tunnel	*Chesapeake Bay Bridge-Tunnel, Virginia Beach VA*
VA	Virginia Beach	Forbes Candies	*2800 Atlantic Ave A, Virginia Beach VA 23451*
VA	Virginia Beach	Virginia Aquarium & Marine Science Center	*717 General Booth Blvd, Virginia Beach VA 23451*

VA	Virginia Beach	Virginia Aquarium & Marine Science Center (Marsh P	*Virginia Aquarium & Marine Science Center (Marsh Pavilion), Virginia Beach VA 23451*
VA	Virginia Beach	Virginia Originals & Chesapeake Grill	*XV8P+CR Virginia Beach, Virginia Beach VA*
VA	Virginia Beach	Virginia Originals & Chesapeake Grill	*Northampton Blvd, Virginia Beach VA*
VA	Washington	The Pentagon	*1400 Defense Blvd, Washington VA 20301*
VA	White Post	Dinosaur Land	*3848 Stonewall Jackson Hwy, White Post VA 22663*
VA	White Post	Dinosaur Land	*3848 Stonewall Jackson Hwy, White Post VA 22663*
VA	Williamsburg	Busch Gardens Williamsburg	*1 Busch Gardens Blvd, Williamsburg VA 23185*
VA	Williamsburg	Busch Gardens Williamsburg	*1 Busch Gardens Blvd, Williamsburg VA 23185*
VA	Williamsburg	Colonial Williamsburg	*101A Visitor Ctr Dr, Williamsburg VA 23185*
VA	Williamsburg	Colonial Williamsburg Visitor Center	*101A Visitor Ctr Dr, Williamsburg VA 23185*
VA	Williamsburg	Great Wolf Lodge Williamsburg	*549 E Rochambeau Dr, Williamsburg VA 23188*
VA	Williamsburg	Great Wolf Lodge Williamsburg	*549 E Rochambeau Dr, Williamsburg VA 23188*
VA	Williamsburg	Historic Jamestowne	*1368 Colonial Nat'l Historical Pkwy, Williamsburg VA 23185*
VA	Williamsburg	Jamestown Settlement	*1760 Jamestown Rd, Williamsburg VA 23185*
VA	Williamsburg	King's Treasure	*424 W Duke of Gloucester St, Williamsburg VA 23185*
VA	Williamsburg	Kings Treasure	*424 W Duke of Gloucester St, Williamsburg VA 23185*
VA	Williamsburg	Ripley's Believe It or Not	*1735 Richmond Rd, Williamsburg VA 23185*

VA	Williamsburg	Ripley's Believe It or Not! Williamsburg	*1735 Richmond Rd, Williamsburg VA 23185*
VA	Williamsburg	Wallace's Trading Post	*1851 Richmond Rd, Williamsburg VA 23185*
VA	Williamsburg	Wallace's Trading Post	*1851 Richmond Rd, Williamsburg VA 23185*
VA	Williamsburg	William Pitt Store	*401 E E Duke of Gloucester St, Williamsburg VA 23185*
VA	Williamsburg	Williamsburg General Store	*1656 Richmond Rd, Williamsburg VA 23185*
VA	Williamsburg	Williamsburg General Store	*1656 Richmond Rd, Williamsburg VA 23185*
VA	Yorktown	American Revolution Museum at Yorktown	*200 Water St, Yorktown VA 23690*
VA	Yorktown	American Revolution Museum at Yorktown	*100 Water St, Yorktown VA 23690*

Vermont			
VT	Burlington	ECHO Leahy Center for Lake Champlain	*1 College St, Burlington VT 05401*
VT	Hartford	Quechee Gorge Vistors Center	*5966 Woodstock Rd, White River Junction, VT 05001, Hartford VT 05059*
VT	Morristown	Saxony Imports	*10 Railroad St, Morristown VT 05661*
VT	Shelburne	Shelburne Museum	*42 Shelburne Museum 2, Shelburne VT 05482*
VT	Shelburne	Vermont Teddy Bear	*6655 Shelburne Rd, Shelburne VT 05482*
VT	Waterbury	Ben & Jerry's	*1281 Waterbury-Stowe Rd Route 100, Waterbury VT 05676*

			Washington
WA	Bainbridge Island	Calico Toy Shoppe	*Winslow Way at Ericksen (Town & Country), Bainbridge Island WA 98110*
WA	Blaine	Horseshoe Coins & Antiques	*810 Peace Portal Dr, Blaine WA 98230*
WA	Castle Rock	Mount St. Helens Visitor Center	*3029 Spirit Lake Hwy, Castle Rock WA 98611*
WA	Centralia	Great Wolf Lodge Grand Mound	*1 Grand Mound Loop SW, Centralia WA 98531*
WA	Chelan	Lake Chelan	*109 E Woodin Ave, Chelan WA 98816*
WA	Chelan	Swim World	*114 S Emerson St, Chelan WA 98816*
WA	Cougar	Mount St. Helens National Volcanic Monument	*84RV5RR3+HQ, Cougar WA 98616*
WA	Eastsound	Cottage Gift Shop	*5372 Orcas Rd, Eastsound WA 98245*
WA	Eatonville	Northwest Trek Wildlife Park	*11610 Trek Dr E, Eatonville WA 98328*
WA	Eatonville	Northwest Trek Wildlife Park	*11610 Trek Dr E, Eatonville WA 98328*
WA	Fall City	Falls Gift Shop	*6351 Railroad Ave, Fall City WA 98024*
WA	Forks	Native To Forks	*10 S Forks Ave, Forks WA 98331*
WA	Friday Harbor	Dockside Treasures	*91 Front St S, Friday Harbor WA 98250*
WA	Friday Harbor	Dockside-Treasures	*100 Front St # 6, Friday Harbor WA 98250*
WA	Friday Harbor	The Whale Museum at Friday Harbor	*62 First St N, Friday Harbor WA 98250*
WA	Kennewick	Gesa Carousel of Dreams	*2901-F Southridge Blvd, Kennewick WA 99338*

WA	Lacey	Cabela's	*1600 Gateway Blvd NE, Lacey WA 98516*
WA	Leavenworth	Hat Shop	*721 Front St, Leavenworth WA 98826*
WA	Leavenworth	Leavenworth Shirt Company	*929 Front St, Leavenworth WA 98826*
WA	Leavenworth	Simple Treasures	*805 Front St, Leavenworth WA 98826*
WA	Leavenworth	Smallwood's Harvest	*10461 Stemm Rd, Leavenworth WA 98826*
WA	Long Beach	Marsh's Free Museum	*409 Pacific Ave, Long Beach WA 98631*
WA	Moclips	Museum of the North Beach	*4658 WA-109, Moclips WA 98562*
WA	Mukilteo	Future of Flight Aviation Center & Boeing Tour	*8415 Paine Field Blvd, Mukilteo WA 98275*
WA	Newport	Owen Grocery & Deli	*337 S Washington Ave, Newport WA 99156*
WA	Ocean Shores	First Cabin	*698 Ocean Shores Blvd NW # 1, Ocean Shores WA 98569*
WA	Olympia	Hands On Children's Museum	*414 Jefferson St NE, Olympia WA 98501*
WA	Olympia	Legislative Gift Center	*416 Sid Snyder Ave SW, Olympia WA 98501*
WA	Olympia	Olympia, Lacey, Tumwater	*103 Sid Snyder Ave SW, Olympia WA 98501*
WA	Olympia	Washington State Capitol Campus	*1225 Capitol Way S, Olympia WA 98501*
WA	Pacific Beach	Seabrook Front Street	*41 Fireside Ln, Pacific Beach WA 98571*
WA	Packwood	Blanton's Market	*13040 US-12, Packwood WA 98361*
WA	Port Townsend	Wandering Angus	*914 Water St, Port Townsend WA 98368*
WA	Puyallup	Washington State Fair	*110 9th Ave SW, Puyallup WA 98371*

WA	Quinault	Lake Quinault Lodge	*345 S Shore Rd, Quinault WA 98575*
WA	Seattle	Archie McPhee Novelty Shop	*1300 N 45th St, Seattle WA 98103*
WA	Seattle	Bill Speidel's Underground Tour	*614 1st Ave, Seattle WA 98104*
WA	Seattle	EMP Museum	*325 5th Ave N, Seattle WA 98109*
WA	Seattle	Hat Shop	*1409 1st Ave, Seattle WA 98101*
WA	Seattle	Hiram M Chittenden Locks	*Ballard (Hiram M. Chittenden) Locks, Seattle WA 98107*
WA	Seattle	Market Magic & Novelty Shop	*1501 Western Ave, Seattle WA 98101*
WA	Seattle	Norwegian Cruise Line	*Bell Street at Pier 66, Seattle WA 98121*
WA	Seattle	Pier 55 Shirt Company	*1101 Alaskan Wy, Seattle WA 98101*
WA	Seattle	Pike Place Market	*1901-1919 Post Alley, Seattle WA 98101*
WA	Seattle	Pirates Plunder	*1301 Alaskan Wy, Seattle WA 98101*
WA	Seattle	Public market	*85 Pike St, Seattle WA 98101*
WA	Seattle	Seattle Aquarium	*1483 Alaskan Wy Pier 59, Seattle WA 98101*
WA	Seattle	Seattle Great Wheel	*1301 Alaskan Wy, Seattle WA 98101*
WA	Seattle	Seattle Mariners	*1250 1st Ave S, Seattle WA 98134*
WA	Seattle	Seattle Shirt Co	*105 1/2 Pike St, Seattle WA 98101*
WA	Seattle	Simply Seattle	*1610 1st Ave, Seattle WA 98101*
WA	Seattle	Space Needle	*400 Broad St, Seattle WA 98109*

WA	Seattle	Wings Over Washington	*1301 Alaskan Wy, Seattle, WA 98101, Seattle WA 98101*
WA	Seattle	Ye Olde Curiosity Shop	*1001 Alaskan Wy, Seattle WA 98104*
WA	Seattle	Zoomazium (Woodland Park Zoo)	*5500 Phinney Ave N, Seattle WA 98103*
WA	Sequim	Olympic Game Farm	*1423 Ward Rd, Sequim WA 98382*
WA	Snoqualmie	Northwest Railway Museum	*38625 SE King St, Snoqualmie WA 98065*
WA	Spokane	IMAX	*574 West N Howard St, Spokane WA 99201*
WA	Spokane	Looff Carousel	*Clocktower Meadow, Spokane WA 99201*
WA	Spokane	SkyRide at Riverfront Spokane	*720 W Spokane Falls Blvd, Spokane WA 99201*
WA	Tacoma	Point Defiance Zoo & Aquarium	*5400 N Pearl St, Tacoma WA 98407*
WA	Tacoma	Point Defiance Zoo & Aquarium	*5605 Five mile Rd, Tacoma WA 98407*
WA	Tacoma	Steamer's Seafood Cafe	*8802 6th Ave, Tacoma WA 98465*
WA	Toutle	Johnston Ridge Observatory	*24000 Spirit Lake Hwy, Toutle WA 98649*
WA	Toutle	Mount St. Helens Forest Learning Center	*17000 Spirit Lake Hwy, Toutle WA 98649*
WA	Tukwila	The Museum of Flight	*9404 E Marginal Wy S, Tukwila WA 98108*
WA	Union	Alderbrook Resort and Spa	*10 E Alderbrook Dr, Union WA 98592*
WA	Union Gap	Cabela's	*1400 E Washington Ave, Union Gap WA 98903*
WA	Westport	Granny Hazel's Candy Inc.	*2329 Westhaven Dr, Westport WA 98595*
WA	Winthrop	Sheri's Sweet Shop	*Main Deck, Winthrop WA 98862*

			Wisconsin
WI	Appleton	Appleton International Airport	*Appleton International Airport (ATW), Appleton WI 54914*
WI	Appleton	Outagamie Airport	*330 E College Ave, Appleton WI 54911*
WI	Appleton	Outagamie County Regional Airport	*330 E College Ave, Appleton WI 54911*
WI	Appleton	The History Museum at the Castle, East College Ave	*330 E College Ave, Appleton WI 54911*
WI	Ashwaubenon	Cabela's	*1499 Lombardi Ave, Ashwaubenon WI 54304*
WI	Ashwaubenon	Cabela's	*1499 Lombardi Ave, Ashwaubenon WI 54304*
WI	Bagley	Yogi Bear Jellystone	*11354 County X, Bagley WI 53801*
WI	Bagley	Yogi Bear's Jellystone Camp	*11354 County X, Bagley WI 53801*
WI	Baraboo	Buffalo Phil's	*150 Gasser Rd, Baraboo WI 53913*
WI	Baraboo	Circus World	*550 Water St, Baraboo WI 53913*
WI	Baraboo	Circus World Museum	*550 Water St, Baraboo WI 53913*
WI	Baraboo	Devil's Lake	*Visitor Center North Shore, Baraboo WI 53913*
WI	Baraboo	Great Wolf Lodge	*1400 Great Wolf Dr, Baraboo WI 53913*
WI	Baraboo	Kalahari Resort	*1305 Kalahari Dr, Baraboo WI 53913*
WI	Baraboo	Wilderness Resort	*511 E Adams St, Baraboo WI 53913*
WI	Bay City	Flat Pennies Ice Cream	*6442 WI-35, Bay City WI 54723*
WI	Bay City	Flat Pennies Ice Cream	*6442 WI-35, Bay City WI 54723*
WI	Bayfield	Keeper of the Light	*2 Front St, Bayfield WI 54814*

WI	Blue Mounds	Cave of the Mounds	*2975 Cave of the Mounds Rd, Blue Mounds WI 53517*
WI	Blue Mounds	Cave of the Mounds	*2975 Cave of the Mounds Rd, Blue Mounds WI 53517*
WI	Deerfield	Schuster's Farm	*1326 US-12, Deerfield WI 53531*
WI	Egg Harbor	From the Forty	*7828 WI-42, Egg Harbor WI 54209*
WI	Elroy	Elroy Commons Trail Shop	*314 Railroad St, Elroy WI 53929*
WI	Fish Creek	Alpaca to Apparel	*4185 Main St, Fish Creek WI 54212*
WI	Fremont	Yogi Bear Jellystone Campground	*87 Northern Ave, Fremont WI 54940*
WI	Green Bay	Bay Beach Wildlife Sanctuary	*G2HF+H3 Green Bay, Green Bay WI 54302*
WI	Green Bay	Lambeau Field	*1265 Lombardi Ave, Green Bay WI 54304*
WI	Green Bay	NEW Zoo	*4378 Reforestation Rd, Green Bay WI 54313*
WI	Green Bay	NEW Zoo	*4378 Reforestation Rd, Green Bay WI 54313*
WI	Hayward	Lake Chippewa Campground	*8380 N County Rd CC, Hayward WI 54843*
WI	Hayward	Wilderness Walk	*9545 WI-27, Hayward WI 54843*
WI	Kenosha	Civil War Museum	*5400 1st Ave, Kenosha WI 53140*
WI	Kenosha	Dinosaur Discovery Museum	*5608 10th Ave, Kenosha WI 53140*
WI	Kenosha	Dinosaur Discovery Museum 3p	*5608 10th Ave, Kenosha WI 53140*
WI	Kenosha	Kenosha History Center	*220 51st Pl, Kenosha WI 53140*
WI	Kenosha	Kenosha Public Museum	*5500 1st Ave, Kenosha WI 53140*
WI	Lake Geneva	Geneva Gifts	*150 Broad St, Lake Geneva WI 53147*

WI	Lake Geneva	Timber Ridge Lodge and Waterpark	*7020 Grand Geneva Way, Lake Geneva WI 53147*
WI	Madison	Henry Vilas Zoo	*702 S Randall Ave, Madison WI 53715*
WI	Madison	Olbrich Botanical Gardens	*3330 Atwood Ave, Madison WI 53704*
WI	Manitowoc	Lincoln Park Zoo	*1215 N 8th St, Manitowoc WI 54220*
WI	Manitowoc	S.S. Badger	*Manitowoc Dock, Manitowoc WI 54220*
WI	Marinette	Seguin's House of Cheese	*1968 US-41, Marinette WI 54143*
WI	Menomonee Falls	Harley-Davidson Powertrain Operations	*W156N9000 Pilgrim Rd, Menomonee Falls WI 53051*
WI	Menomonie	Dunn County Historical Society Rassbach Museum	*1820 John Russell Rd, Menomonie WI 54751*
WI	Milwaukee	Discovery World	*500 N Harbor Dr, Milwaukee WI 53202*
WI	Milwaukee	Grohmann Museum	*Grohmann Museum, Milwaukee WI 53202*
WI	Milwaukee	Harley Davidson Museum 8p	*126 N 6th St, Milwaukee WI 53203*
WI	Milwaukee	Miller Brewery Tour	*4251 W State St, Milwaukee WI 53208*
WI	Milwaukee	Milwaukee County Zoo	*Pachyderm Exhibit Building (East), Milwaukee WI 53226*
WI	Milwaukee	Milwaukee Public Museum	*800 W Wells St, Milwaukee WI 53233*
WI	Milwaukee	Mitchell Park Horticultural Conservatory (Mitchell	*524 S Layton Blvd, Milwaukee WI 53215*
WI	Milwaukee	National Bobblehead Hall of Fame and Museum	*170 S 1st St, Milwaukee WI 53204*
WI	Minocqua	Elements	*518 Oneida St, Minocqua WI 54548*
WI	Minocqua	Gaslight Antiques	*415 Oneida St, Minocqua WI 54548*

WI	Minocqua	Minocqua (Gaslight Square)	*415 Oneida St, Minocqua WI 54548*
WI	Minocqua	Monkey Business	*518 Oneida St, Minocqua WI 54548*
WI	Minocqua	Monkey Business	*518 Oneida St, Minocqua WI 54548*
WI	Minocqua	Wildwood Wildlife Park and Nature Center	*10094 WI-70, Minocqua WI 54548*
WI	Oshkosh	EAA AirVenture Museum	*3000 Poberezny Rd, Oshkosh WI 54902*
WI	Oshkosh	EAA Aviation Museum, Poberezny Road, Oshkosh, WI,	*3000 Poberezny Rd, Oshkosh WI 54902*
WI	Pepin	Laura Ingalls Wilder Museum	*312 Great River Rd, Pepin WI 54759*
WI	Pleasant Prairie	Jelly Belly	*10100 Jelly Belly Ln, Pleasant Prairie WI 53158*
WI	Pleasant Prairie	Jelly Belly Factory	*10100 Jelly Belly Ln, Pleasant Prairie WI 53158*
WI	Port Washington	Vines To Cellars, East Main Street, Port Washingto	*114 E Main St, Port Washington WI 53074*
WI	Racine	Racine Zoological Gardens	*2131 N Main St, Racine WI 53402*
WI	Richfield	Cabela's Outdoor Gear	*1 Cabela Way, Richfield WI 53076*
WI	Sauk City	Wollersheim Winery	*7876 WI-188, Sauk City WI 53583*
WI	Shawano	Twig's Beverage	*920 South Franklin Street 711 S. Washington, Shawano WI 54166*
WI	Spring Valley	Crystal Cave	*W965 WI-29, Spring Valley WI 54767*
WI	Sturgeon Bay	Door Peninsula Winery	*5806 WI-42, Sturgeon Bay WI 54235*
WI	Sturgeon Bay	Door Peninsula Winery, Wisconsin 42, Sturgeon Bay,	*5806 WI-42, Sturgeon Bay WI 54235*

WI	Tomahawk	Harley Davidson - Tomahawk Operations	*488 Kaphaem Rd, Tomahawk WI 54487*
WI	Tomahawk	Harley-Davidson Motor Co	*611 Kaphaem Rd, Tomahawk WI 54487*
WI	Warrens	Yogi Bear Jellystone Park	*1500 Jellystone Park Drive, Warrens WI 54666*
WI	Washington	Susie's Sweets and Souvenirs	*1219 Main Rd, Washington WI 54246*
WI	West Bend	Shalom Wildlife Zoo	*1901 Shalom Dr, West Bend WI 53090*
WI	Wisconsin Dells	Chula Vista	*2501 River Rd, Wisconsin Dells WI 53965*
WI	Wisconsin Dells	Dells Deals Store	*119 WI-16 Trunk, Wisconsin Dells WI 53965*
WI	Wisconsin Dells	Dockside Shops/Gifts	*452 US-12, Wisconsin Dells WI 53965*
WI	Wisconsin Dells	Gilly's Island	*400 Broadway, Wisconsin Dells WI 53965*
WI	Wisconsin Dells	H.H. Bennett Studio & History Center	*217 Broadway, Wisconsin Dells WI 53965*
WI	Wisconsin Dells	Moosejaw Pizza & Dells Brewing Co	*110 Wisconsin Dells Pkwy S, Wisconsin Dells WI 53965*
WI	Wisconsin Dells	Mt. Olympus	*1701 Wisconsin Dells Pkwy, Wisconsin Dells WI 53965*
WI	Wisconsin Dells	Paul Bunyan's Cook Shanty	*411 State Hwy 13, Wisconsin Dells WI 53965*
WI	Wisconsin Dells	Polynesian Resort	*855 N Frontage Rd, Wisconsin Dells WI 53965*
WI	Wisconsin Dells	Ripley's Believe It or Not!	*115 Broadway, Wisconsin Dells WI 53965*
WI	Wisconsin Dells	Riverside and Great Northern Preservation Society Inc	*1561 Brew Farm Rd, Wisconsin Dells WI 53965*
WI	Wisconsin Dells	Timbavati Wildlife Park	*2020 Wisconsin Dells Pkwy, Wisconsin Dells WI 53965*

WI	Wisconsin Dells	Timber Falls Adventure Park	*1000 Stand Rock Rd, Wisconsin Dells WI 53965*
WI	Wisconsin Dells	Tommy Bartlett Exploratory	*560 Wisconsin Dells Pkwy, Wisconsin Dells WI 53965*
WI	Wisconsin Dells	Wally World	*301 Broadway, Wisconsin Dells WI 53965*
WI	Wisconsin Dells	Wizard Quest	*105 Broadway, Wisconsin Dells WI 53965*

			West Virginia
WV	Beckley	Beckley Exhibition Coal Mine	*124 Mahan Ave, Beckley WV 25927*
WV	Beckley	Exhibition Coal Mine	*513 Ewart Ave, Beckley WV 25801*
WV	Beckley	Tamarack	*1 Tamarack Pl, Beckley WV 25801*
WV	Big Bend	Oglebay Good Children's Zoo	*XR9H+F3 Big Bend, Big Bend WV 26136*
WV	Cass	Cass Scenic Railroad State Park	*165 Main St, Cass WV 24927*
WV	Charles Town	Shepherdstown Visitors Center	*23 E Georgia Ave, Charles Town WV 25414*
WV	Charleston	Department of Environmental Protection	*57TH Kanawha Ave SE, Charleston WV 25304*
WV	Charleston	West Virginia State Museum	*1900 Kanawha Blvd E #435, Charleston WV 25305*
WV	Davis	Big John's Family Fixin's	*6438 Appalachian Hwy, Davis WV 26260*
WV	Glen Jean	New River Gorge National Park	*104 Co Rte 25/9, Glen Jean WV 25846*
WV	Harpers Ferry	Hodge Podge Antiques/Country Treasures Gifts & Sou	*144a High St, Harpers Ferry WV 25425*
WV	Harpers Ferry	River Riders Inc	*408 Alstadts Hill Rd, Harpers Ferry WV 25425*
WV	Omps	Cacapon Resort State Park	*GM4M+49 Omps, Omps WV 25411*
WV	Point Pleasant	Mothman Museum	*400 Main St, Point Pleasant WV 25550*
WV	Prosperity	Beckley Travel Plaza	*127 Teresas Pl, Prosperity WV 25909*
WV	Rock Cave	West Virginia State Wildlife Center	*VM4R+72 Rock Cave, Rock Cave WV 26234*
WV	Seneca Rocks	Yokum's Grocery and Deli	*925 Freeland Dr, Seneca Rocks WV 26884*

WV	Sutton	Flatwoods Monster Museum	*208 N Main St, Sutton WV 26601*
WV	Thomas	Blackwater Falls State Park	*4G55+H9 Thomas, Thomas WV 26260*
WV	Wheeling	Oglebay - The Good Zoo	*465 Lodge Dr, Wheeling WV 26003*
WV	Wheeling	Oglebay Resort - Arcade in the Lodge	*465 Lodge Dr, Wheeling WV 26003*
WV	Wheeling	The Carriage House at Oglebay Resort	*83 Mansion Dr, Wheeling WV 26003*

			Wyoming
WY	Canyon Village	Canyon Village - General Store	*PGM5+CF Canyon Village, Canyon Village WY 82190*
WY	Casper	Fort Caspar Museum	*4001 Fort Caspar Rd, Casper WY 82604*
WY	Casper	National Historic Trails Interpretive Center	*1501 N Poplar St, Casper WY 82601*
WY	Casper	Tate Geological Museum	*2332 Lisco Dr, Casper WY 82601*
WY	Cheyenne	Cheyenne Depot Museum	*121 W 15th St #304, Cheyenne WY 82001*
WY	Cheyenne	Cheyenne Frontier Days Old West Museum	*4610 Carey Ave, Cheyenne WY 82001*
WY	Cheyenne	KOA	*8800 Hutchins Dr, Cheyenne WY 82007*
WY	Cheyenne	Little America - Gas Station	*2800 W Lincolnway, Cheyenne WY 82001*
WY	Cheyenne	Wyoming State Museum	*2301 CanAm Hwy, Cheyenne WY 82001*
WY	Cody	Buffalo Bill Dam Visitor Center	*4808 N Fork Hwy, Cody WY 82414*
WY	Cody	Top of the World Resort	*1699 US-212, Cody WY 82414*
WY	Cody	Yellowstone Gift Shop	*1241 Sheridan Ave, Cody WY 82414*
WY	Devils Den	Tower General Store	*VJR7+R5 Devils Den, Devils Den WY 82190*
WY	Devils Tower	Devils Tower Trading Post	*57 WY-110, Devils Tower WY 82714*
WY	Douglas	Camp Douglas Officers Club State Historic Site	*115 S Riverbend Dr, Douglas WY 82633*
WY	Douglas	Ft. Fetterman State Historic Site	*752 WY-93, Douglas WY 82633*
WY	Douglas	Wyoming Pioneer Memorial Museum	*400 W Center St, Douglas WY 82633*
WY	Fort Bridger	Fort Bridger	*37000 I-80BL, Fort Bridger WY 82933*

WY	Green River	Green River Chamber of Commerce & Visitor Center	*1155 W Flaming Gorge Way, Green River WY 82935*
WY	Hartville	Guernsey State Park CCC Museum	*Museum Rd, Hartville WY 82215*
WY	Jackson	National Elk Refuge Sleigh	*790 E Kelly Ave, Jackson WY 83001*
WY	Laramie	Lincoln Monument	*6HP7+QF Laramie, Laramie WY 82070*
WY	Laramie	Wyoming Territorial Prison State Historic Site	*975 Snowy Range Rd, Laramie WY 82070*
WY	Little America	Little America Truck Stop and Travel Center	*6945 80, Little America WY 82929*
WY	Moose	Craig Thomas Discovery and Visitor Center	*100 Discovery Way, Moose WY 83012*
WY	Moran	Colter Bay Village General Store	*100 Colter Bay Village Rd, Moran WY 83013*
WY	Moran	Colter Bay Visitor Center	*640 Cottonwood Way, Moran WY 83013*
WY	South Pass City	South Pass City State Historic Site	*125 S Pass Main St, South Pass City WY 82520*
WY	Thermopolis	Hot Springs State Park	*Hot Springs State Park Bath House, Thermopolis WY 82443*
WY	Thermopolis	Star Plunge	*3 Big Springs Dr, Thermopolis WY 82443*
WY	Thermopolis	The Wyoming Dinosaur Center	*110 Carter Ranch Rd, Thermopolis WY 82443*
WY	Yellowstone National Park	Grant General Store	*2 Grant Village Rd, Yellowstone National Park WY 82190*
WY	Yellowstone National Park	Grant General Store	*2 Grant Village Rd, Yellowstone National Park WY 82190*
WY	Yellowstone National Park	Old Faithful Basin Store	*1 Old Faithful Rd, Yellowstone National Park WY 82190*
WY	Yellowstone National Park	Old Faithful General Store	*2 Old Faithful Rd, Yellowstone National Park WY 82190*

WY	Yellowstone National Park	Yellowstone National Park	*CCH6+5J Yellowstone National Park, Yellowstone National Park WY 82190*

Notes:

Notes:

Notes:

Notes:

Notes:

www.ingramcontent.com/pod-product-compliance
Ingram Content Group UK Ltd.
Pitfield, Milton Keynes, MK11 3LW, UK
UKHW021906190726
13853UKWH00002B/540

9 798218 146962